Voyage to
a Thousand Cares

Voyage to a Thousand Cares

Master's Mate Lawrence with
the African Squadron, 1844–1846

C. Herbert Gilliland

C. Herbert Gilliland

Naval Institute Press
Annapolis, Maryland

Naval Institute Press
291 Wood Road
Annapolis, MD 21402

Library of Congress Cataloging-in-Publication Data

Lawrence, John C., d. 1846.

Voyage to a thousand cares : master's mate Lawrence with the African Squadron, 1844–1846 / [compiled by] C. Herbert Gilliland.

　　p. cm.

ISBN 1-59114-320-9 (hardcover)

1. Slavery—Africa, West—History—19th century. 2. Antislavery movements—United States—History—19th century. 3. United States. Navy. African Squadron—Officers—Diaries. 4. Lawrence, John C., d. 1846—Journeys. 5. Atlantic Coast (Africa)—Description and travel. I. Gilliland, C. Herbert. II. Title.

　　HT1332.L385 2003

　　306.3'62'0966—dc21

2003005263

Printed in the United States of America on acid-free paper ∞

11　10　09　08　07　06　05　04　　9　8　7　6　5　4　3　2

First printing

Contents

Preface

John C. Lawrence's journal was kept in a single ordinary bound blank book with ruled 33.5-by-21.5 centimeter pages, now held in the special collections of the Nimitz Library at the U.S. Naval Academy in Annapolis, Maryland. The journal was donated to the Naval Academy in 1995 by Mrs. Louise M. Royall, a descendant of John Lawrence's younger sister. Fifty-four leaves remain, of which the last two have been cut from the binding. At least seven leaves have been cut or torn from the beginning of the book, and at least eighteen or twenty from the back. Additionally, most of one page adjacent to the entry for 4 July 1845 has been cut out. Such is the journal that has been edited for the present volume.

From internal remarks Lawrence made it seems likely that he anticipated others might read his journal (though perhaps only his friends), but there is no particular reason to think he intended it for publication. I have thought it appropriate, therefore, to make certain assumptions and modifications in preparing the manuscript for the press. My principles have been: (1) to make such textual changes as might have been made had Lawrence himself taken the journal to a publisher—that is, minor changes, chiefly of punctuation and in the spelling out of numerals and abbreviated forms to make the resulting text correct, clear, and conventional; (2) to add such remarks and notes of my own as would help the twenty-first-century reader understand and enjoy this work of the mid–nineteenth century; and (3) to subtract nothing meaningful.

Other editorial matters:

Punctuation: Lawrence only occasionally marked off distinct sentences; his most common punctuation mark is one resembling a short dash, which seems to fill almost all purposes. I have silently replaced many of these dashes with commas, periods, and the like, as Lawrence himself might have done were he seeing his work through to publication. More often than not the word following a dash is not capitalized, even when it clearly should be the first word in a new sentence. I have therefore capitalized where it seemed appropriate. Conversely, I have in some cases converted Lawrence's capitals to lowercase, all the while retaining many capitals where they would not appear in a modern text (for example, he and his shipmates regularly capitalize the word "Topsail"). At times I have also broken what might have been very long compound sentences into shorter ones. I have made various other changes to punctuation to accord with standard practice. Words underlined by Lawrence are printed in italics here.

Words: I have in a few places added words in brackets to clarify the sense of a passage or make it grammatically correct. I have often silently expanded abbreviations, such as "fathoms" for "fms," "account" for "acc't," or "and" for "&," as I think would have been done by any publisher in Lawrence's day. I have deleted no words from the original text except in three or four instances where Lawrence has clearly inadvertently written the same word or phrase twice; Lawrence crossed out a word or phrase and substituted another, or made brief additions, where I have incorporated his corrections. Some uneventful entries have been deleted. Lawrence uses the old form "Ye" specifically when referring to topmasts; I cannot explain this choice but have retained it.

Numerals: In keeping with standard editorial practice of his day and ours, I have changed many numerals to their word equivalent. For example, "8" appears as "eight."

Spelling: I have silently corrected everyday words but retained Lawrence's spelling for place names, often entering the correct or today's accepted spelling in brackets after the first mention. I have normalized some of Lawrence's spellings, such as "agreeable" for "agreable," but I have retained some spellings that today would seem "British" rather than "American." I have combined some word pairs, such as "today" for "to day."

Daily labels: At the top of each manuscript page and at some places within pages Lawrence provides running titles such as "At Sea November," or "Settra Krou, December 1844." Often in the manuscript a title at the top of the page is placed in the middle of a day's entry. To replicate these would be obtrusive in any edition with a different pagination, like the present one. I have therefore deleted, modified, or added labels to fit the new pagination and to assist the reader.

Additional remarks and notes: I have added these in considerable quantity to fill in details, to explain things not obvious to a modern reader, and, most important, to complete the story. The last few leaves of the journal, where Lawrence may have recorded the dreadful though splendid final weeks of his life, are missing. Archival materials have yielded much here, permitting a substantial and vivid reconstruction.

Finally, it should be noted that contemporaneous logs, letters, and records all agree with Lawrence's account, and nothing I have found disagrees in any substantial way. These sources include the official logs of the *Yorktown*, Midn. Francis A. Roe's journal of the same cruise, and official correspondence from Captain Bell, Commodores Perry and Skinner, and others.

Acknowledgments

One of the little-advertised pleasures of making a book is sharing the process with those who help and support it. I owe particular thanks to Louise Royall for permission to publish John Lawrence's journal. Her donation to the Naval Academy's Nimitz Library of the manuscript, which had descended to her from Lawrence's sister, was the event that first brought it to my attention. I am very grateful to her and her cousin, Anne Wilson, for their enthusiastic interest in the project. Credit is due also to the late Rear Adm. William F. Royall for having prepared a typescript copy of the journal, which eased the early stages of my work.

Alice Creighton, prior to her retirement as director of special collections at the Nimitz Library, also took what I can only describe as a gleeful interest in the work, and could not have been more helpful. Thanks go also to her assistant, Mary Catalfamo.

I thank the Naval Academy Research Council for generous support during the several years of research.

The staffs of various branches of the National Archives and Record Administration—in New York, Philadelphia, and Washington—were invariably helpful and remarkably efficient. So, too, was the staff of the Library of Congress.

Ann Baker was all that one could want in a copy editor—sensible, sensitive, and diligent.

My colleagues at the Naval Academy—Eric Bowman and Ron Kyhos—read and commented on the manuscript. Bob Madison not only directed me to Horatio Bridge's book, the most similar previous publication, but also loaned me his copy for five years without ever asking for its return.

The Naval Academy Research Council has supported the research with repeated grants, for which I thank them.

Thanks to the Maryland Historical Society for permission to quote from the Lewis S. Williams Papers; to the Historical Society of Pennsylvania for permission to quote from Joseph Z. Sill's diary; and to the Smithsonian Institution (National Portrait Gallery) for permission to use the portrait of Captain Bell.

My wife, Carol Gilliland, thought this was a pretty good project and was willing to let me play hooky from household chores when the work repeatedly took me out of town. My daughters, Anne-Marie, Alexandra, Elizabeth, and Alice, were understanding of such absences too.

Voyage to
a Thousand Cares

Introduction

In 1844 John C. Lawrence became part of the American effort to stop the slave trade. A young officer aboard the U.S. Navy sloop *Yorktown,* Lawrence kept a personal journal that lets the reader inside his thoughts and feelings as his ship patrols the coast of western Africa, showing its flag and pursuing the practitioners of that odious trade. Many extant narratives tell the story of the Middle Passage in various ways; the literature of the transatlantic slave trade is massive and growing. Lawrence's story is remarkable in its combination of freely expressed opinion and dramatic circumstances.

Antislavery sentiments in the north (Lawrence was a New Yorker) were strong and vehemently expressed. Commodore Matthew Perry, under whom the African Squadron sailed, and Commander Charles Bell, captain of the *Yorktown,* both acted aggressively against slaving. However, Lawrence himself, probably like most of his shipmates, was not motivated by any such strong passion. An early comment of his on the benign nature of slavery in the American South will to the charitable reader sound naïve, though of course it echoes sentiments expressed by others in his day. The comment also probably emanates more from his annoyance with the British than anything else, as Lawrence elsewhere makes clear his antislavery sympathies. However, those sympathies seem more of a theoretical sort, of the kind held by someone humane in nature but with little personal experience with the "peculiar institution" itself. For him sailing with the African Squadron meant employment, a professional step up, and the chance to see new and perhaps interesting things. So much more powerful then will be the reaction when Lawrence steps aboard a ship full of slaves and sees and smells and touches slavery at its hideous root.

The slave traffic of the early nineteenth century much resembles the drug traffic of the early twenty-first. The profits were huge, the human cost immeasurable, and the end came only when the markets dried up. A slave bought for thirty dollars on the African coast could bring three hundred dollars on the other side of the Atlantic, so a successful voyage could net tens of thousands of dollars in a day when a navy master's mate like Lawrence earned four hundred dollars a year.

Though it was politically impossible for the United States to eliminate slavery within its borders prior to the conclusion of the Civil War, Congress did proscribe the importation of slaves as of 1 January 1808. That act was followed by one with stronger provisions in 1819. The act of 1819 authorized the president to use the armed vessels of the United States to seize any American ship that either was actually transporting slaves or was intended to be used to transport slaves. By 1820 Congress had declared the transport of slaves by any American citizen or aboard any American ship to be piracy, with death as the penalty. (Thus in the 1840s bringing slaves into the United States had been illegal for decades and smuggling them was a risky undertaking.) The chief demand for slaves from Africa was on the sugar plantations of Brazil, Cuba, and Puerto Rico. However, American ships, owners, and crews were inevitably drawn into the trade.

The U.S. Navy sent the corvette *Cyane,* under command of Lt. Edward Trenchard, to the west coast of Africa in 1820, marking the beginning of American naval presence in the region. The *Cyane* was escorting the *Elizabeth,* which carried the first group of freed slaves being sent back to resettle in Africa. After a bad start on Sherbro Island in Sierra Leone, the settlers moved south to Cape Mesurado, a spot recommended by the *Cyane*'s first lieutenant, Matthew Calbraith Perry. The *Cyane* also captured a number of ships suspected of intent to carry slaves. In following years the navy sent a few ships to visit the coast of western Africa, to pursue slavers and look after the growing American interests in the area, which included missionaries and trade.

The real beginnings of the African Squadron, though, came with the signing of the Webster-Ashburton Treaty in 1842. Though importation of slaves into the United States had been banned in 1808, Americans and American ships continued to be deeply involved in the trade, which by 1842 transported its annual thousands of victims mostly to Brazil and the Caribbean, especially Cuba. Not only were American ships among the world's finest, hewn from primeval forests by skilled craftsmen, but the American flag had special value. Britain by this time led the world's efforts to stop the slave trade. The British not only declared it illegal within their empire in 1807, but encouraged similar declarations by other nations and arranged antislavery treaties with the other European maritime powers. Britain, with the world's largest navy, also maintained on the African coast a sizable and effective naval squadron that constantly patrolled against slave ships. A treaty with France in 1831 and the Quintuple Treaty of 1841 (signed by Great Britain, Portugal, Austria, and Prussia—with France backing out) gave mutual right of search and permitted the Royal Navy to board, examine, and seize (if appropriate) any ships operating under those major flags. The important exceptions of maritime powers not signing these treaties were Brazil (a major slave destination) and the United States. The United States had fought the War of 1812 against Britain in considerable measure over the very issue of the British boarding American ships and impressing U.S. seamen. The British nevertheless boarded some American vessels in African waters on the theory that it was necessary to verify that they were in fact American. The resultant discord, plus a desire on the part of the U.S. administration to support the growing legitimate American trade with Africa, led to discussions between Secretary of State Daniel Webster and Britain's Lord Ashburton. The result was the Webster-Ashburton Treaty (also called the Washington Treaty) of 1842, which not only established the eastern border between the United States and Canada but also sought cooperation between Britain and the United States in suppressing the slave trade. It was agreed each would maintain off the coast of Africa a naval force of not fewer than eighty guns.

As the Royal Navy was ten times the size of the U.S. Navy, and had been patrolling the African coast for years, the bargain was an easier one for Britain to keep. Not until 1843 was the U.S. African Squadron under way, arriving that August at Monrovia, Liberia, under the command of Commodore M. C. Perry. The U.S. Navy had been given no additional resources for the task. With about three dozen deployable ships (subtracting from the total of sixty those laid up in ordinary, receiving ships, experimental, or otherwise nondeployable) the navy was already maintaining a presence in the Pacific, in the Mediterranean, along the South American coast, and in the Caribbean, as well as in home waters. Perry's initial squadron consisted of four ships, the flagship *Macedonian* (a 6-gun frigate) and three smaller sailing vessels. Though its arms met the eighty-gun treaty obligation, the squadron was not optimally configured for interdicting slavers. The British squadron included some steamers, whereas the Americans had none. And two 16-gun sloops would have been twice as good as one 6-gun frigate because slavers tended to have few guns and small crews. Subsequently the squadron did generally employ ships of eighteen guns or less, and in the late 1850s it was given steamers. Throughout its existence, though, the African Squadron was hampered by other difficulties, especially the fact that its squadron rendezvous (or base of operations) was at Porto Praya in the Cape Verde Islands, a thousand miles from the coast that was being patrolled. Also, because the United States would not agree to reciprocity, the American squadron could capture only American ships. During the squadron's existence, from 1843 until the early part of the Civil War, it did capture dozens of slavers; in the same period, however, the British took hundreds.

Nevertheless, the African Squadron (referred to officially under that title or as "U.S. Naval Forces, West Coast of Africa") did constitute an American naval presence on the African coast, and an answer of sorts to the slavers' abuse of the American flag.

American-built ships, being well regarded and abundant, were often simply bought or leased by slavers. Frequently, though, by the time Lawrence and the *Yorktown* began their voyage, a more elaborate practice was common. Although by 1844 most maritime powers condemned slavery, U.S. law in addition defined slavery as a form of piracy and provided that any American citizen caught aboard a ship actually transporting slaves could be convicted of piracy and punished by death. Slavers soon adapted their activities, finding ways to make American involvement indirect. An American crew might sail an American-flag ship to Africa, taking along as passengers a second crew composed of Portuguese, Spaniards, or other non-U.S. citizens. Then, as slaves were about to be loaded, a prearranged "sale" would be transacted, turning the ship over to the second crew under a new flag. The first (American) crew would go ashore or to another ship to find their way home. The second (non-American) crew would take the ship and slaves back across the Atlantic. Thus the first crew avoided the risk of being stopped by any but the thinly spread U.S. squadron (and, if stopped, were safe from the charge of piracy since no slaves were aboard), while the second crew was immune from arrest by

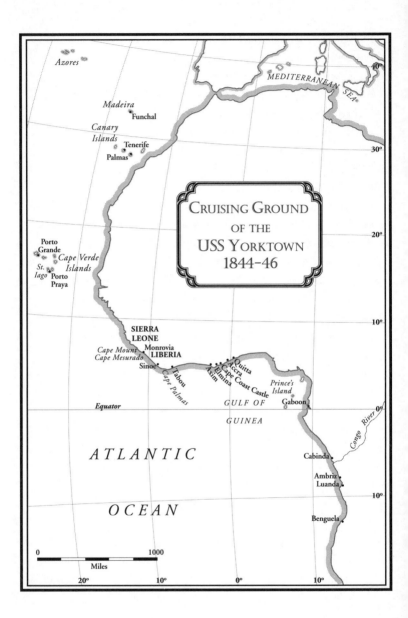

Azores

MEDITERRANEAN SEA

40°

Madeira
•Funchal

Canary
Islands   •Tenerife
Palmas•

30°

CRUISING GROUND
OF THE
USS YORKTOWN
1844–46

20°

Porto
Grande
•Cape Verde
St.•• Islands
Iago•Porto
Praya

10°

SIERRA
LEONE
Cape Mount Monrovia
Cape Mesurado LIBERIA
Sinoe•   Quitta
                   •Accra
              Cape Coast Castle
           Axim•Elmina
                        Prince's
                        Island
Equator   GULF OF   Gaboon
                GUINEA

Congo River

0°

ATLANTIC
                              Cabinda•

                              Ambriz•
                              Luanda•

10°

OCEAN
                              Benguela•

0 ━━━━━━━ 1000
        Miles
20°   10°   0°   10°

the U.S. Navy and, if taken by another navy, also did not risk prosecution for piracy.

Lawrence himself, a young white New Yorker of the early nineteenth century, is thoughtful and observant, but also can show brashness, vehemence, and cultural arrogance that may startle today's reader. It is only fair to remember not only the times in which he wrote but that he wrote his journal for his own private ends. Though he may have imagined sharing it later with friends, he never had that opportunity and did not publish it. Some of his comments have at best a blatant tastelessness that might find their equivalents today only in certain television and radio shows catering to low instincts, if anywhere. He can be shallow and unfair and crude; missionaries, for example, were not as universally hypocritical as he takes them to be. The physical appearance of the Kroo tribesmen no more deserved the treatment he gives it than did that of some of his own New York neighbors, had it been similarly displayed. Sometimes, too, as in the case of the missionary Mr. Wilson, he is simply misinformed. However, Lawrence can also be an unusually thoughtful and observant and eloquent writer. His lively style and his personality are ultimately engaging.

Prologue

THE CAPTAIN

In a light breeze under passing clouds the thirteen stripes and twenty-six stars of the American flag rose over the stern of a 16-gun sloop in the Brooklyn Navy Yard. It was 7 August 1844. Cdr. Charles Heyer Bell, USN, had placed the *Yorktown* back into commission and assumed its command.[1]

Bell had not wanted the job. A New Yorker a week shy of his forty-sixth birthday, Bell had begun his career as a thirteen-year-old midshipman under Commodore Decatur aboard the frigate *Macedonian* in the War of 1812. Three years later, again with Decatur on the *Macedonian,* Bell had operated against Algiers. As a lieutenant he commanded the *Ferret* when that vessel capsized off the coast of Cuba; with his surviving crewmen he clung to wreckage for twenty-one hours until rescued. He had operated against Caribbean pirates, and cut out a ship from under the guns of Fort Guadeloupe. More relevant to the impending cruise of the *Yorktown,* though, was that his two most recent sea tours had been to Africa. Therein lay much of Bell's reluctance, for none knew better than he the possible difficulties and danger.

Still, one could almost say that in taking the *Yorktown* to Africa Bell would be following his own advice. In late 1839 and again in 1840 he had been sent in command of the 10-gun brig *Dolphin* to patrol the African coast. At the same time, though independently, Lt. John S. Paine was sent with the sloop *Grampus*. The two lieutenants had been aggressive and resourceful. Paine had struck a cooperative arrangement with the local British naval senior officer, agreeing that each could stop vessels flying the other's flag, seize any slavers, and turn them over to the other navy. The plan made sense locally but raised a furor in Washington. It impinged on issues of sovereignty far beyond the accepted powers of a navy lieutenant, and drew Paine a strong reprimand from then– Secretary of the Navy James K. Paulding.[2] For his part Bell (at Liberian urging) had formally threatened to destroy the slaver settlement of New Sester, located north of Cape Palmas and run by the notorious slaver Theodore Canot. It proved impossible for Bell to make good on his threat. However, he did write a strong letter to the secretary of the navy advocating the use of a frigate's landing party to wipe out some of the main slave stations, and he volunteered to extend his stay.[3] Some of Bell's antislavery correspondence also found its way into the newspapers.

In 1842 Secretary of State Daniel Webster found himself negotiating, with Britain's Lord Ashburton, what came to be known as the Webster-Ashburton Treaty. The treaty would settle the northeastern boundary of the United States between Maine and British North America, but another major topic of discussion was the slave trade. Britain had for many years exerted its diplomacy toward extinction of the trade. Webster turned to the two lieutenants (now commanders) as consultants, giving them a detailed questionnaire. Their response, the Paine-Bell Report, surveyed the situation on the West African coast and gave precise recommendations. The report played a significant role in shaping the antislavery provisions of the treaty, which was signed that August. One provision was that the United States and Great Britain each would maintain on the African coast a naval force of not fewer than eighty guns. In June 1843 the United States sent several ships to

Africa under the command of Commo. Matthew C. Perry. Now the *Yorktown* was going to take a turn as part of that force—the U.S. Navy's African Squadron.

Clearly Charles Bell was energetic, courageous, experienced, and a man with a genuine antipathy to the slave trade. No one was better qualified—he had literally "written the book" on the subject. But he did not want the job. In attempting to decline command of the *Yorktown* he gave two reasons. First, his last two cruises had been to Africa, the least popular station the U.S. Navy offered and with some reason regarded as the least healthy. In a conversation with the secretary of the navy when the question of his commanding the *Yorktown* had first come up, Bell had suggested it would be fair to let someone else take a turn. He had gone so far as to tell Paulding explicitly that he "would not volunteer for any ship he knew was going to Africa." Second, he had hoped by this point in his career to obtain command of a larger ship—indeed, others junior to him had already done so. Paulding's successor John Y. Mason was firm and direct: if Bell wanted any assignment at all he must take the *Yorktown*. At this time the navy had more commanders than assignments; Bell had been without orders for three years. He took the *Yorktown*. The position held so little attraction, though, that even while preparing the ship for sea he tried again to get another assignment. In rejecting his appeal Mason offered the sop that he hoped no deployment to Africa would last longer than twelve months.[4] In the end Bell was gone for twenty.

THE SHIP

Much had to be done to get the *Yorktown* ready for sea. A ship "in ordinary" between commissionings was little more than a hull. A third-rate sloop of the *Dale* class, the *Yorktown* was first commissioned in 1840. With three masts, a length of 118 feet, beam of 33 feet, and 566 tons displacement, she carried fourteen 32-pounder carronades (of which two were the new Paixhans guns firing shells rather than shot) and two long 12-pounders. She was rated for a crew of 150.

When Captain Bell first hoisted the *Yorktown*'s flag his crew was a mere handful; over the next few weeks the remainder reported on board in ones and twos and scores—a total of about 120, including several musicians and twenty marines plus their own fifer and drummer. This number left room for augmenting the crew later, once the ship reached Africa. The *Yorktown* began to wake from her hibernation: the masts were stayed, the rigging put up. Sails, navigational equipment, charts, tables, and chairs—all the paraphernalia of daily life at sea had to be selected and brought aboard. Day by day tons of bread, salt pork, and salt beef came aboard in barrels to be laid below. Thousands of gallons of water filled metal tanks on the lowest deck. Lamp oil, ledgers, lumber, pencils and quill pens, paint, powder, shot, bales of trousers and pea coats, and much more had to be stowed securely. Secretary of the Navy John Y. Mason urged alacrity on the *Yorktown* and the *Preble,* sister ships on the same mission. One of the greatest difficulties was getting enough officers; Bell remarked that he could have been ready for sea in less than three weeks had it not been for the shortage of officers. Lieutenants and midshipmen did not seem eager for Africa, did not always answer messages, and were disproportionately unhealthy. Some of the more dutiful reported aboard and then mailed requests to the secretary asking for another assignment for reasons of health. Midn. William Cushman supported his unsuccessful plea with a letter from his father. Lt. Henry Steele, with eighteen years in the navy and having just completed two three-year cruises, asked only that he be able to return home within "15 or 18 months, should I survive the effects of the climate of the coast of Africa." Despite distracting health problems Steele would serve as Bell's first lieutenant (second in command) for the entire voyage. Midn. Francis Roe, for some reason believing the ship bound for the Mediterranean, actually requested assignment to the *Yorktown.*[5] Without comment the secretary gave it to him.

Meantime, the two long 12-pounders in the bows were exchanged for 18-pounders. Workmen from the yard painted the ship inside and out. After the upper two sections of the masts were in place the crew slushed the masts, greasing them so the yards would slide smoothly up and down. They prepared the rigging, scrubbed the decks, and loaded stores. Purser John Hambleton filled his iron strongbox with thousands of Spanish milled dollars, the currency of the African coast.

Lieutenant Steele, responsible for furnishing the wardroom, noted to his fellow officers that chairs with arms rather than plain straight chairs could be had for anyone willing to chip in a dollar more per chair. The other officers were content with regular chairs, but Steele, beset with chronic pains and seeking what comfort he could, paid the dollar to get arms on his. The wardroom of the *Yorktown,* where the dozen commissioned and noncommissioned officers (other than the captain) dined, had two tables with six chairs each. As the senior in the mess Steele placed his armchair in the traditionally senior location, at the starboard end of the after table. Most of the officers slept in staterooms adjacent to the wardroom. Forward of the wardroom the enlisted crew slept and ate in the great open space of the berth deck, without benefit of tables and chairs or staterooms. At meals each mess of six or eight gathered round a piece of canvas laid on the deck or over a chest, and at night each man slung his hammock from a pair of hooks.

With the solitude of command Commander Bell slept and dined in his own quarters above the wardroom in the poop deck. The *Yorktown* rated three lieutenants, the next rank below commander. Next below them were the passed midshipmen, each of whom had perhaps five or ten or more years of service and had passed an examination. Most junior of the commissioned deck officers were the midshipmen, who might be newly commissioned with little or no seagoing experience; or, if they had some years at sea, they had yet to pass the examination. Other officers included the surgeon, the purser, the gunner, the boatswain, and the carpenter. Also dining at the junior ("steerage") table would be the master's mate.

THE MASTER'S MATE

Sometime during the final weeks of preparation Master's Mate John C. Lawrence reported aboard. About twenty-two years old and a native of Long Island, New York, Lawrence had first gone to sea as a merchant seaman, making several voyages. Then in 1842 his brother-in-law, Navy captain John Gallagher, invited Lawrence to join the navy aboard the ship he commanded, the razee frigate *Independence.* Assigned to the Home Squadron, the *Independence* had spent its time in New York and Boston and the waters of the East Coast and the Caribbean. Gallagher died in November 1842, and six months later Lawrence left the navy to seek better opportunities in the merchant marine. Those opportunities proved limited, and in January 1844 he rejoined the navy as an acting master's mate aboard the receiving ship *North Carolina* at the New York Navy Yard in Brooklyn.[6] With assignment to the *Yorktown* the following October came full status as master's mate.

As Lawrence awaited that assignment New York offered a variety of entertainments. At the Park Theater the great English Shakespearean actor William Charles Macready played Hamlet. Niblo's Garden offered minstrel shows, bellringers, and acrobats, and Palmo's Opera House showed Bellini's *Il Pirata.* However, New York and the whole country were caught up in the fervor of a presidential election.[7] The incumbent John Tyler had left the Democrats in 1833 to serve as an independent before being chosen by the Whigs as Harrison's running mate in 1840. After succeeding Harrison in 1841, by 1844 he was supported for reelection by neither party. Democrats met in Baltimore, and over a line that stretched from there to Washington, Samuel Morse's recently invented telegraph clicked out the world's first electrically transmitted news item: the nomination of James K. Polk, a dark horse from Tennessee. Polk favored aggressive expansion of U.S. territory, and the Republic of Texas, having recently created itself from the northeastern part of Mexico, wanted to be annexed.

Polk's opponent, Whig Henry Clay of Kentucky, was against annexation of Texas, which he saw as an action likely to provoke a war with Mexico, possibly drawing in Britain or France on the Mexican side. Behind the Mexican question also loomed the specter that had shadowed national politics since the creation of the republic: slavery and its possible destruction of the union. The pending statehood of Iowa (free) and Florida (slave) was safe enough, as together they would keep the delicate balance of slave and free states. Texas, though, threatened that balance.

The country faced yet another challenge in the Oregon Territory. The United States unquestionably owned Oregon, but what *was* Oregon? That is, just where was the border between American and British territory in the Pacific Northwest? "Fifty-four forty or fight!" thundered Polk, claiming territory hundreds of miles farther north than he would eventually settle for after the election, without a fight.

In New York, as elsewhere across the nation, rallies and speeches proliferated and newspaper editors filled their pages with material of one bias or the other. Lawrence might have attended a rally like the one held near Tammany Hall that a British correspondent described as having a "wild oriental beauty." Powerful limelights mounted on poles high above the buildings "shed a silvery radiance" over the crowd of thousands, while Roman candles and rockets shot up over City Hall and the speakers, and a procession bearing countless banners and lanterns wound through the trees of the adjacent park.[8] In any event, scanning his newspapers in the autumn of 1844 and perhaps noting Polk banners or Clay placards or spotting daguerreotype campaign badges on a coat or two, John Lawrence anticipated a Polk victory. Might he and the *Yorktown* be exchanging shots with the British, the Mexicans, or even the French, before his cruise was over? Such considerations aside, Africa waited with its own dangers as well as attractions. Lawrence had never been there.

Lawrence crossed the *Yorktown*'s gangplank with a blank new journal in hand, resolved to write something in it every day. Midshipmen who had not yet passed the examination to become passed midshipmen were required to keep journals, but these were homework reviewed by their commanding officers and closely resembled official logs. Under no such requirement, Lawrence was free to write what he thought and felt, for his own pleasure and perhaps that of friends when he returned.

On 11 October 1844, after weeks of delay, the bow of the *Yorktown* at last cut the waters of the North Atlantic, heading east and south. The continent quickly fell beneath the horizon, but the *Yorktown* sailed as the instrument of the nation she left behind. However unsettled that nation was on the issue of slavery, the ship's mission along the African coast was clear. Her first stop would be Madeira.

1

November 1844

It took twenty-eight fairly uneventful days to cross the Atlantic. Captain Bell's officers thought well of him, and generally got along with each other. As in the wardrooms of every U.S. Navy ship at the time, officers perused the pages of Prescott's *History of the Conquest of Mexico* in anticipation of their own involvement in a new conquest.

The weather after leaving New York had at first been cold with easterly winds and occasional storms. As the ship sailed further south the weather became pleasant, and the wind generally favorable; the *Yorktown* dropped anchor off Funchal on the island of Madeira on the afternoon of 10 November. The next day, assisted by boats from the Portuguese frigate *Diana,* the *Yorktown* was towed to a better anchorage. Gun salutes between the American warship and the local authorities boomed across the harbor. Bumboats brought fresh vegetables and meat for the crew. The next couple of days were taken with loading twenty-seven tons of water, painting the outside of the ship, and blacking the rigging.[1]

The *Yorktown*'s crew did not have liberty, but some of the officers, including Lawrence, were able to take a boat ashore and play the tourist. It seems likely that Lawrence had been keeping his journal for some weeks, probably since departing New York. Unfortunately the journal as we have it today is missing some leaves at the beginning and end, so for us Lawrence's remarks

begin upon his arrival at Madeira. On the first surviving page of
his journal, which begins in mid-entry, we find him there on
13 November 1844. He has been visiting with the Portuguese gar-
rison and is interested in their pay and living conditions.

FUNCHAL, MADEIRA

13 November 1844 (continued)

*The sergeant gets 10 cents per diem, sans ration, and a
room in the barracks—the drummers receive the same
pay—and if I remember aright a lieutenant get[s] $8.00
per month with the ration improved upon.*

　　*The accommodations for the Sergeants' families in
the barrack seemed very comfortable. Many of the females
were washing away at foul clothes like good fellows; perhaps this is another source of revenue to the sergeants'
funds. We tried the effects of a few pert queries in English
to these soldiers' wives etc.—but not understanding the
tongue in which we spoke, we might as well have sung
Icelandic Madrigals to them as far as the effect went. After
scouring various noted parts of the town (population
Madeira is 120,000—ditto of Funchal 28,000) such as
those where abide vice in the female form (horrid to think
of) etc. etc., we hired a horse apiece. But before going farther I feel it an incumbent duty I owe to myself to mention
(in case some of my moral friends might get hold of this
journal) that our object in going in the vicinity of Rica del
Forno was really from a species of sad and I might say
pious curiosity to ascertain the amount of sin in petticoats
and underdrawers that actually did exist in this town: but
for no other reason. Can culpability or criminality be*

attached to such a visit when actuated by such noble incen-
tives? I calculate no, decidedly! Not exactly, god be
praised!—at least so goes my opinion. As aforesaid, we
hired horses and went beyond the precincts of the town,
perhaps to the distance of five miles. But the great incon-
venience to this kind of excursion is, you are compelled to
have either a good sized boy or man following all the way
behind you on foot, at the same time clinging to your
horse's tail for assistance, which is a great impediment to
the horse especially while ascending hills, which abound
here. However, it is the custom of the country and you
must bear it; these people consider that they add a large
amount to your felicity, instead of which they are actually
producing a violent state of irritation in one's mind. From
the summit of the hills, the roadstead and vicinity of
Funchal form one of the most picturesque scenes that I
remember of ever having seen. After gazing at this
panorama-like view, we descended to the town, got clear of
our horses, sought rest and repose at the London Hotel,
which Hotel does furnish most delicious wines at very rea-
sonable prices. I shall not forget their various flavors of the
various qualities that I partook of on this eventful night I
know! But as I should not succeed in conveying an ade-
quate idea of their delicacy of relish of any of them if I
were to attempt it but shall drop the matter abruptly—
likewise avoid the other events of the night—for they were
decidedly queerish in their nature. Next morning went on
board—an abominable sea on—some expectation of being
swamped.

Some of the "queerish" events of the night probably involved
Passed Midshipman Neville, of whose drunkenness Captain Bell

took particular note (and of whom more later). Three crewmen were flogged for drunkenness the next day, but as an officer Neville could not be flogged.

14 November 1844

Pleasant breezes, without the usual serenity of atmosphere. After I had got on board, I remembered that I had neglected to make some purchases from the nunneries, although I had passed several of these establishments, and saw the female inmates, looking out like so many unhappy immured [imprisoned] delinquents. Never mind; will see Madeira soon again, I hope.

One souvenir of Funchal was a sort of flower display the local nuns made from feathers. Among the various vessels stopping at Funchal, *Yorktown* officers notice an American barque, the *Pons* of Philadelphia. The strikingly handsome *Pons,* captained by her owner, John Graham, is employed in legitimate trade, chiefly between Africa and Brazil, and is now on her way to Rio de Janeiro. Lieutenant Steele remembers seeing her in Norfolk a year earlier. She had then been under navy charter, bringing back from Gibraltar the crew and salvaged metal parts of the unfortunate USS *Missouri.* One of the American navy's two new steam frigates (of the total four steamers), the *Missouri* was destroyed by fire after a crewman dropped a demijohn of turpentine onto a hot engine part. A year from now the *Yorktown* (and Lawrence) will encounter the *Pons* again, under very different circumstances.

15 November 1844

Preparations for getting under way.

16 November 1844

All ready, hove into sixty fathoms cable. At about 5:30 P.M. made sail, hove up our anchor, and stood out to Sea bound for Teneriffe [Tenerife].

AT SEA

17 November 1844

Weather mild and agreeable, wind from Northward and Eastward (trades).

Doubtless a very heavy gale or even a hurricane has within a day or two swept the sea from the coast of Africa as far West as eight or ten degrees; the sea is literally covered with grasshoppers that have been blown from the land—Red they are—as fresh born babies—look queer, no two ways about it.

18 November 1844

Glorious breezes; but to tell the truth I do not know from what direction, whether fair for us, or foul, the weather being so delicious that it renders us so voluptuously listless as to make us totally regardless as to our course, destination, or rate of going—just as good as being in a Turkish bath or under the influence of Opium. But still a little ice would be none the worse, never mind how jagged in form, how small in quantity allowing it to be no smaller than a reasonably sized man's head. T'would be cheap at 25 cents per pound—think of the Iced wines that we would enjoy!

This is an enjoyment sometimes indulged in at Madeira, the ice being procured from the Mountaintops.

It is a temptation to think of (but after all perhaps we are better without it) "lead us not into temptation"! as the old prayer says.

19 November 1844

After being refreshed with a night's slumber, I arose, put on my garments, went on deck and encountered a delightful breeze and pleasant weather. The day was not marked by any extraordinary transaction. A few lighthearted fish, well grown, at the age of puberty probably, played a few old fashioned gambols that have been in vogue amongst the scaly tribe for countless years back.

20 November 1844

Fine weather still. Nothing occurred until about 4 P.M. when the far famed Peak of Teneriffe appeared to view in all the lofty grandeur that has ever been ascribed to it—as regular and even it seems in formation as if it had been the stupendous work of man. At the distance of fifteen or twenty miles from the Westward it appears like a perfect cone. At 11 close in by the land; we are allowed consequently a fine view of its general aspect, which resembles a good deal that of Madeira, though all islands of volcanic formation are generally pretty much all alike—but the difference between this island and Madeira is that the latter affords a far greater degree of verdure.

SANTA CRUZ, TENERIFE, CANARY ISLES

Tenerife often charms visitors. Surgeon Williams notes the tidy streets, women wearing white mantillas, and many camels used as beasts of burden. Lawrence, too, finds much to admire.

21 *November 1844*

After taking in all sail and letting go our anchor we were at leisure to view the town of Santa Cruz, abreast of which we are lying. It is a remarkably neat and beautifully built town; most of the dwellings are white, giving it a very light and lively appearance. The bumboat men that come off with fruits and vegetables to the ship show the most inordinate avidity to acquire money by the sale of their stock in trade, so much so as actually to heave each other overboard and fight like clawless cats while in the water. The anchoring ground here is very fair; we are lying in about twenty-five fathoms water, mixed bottom unlike Funchal. This place bears some semblance to a harbor, though not a very safe one. Now in my breast rise useless and vain, but choking regrets to think that I cannot draw, "when I view these scenes so charming"—but might not with as much reason, a barren wife bewail her unfruitfulness, as for me to sigh for the want of the above accomplishment when like the above mentioned wife, I know it isn't in me. A delightful breeze from the Eastward is refreshing us. Upon the information of two visitors who came on board of us today, the one a Captain of a smuggler, and also as I suspect, a slaver, held in durance but not very vile (being on large gaol [jail] liberties) by the Spanish government for some violation of

revenue law or other—the other one his bail (and a devil-
ish acute fellow too I guess)—we find amongst other things
that the insect that we have taken all along for
Grasshoppers prove to be the African Locust. Millions are
ashore—people are destroying them as fast as they can.
Laguna is a delightfully romantic situated town five miles
in the interior amongst the mountains: fourteen windmills
all in a row, and all at a time in operation; two or three
cathedrals; one or two monasteries; besides several public
squares, serve to give this place a very interesting and
pretty appearance. But a more extensive account of this
place must be postponed until we visit the Island again. It
is now all hands up anchor; hour 7 P.M. and fair wind.
After the anchor was tripped, the wind not being strong
enough to pay her off short, around we came within our
length of falling foul of a brig (Spanish) at anchor, which
however was prevented by heaving all three topsails to the
mast and flatting in our jibs, which gave her sternway, at
the same time paying her off to starboard. Consequently we
cleared the brig and then braced round, filled away and
stood out to sea—all sail set upon the ship to studding sails
(topsails), course ESE.

AT SEA

22 November 1844

Wind fair and plenty of it. Thus far no sickness has
occurred on board of us. May it continue so on that accurs-
edly infectious coast of Africa—"Mais nous verrons, n'im-
porte"—we are enjoying the "trades" now in their fullest

*blasts. Our good ship is amongst other gambols showing
her bright red bottom at the rate of ten knots per hour—all
sail set from Topgallant Studding sails to courses. At about
2 P.M. we came into green water, a peculiarity of this latitude (22° N) whose cause has as yet remained undiscov-
ered, no shoals being noticeable by the lead. But nevertheless that must be the reason of this alteration from the
general colour. Green sand may be the bottom! This part or
rather eight or ten degrees further south of this the Atlantic
Ocean abounds with rocks and shoals. With this wind we
may soon expect to be in Porto Praya, our next port of destination. And after that—I hate to utter it—that baleful,
and most deleterious of all regions, that most pestilential
bower from which so few white men return that are induced to visit it—or if they return, they only reappear as
shadows and phantoms of their former selves. The being
who ventures into these insidious realms, upon his first
arrival, suddenly feels his soul disencumbered of all his former apprehensions in regard to the latent dangers in shape
of pestilence that beset him, when his eye meets the magnificent array of vegetation that advances to the very
water's edge and seems to invite him to their depths as a
delightful retreat from his late toils and anxiety upon the
sea, and the burning heat that pervades everywhere without its precincts. He yields to the temptation, leaps upon
the strand, and seems suddenly to have become inspired
with an elastic delight—when he perceives himself surrounded with the glorious and profuse variety of verdure in
every shape and on every side. The long and glossy leaved
Plantain, Mango and Orange trees offer their inviting
golden fruits to his appetite. The tall and solemn cocoanut
and Palm trees seem to look down as in welcome of his*

*advent. At length wearied with gazing at these novelties
and of tasting the luscious fruits, he yields to an overpowering inclination to sleep—and after a long and heavy
slumber awakes: a heavy pain has settled in his head and
back, soon his pulses quicken, his pains increase, his blood
acquires the heat of molten lead—it is too much for his
brain—frenzy follows, he is held in lingering torments for
an indefinite season, and then, unless fortune proves
unusually kind, dies a raving maniac. Too often alas is this
the fate of many a noble fellow. And then there is the
heat—all enervating heat—you mark the quivering caloric
with almost the density of smoke rising from all things.
Our healthy and solid muscles are reduced to a flaccid state
like that of decomposing flesh. But still we'll endure it—it
is not equal to Hell after all, we will derive comfort from
comparison with worse situations, we will be like merry
Newgate convicts! We will dance to our graves if we are to
die! So here is to ye Messrs Boa Constrictors, Lions, Tigers,
Jackals, Jackasses, Jackanapes, African fever, and the whole
of your damned diabolical, devouring, devastating, and
deplorably detestable crew! As the chap said, when he
mounted the top of his burning house, "hurrah for Hell!
Who is afraid of fire?"*

24 November 1844

*Pleasant but cloudy weather; scarcely any variation in
trade weather. The sea still continues of a greenish colour.
All this fine weather we must expect soon to exchange for
that of a very unpleasant nature, such as direful heat—
only alternated by saturating rain, deaf'ning thunder, daz-*

zling lightning, rending hurricanes, dangerous navigation
to give keenness to our general apprehensions and heighten
the acuteness of our irritability. Perhaps we may be agree-
ably disappointed and meet with only half the above
annoyances. If such should be the case, I shall fervently
thank God if I should remember it five or six months from
now.

Here the reader may imagine Lawrence is demonstrating his
theme that one of these days is much like another. Both the previous entry and the following one read like complete entries for a
day; the date headings are confusing, and Lawrence himself seems
to have lost track. The manuscript offers an entry for 23 November
reporting "wind and weather the same" and "no incidents again
today to mention" followed by one for 24 November, followed by a
"24th contin" corrected to "23th contin," followed by one for 24
November. Lawrence may have momentarily confused "sea time"
and ordinary time. Until 1848 U.S. Navy logs were dated from
noon to noon, so the log dated 24 November would have described
the time that elapsed from noon on 23 November to noon on 24
November. Thus a seaman writing after noon on the twenty-third
might have dated his personal writings as the twenty-third, but log
entries would have been dated the twenty-fourth.

24 November 1844

Wind and weather the same, the color of water same. This
along with the lunar rainbow, that we witnessed about half
passage to Madeira, and which hath had honorable men-
tion in this faithful journal at the time of its occurrence,
are the only two phenomena that have proved new to me.
Baron Humboldt (no mean authority) mentions a lunar

*rainbow as no very common every night spectacle. But the
green water is always open to the inspection of the curious
between the Latitudes of 20° odd N to 17° ditto ditto Long.
15° and 17° Westerly.*

25 November 1844

Weather same. Color of the water changed to a turbid blue.

26 November 1844

*The ship is rolling along with the most indolent and
damme eye complacency that one could conceive of in anything excepting a jack tar after a return from a long voyage. She rolls at the rate too of ten knots per hour. Land ho!
is the cry from the mast head—it is the Island of Mayo
[Maio], one of the Cape De Verde group. The scenery of
this island quite materially differs from any of either the
Madeira or Canary groups: much plain meadow and table
land is afforded here, which is not the case with the other
mentioned ones. Large herds of cattle are discernible, graz-
ing upon the meadows. These last features by the way,
thrown in juxtaposition with those of lofty hills and mountains, form beautiful landscapes.*

*At 5.30 the Isle St. Iago [São Tiago] hove in sight.
The same description of scenery that is given of Mayo will
apply exactly to this one. At 6 P.M. hove to till 5 A.M. next
morning. We are now running along the land for Porto
Praya Roads, hailed a brig standing off and on the harbors.
She proved to be a whaler—sickening to think of it—who*

would go in one that knew the terms of existence aboard?
But I will not dwell on the subject, for it is too hateful to
contemplate!

PORTO PRAYA, ST. IAGO, CAPE VERDE

27 November 1844

Standing in for the anchorage, came to in seven fathoms
water hard bottom veered to thirty-five fathoms chain.
[That is, besides the seven fathoms required to touch bot-
tom, an additional thirty-five fathoms of chain were paid
out, giving sufficient length and weight to keep the anchor
in place. Anchoring was done with the ship moving slowly
forward to set the anchor and to avoid piling up the chain
on the bottom and fouling the anchor. The procedure is the
same today, except navy ships anchor while backing down
to avoid having the chain damage their bow-mounted
sonar domes.] The slight accident of a Jackass hitching in
the chain cable at the hawse hole when we let go our
anchor, was the cause of our Master catching a devil of a
rating. The Jackass in question, I may as well mention for
the information of [the] ignorant, is a no legged Jack made
something like this [see illustration below] and used to
keep the water out of the hawse hole when the cable is bent.

Lawrence's drawing of the jackass, 17 November 1844.
Nimitz Library Special Collections, U.S. Naval Academy, Annapolis, Maryland

One portion of this town Porto Praya is situated upon the verge of a precipitous ledge of rocks which overlooks the small bight which constitutes the roads: there is some similarity to be detected between this portion of the scenery and that of the Palisades on the far famed Hudson River. Taking this section of the island all together, it may be pronounced as being very pretty. At 1 P.M. a salute of twenty-one guns was fired from this ship, which was answered by an equal number from a fort by the Portuguese authorities.

Here the *Yorktown* rendezvouses with the *Macedonian,* flagship of the commodore, Matthew C. Perry. The *Macedonian,* a 38-gun frigate captured from the British during the War of 1812, is now (rebuilt from the keel up in 1832) a 36-gun frigate. She would be razeed (removing her upper deck) and converted to a sloop in 1852 for Perry's expedition to Japan. The *Decatur* and the *Preble,* both soon to appear, are 16-gun *Dale*-class sloops and sisters to the *Yorktown.* Lawrence has friends aboard the *Decatur*—two officers he had served with aboard the *Independence.*

28 November 1844

The American Consul (name unknown) [Lawrence adds "Gardner"] came on board, gave him a salute of seven guns, remained some time with the Captain, and then in company both went ashore. At 3:30 the Commodore's (Perry) ship [Macedonian] hove in sight. We saluted immediately with thirteen guns, answered with seven. At 7 o'clock as may be supposed our ship was overflowing with officers from the Macedonian. *A mutual exchange of intelligence took place, ours being of America, theirs of Africa.*

Commodore Matthew C. Perry
Oil on canvas, William Sidney Mount, 1834
U.S. Naval Academy Museum, Annapolis, Maryland

*This ended the incidents of the day. Next morning at 11:30
the* Decatur *made her appearance and came to anchor.
Her officers as may be supposed were elated measurelessly,
as we are her relief from the station. I met two former shipmates on board of her, Messrs Passed Midshipman (acting
Master) Adams and Midshipman Jouett, looking both as
hearty as bucks. The accounts given by these gentlemen
seem far from dolesome: I feel differently to what I did,
upon the subject some days since.*

As Captain Bell stands on his quarterdeck looking out at Porto
Praya, he remembers the last time he was here. It was January 1841;
he had arrived prostrate with fever, in command of a disease-
ravaged ship. On his second African cruise in command of the
Dolphin, the secretary of the navy had ordered him to settle a dispute between merchants and local kings on the River Nunez (in
modern Guinea, north of Sierra Leone). Doing so required picking
his way through the shoals and flats at the river's mouth, then
going upriver. Bell knew the risk of exposure to disease was great,
but his orders were explicit.

Joined by Lieutenant Paine in the *Grampus,* he had worked the
Dolphin arduously upriver, the men more often than not in the
boats bending over their oars, towing their ship against the current. They toiled eighty miles inland, around bends, through
swamps and forest, past elephants and hippos and the occasional
settlement, sweating and swatting insects. Then it had taken two
weeks more, anchored in the river, to negotiate the dispute. The
American crews began to sicken. By the time Bell had taken his
ship back down the river, gone south to Sierra Leone, and headed
to the offshore refuge of Porto Praya in the Cape Verdes, forty-five
of Bell's crew of eighty men were on the sick list. The first lieutenant, the doctor, and Bell himself were among the victims.
Unable to tolerate the heat below decks, the sick sprawled under

awnings on the main deck. By the time Bell reached Port Praya two delirious men had leapt overboard and perished, and seven more had simply died. To his astonishment and great relief Bell saw in the harbor the American flag flying from the U.S. sloop *Cyane* (of twenty guns) on her way home from the Mediterranean. The *Cyane*'s Captain Latimer sprang into action. He sent his two doctors to nurse the sick, elicited generous aid from the Portuguese authorities, arranged housing and nursing ashore for the most seriously ill, and put his crew to work refurbishing the *Dolphin*. A few days later the *Grampus* also arrived from the coast, in scarcely better shape. Instead of completing their African cruise as scheduled, both fever-ridden brigs lingered at Port Praya for two months, until the end of March. Even then Bell took his ship across the Atlantic to the Caribbean to improve the crew's health before going home to New York, and Paine had to borrow three officers from the *Cyane* to replace losses aboard the *Grampus*.

The cruise could easily be called a disaster. However, Bell and Paine had learned much. They drew upon their experience to write the Paine-Bell Report requested by Secretary of State Daniel Webster as he prepared to negotiate the Webster-Ashburton Treaty. Now, under the terms of that treaty, Bell was unwillingly on his way to Africa again.

29 November 1844

Opens with fine weather and laborious tasks. Not fifteen minutes leisure all today; stow, stow, stow, all day long. The Preble *standing in—came to at 2:30. Accounts from her today in regard to the state of health very bad, 46 on the list (sick). All the blame is attached to the Captain and I should judge very properly too.*

Like Bell's experience aboard the *Dolphin,* the *Preble*'s story illuminates the U.S. Navy's (and Lawrence's own) very great concern about health in connection with African operations. The *Preble* had been sent to Bissao (modern-day Bissau, in Guinea-Bissau) upon report of disturbances there between the natives and the local Portuguese. Her captain, Commander Freelon, had sent men ashore to support and protect the Europeans. In the process and despite warnings from his ship's doctor, Freelon anchored a mere quarter of a mile offshore. The nights spent anchored close ashore, plus the demanding operation of boats at all hours and various other practices, exposed his crew to what the squadron surgeon described (with the best medical knowledge of the time) as "the pestilential miasma" arising from the coastal mangrove swamps and mud flats. Of the forty men (including Freelon himself) seriously ill when the *Preble* came into Porto Praya, at least sixteen subsequently died. Two months later, after making it to Porto Grande for recuperation, the *Preble*'s crew was still too debilitated to continue further.

Commodore Perry had given ships of the African Squadron strict orders to anchor some distance from the shore, never to permit anyone to spend a night ashore anywhere in West Africa, and not to permit sleeping on an open deck. Additionally, charcoal-fueled drying ovens were used to combat the high humidity and everyone was required to wear a flannel undershirt night and day. Crews must often have stifled and sweltered in the interest of health. Of course those efforts, intended to minimize exposure to "bad air," also minimized exposure to the mosquitoes that we now know actually carried the malaria and other diseases wreaking such havoc.[2]

Since the *Macedonian* was going home she could transfer to the *Yorktown* various surplus supplies. Lawrence supervised the stowing of charcoal, cheese, pickles, flannel, molasses, tobacco, raisins, sugar, beef, pork, butter, pine planking, white jackets for the sailors, and pantaloons for the marines. In return the *Macedonian* got some soap and cordage. Additionally, the *Yorktown* took aboard from the shore a boatload of sand (used to scour the decks) and a considerable amount of firewood.[3]

Like every ship operating along the West African coast, the *Yorktown* augmented her crew with a number of men from a coastal ethnic group called the Kru or Kroo. The coast offered little in the way of harbors, and none with piers or wharves suitable for ships; everything had to be lightered to or from the anchorage using small boats. The Kroo, with their own dugout canoes and considerable skill, were ideal for such work. Organized teams would hire on for the duration of a ship's time on the coast. Essentially everything that came or went from West Africa by sea, including slaves, went in Kroo canoes. Distinguished by a blue stripe tattooed from hairline to nose tip, the Kroo were skilled and diligent in their work and were never taken off as slaves. Here the Kroo from the homebound naval vessel simply transfer to her relief. The *Yorktown* had departed New York some twenty men short of her full allowance in order to leave space for the Kroo.

30 November 1844

Wind and weather the same, a gang of five Kroomen joined us today from the Decatur. *They brought with them their canoe, with which they performed many (to us) new and surprising feats, such as clearing her of water when swamped or otherwise filled. They seem a fine tempered set of men. At 1 P.M. Commodore Perry, Captain Mayo and aids came on board, a salute was fired, inspection followed and all soon after this departed. At 4 P.M. hove up and made sail, stood to sea.*

Commodore Perry, an impressive 250-pound bear of a man nicknamed "Old Bruin" by his men, will in a few years achieve fame for opening Japan to American trade. Now fifty, Perry has been involved with U.S. Navy operations on the African coast for years, and played a key role in selecting the site for the American colony at Monrovia. He has been commodore of the African Squadron since its inception in July 1843 when he was sent with the *Macedonian* and two smaller ships to implement the U.S. obligations under the Webster-Ashburton Treaty. His flag captain, Isaac Mayo, has served with Perry before, and the two get along very well despite their quite different attitudes toward slavery. Perry abhors the institution while Mayo has scores of slaves toiling on his Maryland plantation and had strongly opposed the Colonization Movement's effort to send freed American slaves to Africa. Now, however, after visiting the colonies at Monrovia and Cape Palmas, sponsored by the American Colonization Society and the Maryland State Colonization Society, respectively, Mayo has changed his mind. Impressed by the leadership in those colonies and by what has been achieved he enthusiastically supports the policy: "I advocate it to all slaveholders and others."[4] Later himself commodore of the African Squadron, Mayo nevertheless will remain a slave owner until his dying day, and will resign his commission at the outbreak of the Civil War.[5] By the time Lawrence sees him Mayo's face is healed from powder burns suffered in a fracas he and Perry had undergone a year earlier with King Krako in Little Berebee, down the coast from Cape Palmas.

2

December 1844

It appears Captain Bell visited Commodore Perry aboard the flagship *Macedonian* on 28 November, and received oral instructions and a written set of standing orders and circular instructions. Perry followed up with written orders (perhaps delivered during Perry's brief inspection visit to the *Yorktown* on 30 November) in which he instructed Bell to cruise along the African coast, starting at Gallinas (the Kife River in modern Sierra Leone), working south to Cape Mount, Cape Mesurado (Monrovia), and Cape Palmas in Liberia; then along the Gold Coast and the Bights of Benin and Biafra to Gaboon (modern Gabon) where trouble had been reported; and finally as far south as Benguela (in modern Angola) if possible. Bell was then to come back north to Liberia for new orders.

Bell was instructed to look after the welfare of American missionaries and to maintain "the present good feeling between the United States and British vessels of war." Perry made it clear, however, that "the great object of your cruize will be to detect any vessels or citizens of the United States that may be found engaged violating the laws of their country in reference to the Slave Trade and to give general protection and assistance to all American vessels and citizens who may need your aid."[1] Protecting and assisting American vessels and citizens was of course the common mis-

Dale-class sloop of war, circa 1880. No identified pictures of the *Yorktown* are known; this is one of her sisters. U.S. Naval Institute photograph

sion of the U.S. Navy, but Perry placed that role secondary to the specific mission of the African Squadron: to stop slavers. In this he echoed precisely the sentiments expressed in the orders given to him by Secretary of the Navy John Y. Mason.[2]

As the *Yorktown* sails forth to carry out these orders Lawrence offers his own thoughts about slavery. He comments also on the British involvement in the effort to stop it. Though by the Webster-Ashburton Treaty the British and Americans were each obliged to maintain off the coast of Africa the same naval force of eighty guns, the British squadron generally had more ships and its force included steamers. Also, by diplomatic arrangements with the other major trading countries the British could board and detain vessels flying the flags of those nations. The one great exception was the United States. As the secretary of the navy's instructions to the commodore of the African Squadron indicated, after the War of 1812 the British could board a ship flying the American flag only if they had good reason to think it was not really an American ship. Hence a U.S. naval presence was required. Nevertheless, with more ships to board and a more numerous naval force (including steamers) to do the boarding, the British captured many more slave ships than did the Americans.

Lawrence voices skepticism about British motives and results, however, that other American naval men shared, including Captain Bell and Commodore Perry.[3] Some American officers believed that the British sent the many slaves they liberated to their Sierra Leone colony only to ship them on to Britain's Caribbean colonies under indentures that differed little from their former condition. If evidence exists to clarify the matter, it has yet to be made public. American officers also accused their Royal Navy counterparts (though with apparently little justification) of fattening their pockets by waiting until slavers had fully loaded a ship before taking her, thereby increasing the five-pounds-per-head prize money paid by the British government.

AT SEA

1 December 1844

Commences with fine fresh [weather], ship under topgallant sails close hauled heading her course, sailing at the rate of eight and a half and nine knots. Upon further observation of these Kroomen, they prove to be an easy tempered set of men, very respectful in their manners, willing to work and withal very muscular and powerful. Their names are generally furnished them by the people who first employ them; these are called Jack Brown, Tom Nimbly, Jas [James] Grampus, and Dandy Jim. The English have established amongst this tribe, as well as amongst almost all the rest of them on the West Coast of Africa, the idea that they are most humanely striving to arrest the exportation of their country and tribesmen for the purposes of slavery in foreign countries, but it is to be hoped that ere the lapse of many more years even the obtuse and credulous African will be enabled to discern the crafty and deceptive intrigues of Great Britain in this subject. With her factories forsooth! where the Africans who have been captured in battle by some other tribe and intended by the victorious party for the slave-market are again wrested from their hands by the English and sent for a term of three years it is said, to learn useful trades or be made soldiers of. (Sierra Leone is one of these factory stations.) The pursuit of these courses is left, it is set forth by these philanthropists, to their own option, sometimes if these captives themselves think proper [they] are sent to the West Indies or South America, there to be hired out in a state of apprenticeship for three or four years that they may refund to the English government the amount of expenses that their liberation may have cost her. After which time they are allowed to return on board of the ship they have stationed for the purpose at Rio [de] Janeiro, there to remain, or return to their native land as their minds may dictate. After a poor black has been in a state of apprenticeship for four years amongst such people as the Brazilians far into the depths of the forests, there are few apprehensions to be entertained by humane British officers of his ever again making his appearance before them. May revolutions rise from her corrupt heart until their fruits of perfidy, factions and hate produce indiscriminate bloodshed and overflow her confines, and drown every feature of her former self from earth—as a just punishment—for her long practiced and wholesale villainies. The above described plan of operation practiced by Great Britain, bears the air of plausibility so much! Highly philanthropic, nobly disinterested, amiably sympathetic—so characteristic and probable a course for John Bull to pursue without the expectation of reaping a golden harvest! But to drop this tone of irony and speak in real terms of this huge and corrupt hypocrite.

As if the nations were really ignorant of the nature of Britain's policies, she would by these despicable and equivocating pretenses strive to hide from view the shameful and rapacious avarice that betrays itself in all her national treaties and alliances with every nation.

This is the nation that arrogates to herself all the religion and morality of the world! Here is the region to witness English hypocrisy, duplicity, rascality, cupidity, rapacity and in fact villainy in every shape and shade in their

rankest growth; their thrift rivals that of the native vegeta-
tion here, and that is luxuriant enough, god knows!

This is the nation so horrified at the institution of
slavery as it exists in the U.S. (a circumstance at present
unavoidable and ameliorated as much as it possibly can
be) and so strenuous in her exertions to overthrow the
"hateful fabric."

2 December 1844

The "trades" hereabouts begin to decrease in freshness at
the expiration of two or three days more. Having pro-
gressed South four or five degrees we will probably lose the
trade winds altogether, and experience plenty of calms and
sweltering heat. The water hereabouts swarms with fish of
various species, such as Flying Porpoises, Dolphin, Bonitos.
Several poor unfortunate Flying fish, in endeavouring
probably by most desperate flights to escape the rapacity of
Dolphins, came in contact with our sails and consequently
fell into the hands of those who rendered his fate far sev-
erer than it would have been from the Dolphin.

3 December 1844

This day commences with a slight trade breeze far fainter
than that of yesterday—as we lessen our latitude now we
expect to decrease in the same ratio.—Lat. 9°26´ [N] Long.
17°36´ W—at 3 P.M. the wind passed away entirely and a
calm settled upon us leaving us in the enjoyment of a
degree of warmth equal to 82° of Fahrenheit. The monot-
ony of the evening was a little broken in upon by the cap-

*ture of a small shark of some 4 or 5 feet in length. This was
a triumph of dexterity of boatswain in the use of a harpoon. The shark is rather strong in flavour and consequently not a very choice fish for culinary purposes.*

4 December 1844

*Commences very hot and calm weather. The ocean at times
has hardly a perceptible motion—cats' paws tantalizingly
spring up every few minutes, and then all is calm again.*

5 December 1844

*Set in with a very tolerable breeze today enabling us to
make 129 miles—Lat. 8°01´ [N] Long. 10° [W]—The
morning air now is filled with the most delightful odors, of
plants and trees from the aromatic land of Africa.*

*There is a great deal of interesting information to be
gained concerning this caste of Africans at present on board
of us. It seems as if by general though tacit agreement of
those nations engaged in the slave trade, that this tribe of
Africans shall be exempted from the liability of being kidnapped or otherwise reduced to a state of slavery. This
exemption of course has been adopted from the consciousness of the necessity of these people's services on this dangerously insalubrious coast where the constitution of the
white man would fail in the performance of some of the
indispensable labours to be performed here in this peculiar
trade. So that, these facts being considered, it would not be
politic to steal these people, though avarice might ever so
strongly prompt it. It is a strange fact, that these men*

should be so void of all sympathy as to aid the white in the carrying their countrymen into captivity. Such is nevertheless the case. Oh! for a spirit-stirring glass of Rum! to cheer the cockles of my heart, to act as a spur to the dull pace of my genius—for methinks the calm now settled upon us accompanied with heat and fog almost tangible do[es] bear down upon our souls like the nightmares in the breast of a blood guilty man. Oh for a breeze even though gentle as a zephyr to deliver us from this foul oppression of dense vapors. Lord! I rush on deck for relief, if attainable, of a little fresh air!

6 December 1844

This day cannot be considered as superior in point of affording any more remarkable incidents than yesterday. A light zephyr impelled us at the rate of two knots until 4 o'clock when it fainted away and we were rocked into drowsiness by the insinuating ground swell that agitated the ocean's bosom.

The ship's company enjoyed today the transporting and salubrious exercise of an ocean bathe. A studding sail being expanded from the ship's side as a protection from any obtrusive piscatorial visitation in the shape of sharks, that might chance to be made about that time. An impoverished and harassed species of the ornithological tribe sought temporary repose upon one of the extremities of this vessel's spars today and was actually captured in a state of apparent somnolency, by the simple act of a manual extension and simultaneous contraction of the digital termination of the arm by one of the minions. After having been

subjected to a brief examination of his corporeal constitution, he was emancipated and allowed to indulge in any
spontaneous impulse to aerial elevation or exaltation that
might prompt him.

I do love to indulge a Little now and then in a
Learned style.

7 December 1844

Light airs and calm. The lead was frequently hove this day
but no bottom found. A small but insidious current, say a
half knot per hour, sits towards the Southward and
Eastward.

8 December 1844

Pleasant but calm weather—thermometer ranging from 79
to 86°; water ranging generally one or two degrees higher.
The lead hereabouts was hove every hour, bottom at 25
and 28 fathoms (no land in sight) which was of black sand,
mud and fine gravel. Fish seem to be pretty plentiful
around here, but very shy of bait; even the sharks usually
so voracious are quite coy—performing all sorts of gambols, such as cutting circles, shooting at a considerable distance from the ship then diving, and coming up at a
greater [word missing—familiarity?] than ever, just like
some pretty young girls that [I] have known under the
influence of certain feelings, rising from the sight of young
men. A few pilot fish we have caught by line for amusement more than anything else. These fish are a true
emblem of the sycophant of society; they adhere to the

shark through all scenes and adventures, with the view of deriving a portion of the prey that he may capture, thus escaping all exertion themselves that procuring their own food would cost.

9 December 1844

Commences calm and light airs alternately. At 1 P.M. through the lurid atmosphere on the larboard bow was discovered the continent of Africa—the land that (when seen for the first time) fills the mind of a man of even only common information and reading with such a variety of interesting reflections and associations from lofty to bad. It is a land memorable for some of the greatest nations that ever rose up in the then known world. Egypt, Carthage, Tyre, Sidon, Phoenicia, and Morocco are a few whose grandeur we have distinct accounts of and were remarkable above all the rest of the world at that time for their prowess in war, their superiority in the arts of every species, their excellence in architecture, the inexhaustible fertility of their fields, the surpassing skill in the arts of agriculture of their husbandmen, and the intense and extraordinary and even sublime knowledge and learning of their sages in the sciences of Astronomy, and the mathematics and national polity. In another point of view it is remarkable for its peculiar natural features of landscape, such as its vast and terrific deserts, which first strike upon the memory in reviewing this catalogue, upon whose vast flat sandy plains nothing may be discerned but the heat quivering high in air and in such intensity as to lead to the belief of the impracticability of their ever being traversed by man, and again its forests

of thrice interwoven and almost impervious vegetation
teeming with millions of animals, whose match for ferocity
and gigantic size the universe cannot produce; such as the
Lion, Tiger, Elephant, Rhinoceros and Hippopotamus and
amongst reptiles the awful Boa Constrictor. And then
comes the saddening theme for reflection of the long series
of years of slavery, intense suffering and degradation to
which the inhabitants of this vast continent have been sub-
jected, even from time immemorial. We read of the "Black
African Slave" in documents whose antiquity surpasses
that of the Bible by many ages. It would seem that the
world by tacit consent and agreement have selected the
African from all the universe for their slaves, whom they
place upon the footing of dumb creatures, or even ani-
mated machines to do their biddings implicitly without
either demur, hesitation or questioning. Schemes of the
most revolting nature either to morality or of a physical
nature when to be executed the negro is selected for their
performance. Laborious tasks which no white man could
endure are imposed upon the black man without the least
consideration of his sufferings, or capability. Stripes are
dealt to him unsparingly to hasten his exertions, coarse
fare is penuriously dealt to him, the term of sleep allowed
him is unnaturally brief and he is awakened by the lash or
goad and driven to labor. And yet through all this he lives
for years, his heart breaks not; and when the rare occasion
is allowed him of a few extra hours for repose or recreation
he forgets his tasks of labor, his stripes, yea! all his griev-
ances—he laughs, dances, and enjoys the short respite
granted him to its utmost extent without reflection for
either the past or future. And this pliant and yielding

nature of the African procures for him the reputation of having been intended by nature as a slave. Alas! The poor black! When will the time come when you shall stand among the nations of earth and be considered by them as a man—as a free man? I fear, not until your black complexion shall be changed.

10 December 1844

Commences with heavy squalls and abundance of thunder, lightning and rain. At about 10:30 P.M. at night the ship was thrown into an unusual uproar by the approach of a large black vessel astern, which afterwards proved to be one of the numerous English steamers that cruise on the whole extent of this coast (the present one's name was the Ardent, *Commander Russell). The extraordinary commotion into which this ship was thrown was on many accounts ludicrous and at the same time mortifying. The night being very dark the steamer could not be discerned until she was within a very short distance of us, when (being of course ignorant of her character or nature) quarters were quick[ly] beat and orders rapidly passed for the watch below to hurry on deck. Then commenced the rush—some supposing that a desperate slaver not aware of our character was about to open fire upon or board us, others that we were about to engage an English Steamer, still others that we were in danger of going ashore. At all events we were in as unprepared state as an enemy could have wished. The marines rushed to their quarters with wooden flints in their muskets and [except for] the few that happened to think to snatch cartrouche boxes in the general haste, were as guiltless of cartridges as the baby but an hour old is of sexual desires. Several of the guns that should have been relied upon as most effective in case of an action were rendered perfectly useless by being made use of as supports for large turkey and chicken coops. The Captain of one of these guns was heard to utter, after his gun had been partially disencumbered of a large turkey coop—"Damn my eyes eef the powder in this ere gun's touch hole ain't drowned with Turkey shit!"—Several others in attempting to run the guns out, found the side tackle falls to slide through their grasps, and leave them in a prostrate state, which upon examination were found to have been exposed to the lubricating process of certain chickens suffering from Dysentery or Green Sickness. The quarter gunners had their dilemmas to encounter too—the berth deck being so very dark, no lights being allowed (the expense of such necessaries being out of the question), the articles necessary in time of action, such as passing boxes, match rope, hot fires etc. etc., could not be found until the supposed hostile vessel had finished her speaking, got under way and dropped astern half a mile when two match staves were found in a state of readiness all to being lighted, which was done by an old deaf quarter gunner after an elapse of about ten minutes spent in groping about in quest of a light. The man stationed at the shot and wad locker I found was missing, but after I had myself cleared away to that portion of the ammunition the said man made his appearance in great haste asking me if I thought the action would probably last long enough to require the shot and wad locker to be opened, seeing that each gun had a charge in already besides six wads apiece in the nets, and the racks round the hatches were chock full of shot, so he didn't see no use n'openin the locker till them were on deck was used up. Considering the whole affair it might be set down as one of the broadest burlesques, whose equal could not have been produced upon the Park boards. About half an hour after this occurrence, tranquility being restored on ship board, a turmoil anything but celestial was raised in the upper regions, that threatened devastation indeed, storming thunder, blinding lightning, and drowning rain was the order of this elementary conflict. The sail was reduced to treble reefed topsails and Ye Topmast Staysail. At about 9:30 next morning the weather cleared up and the African shore was visible at the distance of ten miles. The appear-ance of the land along the seaboard very much resembles that of Florida, Georgia, the Carolinas and most of the Southern district of the United States. At 10 A.M. another English ship hove in sight; at 11:30 she stopped her way and sent aboard a boat, with a lieutenant who informed us that the name of this vessel was the English Steamer* Growler—*Commander Buckle—and that she had cap-tured within three weeks a slaver containing 300 slaves.*

The official *Yorktown* log entry for the incident involving the *Ardent* reads only "From 8 to midt light breezes and cloudy with lightning. At 10:30 discovered a steamer astern. Beat to quarters and cast loose the guns. Spoke HBMs steamer *Ardent* Commander Russell from Sheban secured the guns."

As was often done the *Growler* gave the *Yorktown* mail for the direction that ship was headed—in this case letters addressed to Governor Roberts in Monrovia, which the *Growler* had received from another ship a few days earlier.[4]

The coast to be patrolled by the *Yorktown* is largely, as Lawrence indicates, rather low and flat. Notable heights occur at two important places: one is Cape Mesurado, site of Liberia's capital Monrovia, and the other is Cape Mount, where Lawrence and his fellow officers will first set foot on the soil of the African continent.

CAPE MOUNT

11 December 1844

Temperature of the weather very pleasant, depth of water varies from twenty-eight to thirty-eight fathoms, black, yellow, white and green sands, sometimes mud, are the qualities of the bottom. At 5 P.M. a light breeze sprung, carrying us along at the rate of four and a half knots the hour. At 5:30 Cape Mount appeared in sight, distance thirty-five miles. Two more English steamers in sight—this coast literally swarms with this kind of vessel—it must be a money making station that so many are ordered here. At 7:00 wore ship to the South and West; appearances very squally; clewed down and treble reefed the Topsail, hauled down Jib and hoisted Ye Topmast staysail. Along the first watch short squalls of wind accompanied with heavy rain, intensely vivid lightning and hoarse bellowing thunder, which taken in conjunction gave the evening a highly poetical character, but the worst of these kind[s] of evenings is that the higher these poetical traits are carried, personal comfort is lessened in an inverse ratio.

12 December 1844

A four and a half knot breeze sprung up this day. At 5

*o'clock when within four miles of the land (Cape Mount)
two canoes came off from the shore to the ship: the first
contained three of the native negroes perfectly innocent of
any shred of dress about their bodies lower than their heads
on which were straw hats, around which were wrapped
cotton handkerchiefs for the purpose of placing round their
middles when they came on board, which they did just
before ascending the side. Their figures were most
admirably muscular, without the least superfluity of fat
about them and consequently well adapted for the performance of any act requiring agility and strength. From
incessant exposures to the elements, that they are accustomed to, a white incrustation of salt was perceptible upon
their hides. Their visages were long, thin and wrinkled—
and altogether highly repulsive to look upon, their teeth
very large, far apart and protruding some to give a very
ferocious aspect, which is rather heightened by a thin
growth of neglected beard about the throat—although they
are actually very mild and amiable. Their salutations to
the Kroomen on board here were very curious, which consisted of an unfriendly push, then an extension of the hand
terminated by snapping the thumb and middle finger in
the palm of the other. Their business on board here was to
bring a document from an English Captain whose vessel
had been blown off the coast the night previously while he
was ashore, but in a few minutes the Captain in question
came on board himself in this second canoe. He proved to
be a large vulgar, thick bluff headed looking Englishman,
without a coat, in a striped undressed cotton shirt, white
flannel pants and straw hat. This worthy was accompanied
by another, apparently a supercargo—and a complete spec-*

imen, a little contemptible but impudent and self-conceited
cockney. His dress was a lead colored sack of worsted, but-
toned up to show to advantage, probably as he though[t] a
complete model of symmetry; pink striped shirt and pantaloons of thick white blanketing, round topped broad
brimmed hat of grey felt and slippers completed his dress.
When addressed this London jackanapes erected himself,
folded his arms, and gave utterance to his ideas in a most
stately style. His general grotesque appearance was heightened by a thistle down colored moustache and beard about
the eighth of an inch long [that] bore more resemblance to
huge sweat drops on a dirty ground (to use a painter's
phrase) than any description of beard that I ever saw. The
third person of this party was a Portuguese settler here; his
appearance and mode of conversing were indicative of his
country, is all that can be remarked of him. It seemed by
the Captain's account that the vessel under his command
as above stated had been obliged to go to sea on account of
heavy weather—and that as she had not made her reap-
pearance, he felt very uneasy lest she have gone to the bottom or elsewhere. She was a brig of three hundred tons
with a crew of thirteen men and two mates, and he came
on board here to ascertain if anything of her description
(which he gave) had been seen by us. We told him no, and
all three departed in the direction of a vessel in sight again
to try his luck. At 5:30 clewed up and came to in sixteen
fathoms water (forty-five chain), Cape Mount looming up
ahead of us magnificently to a height of three thousand feet
and covered to the very pinnacle with the loftiest and otherwise largest sized trees. [In the process of anchoring the
Yorktown is surrounded by a swarm of dugout canoes,

*each about twenty feet long and paddled by three or four
naked but well-proportioned men.]⁵ This bay in which we
are at anchor is called "Sugari Bay." Upon going on the
Forecastle at an early hour in the morning I was struck by
the delightful aromatic odors that were wafted to us by the
light land breeze. As the sun rose and consequently the
light grew stronger, the scenery circumscribing the bay
became fully developed and appeared in all the grandeur
that ever has been ascribed to the scenery of this country.
The distance from which in a line from the shore is perhaps
three quarters of a mile—at which distance the trees which
compose this forest which covers the side of the mount,
seem so uniform in their height as to appear like some of
those artificial groves shaped into models of Grottoes and
Pillared edifices that are to be seen in many of the public
gardens and private estates in England and France. The
trunks of these trees under discussion are perfectly straight
and upright resembling some vast green temple. The shrub-
bery and underwood are very thick and about three feet in
height. The axe of the white man has been at some time
actively employed on the side of this mountain probably for
the purpose of procuring some of the valuable timber with
which these regions abound, such as African Oak, Lignum
Vitae, and Teakwood.*

*Back from the shore to the distance of three hundred
feet on the Sugari River is situated a native village called
Sugari, which is governed and owned by a chief with a
name something like Sandfeese [actually Gaje, also known
as Sanfish or Sandfish].⁶ To this place at about 9 o'clock we
went to visit this personage who happened to be here at the
time, for he does not reside here, and who proved to be a*

very formidable looking savage, aged I should think about fifty-five or sixty years, rather thin, and with a white beard and grizzled head. He welcomed us quite gracefully. He was surrounded by numerous courtiers, as I suppose they must be termed, variously tattooed and decorated. The fashion of some of their tattooing was altogether different from what I had ever before witnessed, which was in white. The ladies of the court are not beauties of a character to please an American or European taste, although their figures in most cases, especially of some of the "virgins," of which there were a large number, were of most perfect symmetry of form. We could judge of them to the utmost limits, as no obstruction to our view in the way of articles of dress encumbered their bodies. A French brig of war being at anchor in the bay, the officers belonging to her were making merry at the House of the gentleman I took for a Portuguese (but who now proves to be an Italian), and which is a very decent habitation for the country, to which is adjoined quite a beautiful and luxuriant garden. The information of this gentleman upon matters pertaining to the country was various and valuable and amusing. After strolling along in several directions, we all went on board. The brig in quest of last night passed under our stern at 2 o'clock—with the Captain J. R. Parker on board—her name the Arabian.

13 December 1844

Weather the same—at about 4 p.m. this day the objectioned supercargo of the Arabian *was again on board of this ship to know if our Captain would ship a man said to*

*be an American sailor who was discontented on board of
his brig. He was brought on board, examined by the doctor,
and received by the Captain. The man as might be
expected gave rather a bad account of things on board,
which account we divided by two to obtain a dividend
something like truth. Amongst other things he said the
Captain of the* Arabian *had complained that he had not
met with respect and notice commensurate with his rank
and standing. This insolence I conceive to be near the
truth—his appearance is an index to the inner man. I
know of no comparison that would produce in one's mind
an adequate notion of this man's vulgar and generally
repulsive appearance than that of a half wild hog in an
upright position. Our Captain when he first noticed the
fellow come on board dressed as before described, with a
large bloated face like a half boiled duff with two black
grapes stuck in it for eyes, very properly asked him his business, gave him the required information and paid no further attention to him. He probably expected to be asked in
the cabin, to bouse out a gallon of Brandy, then be decently
hoisted over the side into his boat; that would have been
whole souled hospitality—"Dam my 'art."*[7]

14 December 1844

*Upon revisiting this small town, which several of us did
this day, I saw and learned much more, respecting this and
the surrounding tribes, modes of living adapted by the settlers, etc. As we came alongside of a little mole erected by
Mr. Carnot, the gentleman twice spoken of, who I now find
to be a retired Italian slave trade Captain, we found the*

Inspection and sale. One of the slavers in this picture
may represent Captain Canot himself.
Brantz Mayer, *Captain Canot: or Twenty Years of an African Slaver*,
New York: D. Appleton & Co., 1856.

*chief Sandfeese in company with another chief very much
of his own appearance and probably of his own age—envi-
roned by their warrior courtiers just upon the eve of departure for their homes. It seems that the object of their visit
here was to have a matter adjusted between Sandfeese and
another chief young and full of vigor. The affair was something like this: the latter individual had been like Romulus
of old guilty in some late incursion of seizing upon and
carrying away to his own country some seventy of this old
chief['s] female subjects—and to judge from the calm and
even scornful indifference with which he treated everything
and everybody about, was as little inclined to make repara-
tion as if he had never been reminded of the small circumstance. The affair was confessed (the young chief being so
far willing to humour the old chap) to Mr. Carnot (who is
a man of vast importance here amongst these savages) who
was to act as umpire in the case. But the old chief accompanied by his ally, and trains, each of the old men with
umbrellas over their heads—had to depart with neither
satisfaction or the least distant hope of it. The young chief
(whose name I can't remember) being the stronger party,
damned all justice in the settlement of the affair, and he
could not be induced to listen to any arrangement—even
the promise of the restoration of the women or any portion
of them was embargoed.*

The second old chief would be Fanatoro, or Fan Tolo. Captain
Bell reports the meeting to the secretary of the navy as follows: "I
met at Canot's the captain of the French Brigantine, the *Eglantine,*
who had come there for the purpose of holding a Palaver with
King Fanatoro the sovereign of Cape Mount, including about 25

miles of coast. Fanatoro soon made his appearance with about a dozen of his suite, principally his grandchildren. He was a venerable looking Negro, his white beard descending a few inches below his chin, had a blue cotton mantle ornamented with red and white embroidery thrown over him which descended a little below his knees; his arms and legs were bare. He said he was 82 years of age and from his appearance I have little doubt of it."[8] The younger chief was Fanatoro's son-in-law, George Cain, who had not been pleased when he learned of the sale of land to Canot. The connection between the controversy Lawrence describes and the palaver with the French captain is not clear.

The dresses of these negroes of the upper society as they consider themselves are really very graceful and I must assert without the highest degree of exaggeration upon the subject that I discover very little if any difference between the Roman Toga and that of these negroes. This may seem perhaps a ridiculous comparison but it is by no means so if the representations that have been handed down to us of the Romans are not false. The drapery that these savages use is gathered and confined at each shoulder—on the one more than on the other and allowed to fall down in large folds as far down as the half length of the leg. The articles of cloths made use of are sometimes Red and Yellow flannel, and Broad Cloths, striped and crossbarred calicoes, the latter giving a resemblance to the style of the Highlander of Scotland's dress, but, the heads of these people are covered with any thing that a fantastical taste may prompt, without regard to any fixed fashion. But in conclusion to this matter, as before stated, to describe the style of these people['s] dress would be but an account of the ancient styles [of] Greece and Rome.

*The personal appearance of old Sandfeese and his
friend deserve[s] a little more notice than has been
bestowed upon as yet. Really a very patriarchal and venerable air is attached to these old men. They are spare and
from age the proportions of their lips and features generally
are much reduced and consequently less disgusting and
sensual in their expressions than the most of negroes.
Besides their beards were white as snow, and trimmed crit-
ically square, imparting a civilised air to them. Their eyes
being quick and bright seemed to give intelligence to their
countenances. Of the wives, daughters, Virgins, maids,
concubines and all the rest of the female portion composing
their trains but little can be said—their dresses in the first
place are of such a simple character as to be unworthy of
description, only consisting of a rag bound round the
pelvis. Of their features the less said the better—the tribute
of praise due their formation has been awarded to them so
nothing more can be said of them. I cannot and never
could lay claim to but a very small amount of modesty,
where women are concerned, but I feel that all of it has
now evaporated, from the prodigal display of the female
form that here meets the eye; from those portions usually
exposed to those that (in most nations) are sacred, and
hidden from vulgar inspection. At home a view of what is
termed the private parts of females is attended with considerable expense—but here—bubbies of all dimensions and
of all consistencies from pumpkin size and jelly soft to goose
eggs bulk and apple hard—Stomachs from rotund to herring like gauntness, all degrees in breadth and description
of pelvis—Buttocks from high peaked to low and flat—
thighs from round and plump to long and scrawny—legs*

from posts to drumsticks—all these proportions are to be seen in such abundance as to cease to be curious; they are a drug to the view. After partaking of refreshments furnished by Mrs. Carnot [Rosaline Smith], who by the bye is a very handsome mulatto and was brought up with one of our officers in Georgia state, and upon recognition of each other[,] embraces of a nature so strong and fervent were exchanged between them that I was afraid they might have been the means of checking the source of our refreshments.[9] For I apprehended the Husband of this lady might become jealous and grow suddenly grave and forget to press us to take any more brandy and water and bread butter and cheese to match. But however after continuing a good hour and a half in relating many past circumstances that had passed between herself and above gentleman and giving a short account of his own parentage, life and advent to this country, we shook hands, received a message from this lady to her mother residing at Monrovia, jumped into our boat and came on board ship. Where we have slept, set Topsails, Topgallant sails, courses and Jib—then tripped our anchor, catted and fished it and stood to sea. [Before modern stockless anchors were developed a ship's anchor was secured by being "catted" or brought up to a protruding timber called a cathead, and "fished," that is, having the flukes hoisted up and stowed onto an anchor bed.] I must mention before closing this day's remarks that the French officers attached to the brig now lying here, and stationed on this coast, called the Eglantine, *have learnt the art of spending the time here agreeably through the means of fishing, gunning, drinking, womaning. We met them here and felt rather flat when our muskets which were carried ashore in case of*

*meeting any game, were contrasted with their splendid
pieces.*

Mr. "Carnot," who at first so little impressed Lawrence, was
indeed a person of considerable importance and historical as well
as literary significance. Born in the Piedmont of northwestern Italy
as Théophile Conneau, he was the son of an Italian mother and a
Napoleonic officer who died at Waterloo. After a rather picaresque
seagoing youth he began his career as a slaver, becoming an agent
for the notorious Pedro Blanco. Apparently feeling the social pres-
sures mounting against slavery, especially as embodied by the
British Navy, Canot (as he and others commonly spelled his name
during his time in Africa) announced his retirement from that line
of work and in 1841 settled at Cape Mount as a legitimate trader
and entrepreneur. There, by treaty with the local chiefs, he
"bought" the entire region—many square miles.

When Lawrence meets him Canot is forty years old, and owns
an establishment (which he calls New Florence) that includes some
twenty-five buildings and perhaps a hundred people, of whom
forty are slaves. The American officers can observe a blacksmith
shop, a sawpit, and a shipyard where a small ship for coastal trade
is under construction. A diverted stream flows through a wicker-
lined perimeter ditch irrigating a neatly square plantation of a
dozen acres. Here flourish corn, cassada, sweet potatoes, figs, plantains, and other fruits, as well as salad greens and even flowers.[10]
This African Xanadu, however, is not without its voices prophecy-
ing war: eight cannon, kept always loaded, protect Canot's fortified
house.[11] Just before the *Yorktown*'s arrival Canot had driven off an
attack by neighboring natives. He is in fact near the peak of his
legitimate career. Within three years the suspicion (already afoot)
that Canot is involving himself in his old ways will cause the local
ruler (George Cain, who has by then succeeded upon the death of
old Fanatoro), at the British Navy's urging, to act against him. Cain

will burn Canot's establishment to the ground during his absence and threaten to shoot him should he return. Leaving Africa for good, Canot goes to South America and then the United States. Living in Baltimore in 1854 he publishes his memoirs simultaneously in Paris, New York, and London. *Captain Canot: or Twenty Years of an African Slaver* is a remarkably detailed and candid account, and a great classic on the Atlantic slave trade. Well connected in France (his brother, Napoleon III's personal physician and close associate, presents the captain to the emperor and empress), in 1855 Canot becomes the French colonial agent in New Caledonia. Invalided to France, Canot dies there in 1860. His new American wife, Eliza McKinley (who trades socially on her false claim to be the sister of William McKinley), outlives him by an incredible seventy-two years, dying in 1932.[12]

At the time of the *Yorktown*'s visit, Canot is flying a modified French flag (the tricolor with a star in the middle) and is at least informally under French protection, as the presence of the French frigate, the *Eglantine,* indicates.[13] At other times he has flown the Union Jack, and in this very period he is negotiating with both the British and the Liberians about placing his territory under the protection of one of their governments.[14]

Canot's present wife Rosaline, now twenty-nine, was born free in Georgia and emigrated to Liberia with a large contingent of relatives in 1835. Though she has been Canot's wife for only a few years, they have a large and heterogeneous household. The 1843 census of Liberia lists her (then living in Monrovia), as the mother of four children aged two to thirteen. Only the youngest is Canot's. Additionally, she and Canot are listed as the parents of eight children aged eleven to sixteen. This second group, however, are probably indigenous Africans adopted by Canot as apprentices.[15]

Though Lawrence may not know it, Captain Bell has encountered Canot before. In 1840, when Bell made his previous visit to Africa as a lieutenant in command of the *Dolphin,* the then-governor of Liberia, Thomas Buchanan, persuaded Bell to visit New Sester where Canot, with other slave traders, was then headquartered. With Buchanan aboard Bell dropped anchor off New Sester and sent a note to the local ruler, urging him to evict the slavers; the request met with refusal. Bell then sent a threatening letter directly to the slavers, telling them "you must break up your establishments at this point, in two weeks from this date; failing to do so, I shall take such measures as I consider necessary to obtain this object." Arriving home a few days later, Canot took it upon himself to reply. Perhaps confident that the crew of a 10-gun ship could hardly do the job against any sort of resistance, Canot thumbed his nose at the idea. Suggesting the hypocrisy of such a threat from the U.S. Navy while slavery still thrived in the American South, and noting that the Liberian colonies had been set up as refuges for people whom the laws of America "cannot protect in their native country," he declared that he would resist "by force of arms." In sending his threat Bell had counted upon Buchanan's proffer of support by the Liberian militia. When Buchanan proved unable to muster enough troops, Bell found himself unable to back up what proved to be an empty threat.[16]

Fluent in at least four languages and literate in Latin as well, Canot is capable of considerable charm and wit. He is accustomed to selling provisions to visiting naval vessels and hosting their officers. On this occasion Canot surely must savor the act of making welcome the officers whose captain he had earlier faced down. Captain Bell, on the other hand, must have had mixed feelings indeed when forced to greet Canot aboard the *Yorktown* and later when he went ashore to New Florence.

Meanwhile, the *Yorktown* purchases no fresh provisions here; the crew dines on the usual salt pork and beef.

AT SEA

15 December 1844

Commences with nearly calm weather, varied by light showers, nothing occurred of any importance today. Cape Mesurado, upon which is built Monrovia, is in sight at the distance twenty-five miles. At about 11 o'clock today appeared from the ship about two hundred yards a huge sea turtle of probably 300 or 400 weight floating on the water, which when perceived by our Kroomen, three of them divested themselves of their clothing in a twinkling and were in the Ocean in chase of him; but the Turtle dived when they got within the space of forty or fifty feet. But the chase did not end here, and a submarine pursuit took place which was astonishing as well as amusing to witness; one would hardly suppose that men could acquire such perfection in swimming as they practice.

The next day the *Yorktown* arrives at Cape Mesurado and Monrovia. Passing the cape she takes aboard twelve additional Kroomen.[17] Officially these men are logged in as Jack Guappo, Poor Fellow, William Walker, Jack West, Jack Brown 2d, Jack Flypan, Ben Grando, Jack Crowbar, Prince of Wales, Black Will, Jack Roberts, and Tom Dollar.[18] As the Kroomen brought their own canoes on board, the *Yorktown* now has several on deck in addition to her own complement of boats—a launch, three cutters, and a gig.

16 December 1844

At 4:30 a sea breeze sprung up and we increased our speed towards Cape Mesurado at the rate of four and a half knots per Hour. At 5:30 we were boarded by four canoes, manned by Kroomen lately discharged from the employ of the Decatur *and now destined for this ship. Most of them had some token, presents from white men as testimonials of good behavior, fidelity and so on on different trying occasions. [When] the character of this caste of Africans is considered, admiration for their very many good traits cannot be withheld even by those most prejudiced against the race (of which there are a great many and often without any reason). They are naturally very tractable, very docile, very obedient, and very abstemious in the use of liquor. They are under the direction of one of their own people called head Krooman, who exercises his authority, which is nearly absolute, with great judgement and discretion. Generally speaking they are inclined to taciturnity, requiring no driving when work is to be dispatched; on the contrary they work cheerfully. Monrovia is their headquarters where they have a large town built of huts. I find a system of apprenticeship is an institution in vogue amongst them.*

At 6:15 clewed up topsails, down Jib, rounded to with the Spanker, let go the Larboard anchor in seven and a half fathoms water twenty-five fathoms chain. We found the U.S. Brig Truxton *at anchor here and learnt that a duel had been fought between Mr. Hurst and Mr. Creighton, the former First Lieutenant, the second acting sailing master; cause of the duel as in most instances grew out of some hair splitting affair of no weight whatever. Upon learning*

> *the particulars out of the hearing of the principals on the*
> *occasion, I was filled with admiration by the cool and pol-*
> *ished bravery displayed—intrepidity that would have*
> *adorned a better cause or more important one.*

Duels were looked upon with considerable disfavor by the naval hierarchy. Such private conflicts did not support good order and discipline and took officers out of action, often when they could ill be spared. The secretary of the navy and the squadron commodores issued stern directives against the practice.[19] In the African Squadron, with its long deployments, grueling operations, and recreation limits set by the sanitary rules that forbade anyone to spend a night ashore, men probably were more irascible than the typical crew at sea. At any rate, the impression was that dueling was more likely to occur among that squadron than elsewhere.

Lawrence's impression of the affair between Hurst and Creighton is borne out in the official record. While the *Truxtun* was anchored off Prince Island on the evening of 15 November, Hurst spoke roughly to Creighton for having made some noise in the room next to the wardroom. One thing led to another, and the next day the two men found themselves preparing for a duel. As Creighton was new to the ship he asked Passed Midshipman McDonough, already Hurst's second, to be his second as well. The antagonists had apparently heretofore been on good terms, and both now sought to avoid the encounter through intermediaries. Apparently largely owing to McDonough's insistence on adherence to the perceived fine points of custom (it appears he was more interested in having the duel proceed properly than in preventing it), these efforts failed. The entire series of events transpired without the captain's knowledge, as he would have stopped the matter at once. The next morning just after dawn, and careful not to awaken the captain, the parties to the dispute quietly took a boat ashore. The group was augmented by the surgeon's mate (tourniquets in hand) and another officer whom Creighton (suspecting McDonough of bias toward Hurst) had at the last minute asked to be his second. The two men, each clutching a "borrowed" *Truxtun* pistol, paced off, turned, and fired. Hurst, who gallantly avoided aiming at Creighton, fell to the latter's bullet—shot through both legs, with one broken. Creighton flew to his fallen adversary, clasped his hand, and apologized, all the while vehemently accusing McDonough of being responsible for the whole thing.[20]

Upon learning of the duel the secretary of the navy took a direct interest in it. Letters and testimony flowed up and down the chain of command for a year and a half. Hurst recovered and stayed in the navy until his death years later. McDonough eventually retired as a captain, and Creighton as a commodore.

Still Hurst was for the time being out of action. The captain of the *Truxtun* felt obliged to cut short his cruise along the African coast and convey his wounded first lieutenant to Monrovia and then to Porto Praya, whence he was sent home. The captain blamed Hurst, believing that as the first lieutenant (second only to the captain) Hurst ought to have followed regulations and avoided the duel. In addition to disease and the need for prize crews, such duels drained officers from the African Squadron.

Lawrence gives a further description of Monrovia, and speculates on the future of this colony of former slaves.

MONROVIA, CAPE MESURADO

17 December 1844

The aspect of this town is really most beautiful and certainly a most eligible site was chosen for it, when facilities for mercantile matters are considered. Its harbor, which is

Street in Monrovia
Anna M. Scott, *Day Dawn in Africa,* New York: Protestant Episcopal Society for
the Promotion of Evangelical Knowledge, 1858.

*large and commodious, is well sheltered from any violent
storms to which the latitude is liable, on account of the
height of the Cape beyond; and upon the most elevated
part of this promontory, there is one grand detraction to
this village and that is the proximity of a marsh. Although
of no very great extent, still it must give rise to pestiferous
malaria, productive of fever. The construction of the houses
here is upon the American plan (as might be supposed),
composed of stone, wood, etc. Who knows but that it may
be destined for the seat of a great nation yet? Doubtless this
colony even though so inconsiderable as it is at present
must, after becoming a nation, have its term of grandeur
like all others. What did the republic of Greece spring from
but a small colony planted originally by Cadmus the
Egyptian? What was the origin of Rome? Where were savages to be found of more obtuse intellects, more intractable,
more averse and displaying less docility in acquiring the
arts and general characteristics of enlightenment than the
ancient English? These people labor under no greater dis-
advantages than other nations in their infancy.*

*Carthage and many oriental cities might be cited as
instances w[h]ere the black race have attained great
national splendor, if their color should be used as an argu-
ment of their never being able to aspire to greatness; I conceive that a black skin and medium intellects in a people
are not always infallible concomitants and insurmountable
barriers to a course of national exaltation. The inhabitants
here, although a race of liberated slaves, possess much
urbanity of manner, much kindness of disposition, which
evinces itself in the hospitality extended towards strangers.
Quite a degree of intelligence is to be met with here to*

which they have begun to give form and embodiment such
as in the issuing of a monthly newspaper and one or two
other small periodicals. All things must have a beginning—
So must this embryo great nation. An army of five hundred
men this place can muster amongst other things—
Colonels, Majors, Captains etc abound, much to the same
extent as they do in all small villages in new settled parts
in the United States.

Monrovia had been established with U.S. government support
in 1822 by the American Colonization Society, which, after a false
start further north, had purchased from local rulers several hundred square miles of territory around Cape Mesurado. Monrovia's
governor was appointed and paid by the Society, which also for
decades underwrote most of the costs of the colony.

Lawrence may already have been ashore the afternoon of
17 December when the boatswain's pipe twittered, sideboys assem-
bled at the gangway, and Joseph J. Roberts, governor of Liberia,
stepped aboard the *Yorktown*. Following a thirteen-gun salute
Roberts, accompanied by Liberian general Lewis, dined in the
cabin with Captain Bell.[21] A light-skinned freeborn mulatto from
Virginia in his thirties, Roberts had come to Liberia fifteen years
earlier and prospered as a trader, becoming one of the wealthiest
men in Monrovia.

The effort of the Colonization Movement to send American
freedmen to settle Africa brought together remarkably disparate
interests. Adherents included abolitionists and philanthropists
who believed free blacks would flourish best in a land of their own,
away from the country where they had been slaves. Supporters also
thought such settlements would hasten the civilization and
Christianization of the native African population, and discourage
the slave trade. However, some of the movement's strongest advo-
cates were southern slaveholders who wished to remove from their

states the destabilizing presence of freedmen and thus strengthen the institution of slavery. Thus, the stated goal of the colonization societies was not to free slaves, but rather to remove to Africa slaves that had been freed. Kentucky slaveholder Henry Clay (who in 1820–21 had engineered the Missouri Compromise, which established an equal balance between free and slave states) was president of the American Colonization Society for years. On the other hand some slaveholders doubted the practicality of colonization and many abolitionists attacked the movement for detracting from the greater goal of eliminating slavery. Freed African-Americans were generally unenthusiastic and even hostile to the idea. To send the millions of American slaves to settle in Africa would never have been remotely practical, and indeed the colonization effort scarcely dented the growing numbers of free people of color in the United States. But the American Colonization Movement did create Liberia and supported it year after year with money, shipments of goods, and occasional infusions of new settlers.

The U.S. government had its own motive for supporting Liberia: following the British model in Sierra Leone, Liberia became the destination for slaves found aboard ships captured by the navy. By 1844 a total of about two hundred fifty such "recaptives," as they were called, had been landed there.

The name "Liberia" was applied to a region approximating the coast of modern Liberia. Along the coast to the south of Monrovia, state colonization societies in Pennsylvania, Mississippi, and Louisiana, and Maryland had sponsored separate settlements at Bassa Cove, Sinoe, and Cape Palmas, respectively. Of these the last, known as "Maryland in Liberia," was the most substantial, with about five hundred nonaboriginal settlers. In 1844 Monrovia itself had a settler population of close to a thousand. In 1847 Governor Roberts would proclaim Liberia an independent state and become its first president. After absorbing the other American colonies and contiguous territories, the Republic of Liberia eventually approximated its modern extent.

On 18 December at noon the *Yorktown* completes its arrival formalities by firing a second thirteen-gun salute, this time returned by the town. Cape Mesurado is a rocky, tree-covered prominence forming a peninsula between the Atlantic Ocean and the Mesurado River. On the highest point of the tree-shrouded cape, two hundred fifty feet above the surf, can be seen a new two-story white-painted wooden lighthouse and a small triangular fort. Commencing three-fourths of a mile down the back slope, Monrovia includes several churches, a large new stone statehouse and stone courthouse and jail, some stone or brick and frame houses built with materials shipped over from the United States, and a good number of thatched huts. Adjacent villages of similar huts are home to several thousand Kroo. Ships must anchor offshore, as the *Yorktown* has done, transferring people and cargo by canoe and boat to a beach landing on the river side of the peninsula.

In the company of two shipmates Lawrence goes ashore for another stroll along the streets of the town, which in their width and vegetation resemble elongated pastures with paths running through them. What little traffic they encounter is all pedestrian, as the colony has no more than one or two horses.

18 December 1844

Delightful weather again or rather a continuation of it. Upon revisiting this place again this day, with more leisure I was enabled to obtain much additional information upon matters generally. Whilst passing the house of the governor of Liberia today, whose name is Roberts, he noticed the two gentlemen and myself and called out to us to ascend to the balcony where he was, and rest ourselves and otherwise refresh. We accepted his kind offer when a very agreeable conversation ensued appertaining to the continent of Africa

or at least that part in which he was interested and conver-
sant. Amongst other matters, he gave a pretty full and I
dare say veracious account of Mr. Carnot before mentioned
as dwelling at Cape Mount. His character and pursuits
coincide exactly with my own conclusions on the subject—
viz. that he is a retired captain of a slaver and now a corre-
spondent and factor of some of the largest slave dealers in
Havana and Rio [de] Janeiro and that by certain deeds
that he himself drew up, he has had conveyed to him by
the chiefs of the district in which he is located a large tract
of land ten miles square, they being under the impression
that about seven or eight acres had been the extent of the
conveyance. As may be supposed there was but one exam-
ining party in this transaction (which was himself) to
inquire into the validity of the deeds when present at the
ceremony of the purchase and exchange of legal documents.
Many cases similar to this gentleman's without the land
transactions are frequently to be met with here on this
coast; to foment Brawls etc. amongst the Chiefs is another
part of this kind of people's occupation. It answers a double
purpose, that of furnishing the slave market (the van-
quished always being sold by the victors to Slave dealers) as
well as affording protection to themselves as the attention
of these savages are diverted from the white residents, their
covert actions and maneuvers, by a continual warfare
existing between each other. This gentleman mentions that
a species of republicanism (although for that matter all
matriarchal governments are a kindred of republicanism)
enters into the mode of government to which these natives
submit, and when a transaction like the above described,
between Mr. Carnot and the Chief Sandfeese at Cape

*Mount, takes place the wills of the individuals compos-
ing the common wealth have to be consulted and of course
the approbation to the measure obtained before a Chief
can act in the case.*

*In speaking of the State of Liberia, the governor
informs me that at present it contains about 4500 emigrants and that as a matter of course all have to pass
through the ordeal of the African fever to become accli-
mated and the averages of deaths from this disease may
equal 8 or 10 percent amongst the newly arrived emigrants. This malady though now is reduced of half its former terrors by a scrutinous study of its character and type;
it seems from all accounts to be a severe form of intermittent fever. Much more of interesting nature was our conversation composed that was indulged in between this gentleman and myself but which would be too prolix a task to
commit to writing. After traversing the town in various
directions, we turned our steps towards the strand. I had
an opportunity of seeing several of those ant hills that are
so celebrated for their magnitude and compactness of
structure, when the size of the insect is considered. Those
that we saw were about four feet high. We called at the
houses of several military and municipal titled gentlemen
who uniformly treated us cordially. We came in contact
also with several of the learned professions all of the same
sombre hue as the rest of the denizens of this republic.
Being so accustomed to witness the ridicule which the
whites are given to indulging towards the negro and
oftener when in the character of a Doctor and Preacher, I
could not deprive my mind of these impressions, so long
since received, when I heard them addressed as Doctor and*

*Parson etc., but for that matter I have no doubt of the
capability of the former in rescuing a man from fever or as
to the latter I would depend upon their exhortations for
salvation as I would to any white rascal of the same profession. About 2 o'clock went to the house of Colonel Hicks
and partook of an excellent dinner and glass of Port to
match. [N. M. Hicks, formerly a slave in Kentucky, was
now in his mid-thirties a prosperous commission-merchant
and community leader.]22 Everything was in most
admirable taste and accordance; Mrs. Hicks did the duties
of hostess faultlessly. The individuals composing our party
were Messrs Lindsay, McDonald (carpenters, the one of the*
Truxtun, *other* Yorktown), *Lawrence M. Mate*
(Yorktown), *Midshipman Truxtun (brig* Truxtun), *Ridley
(Captain's clerk—* Truxtun), *Cushman Midshipman*
(Yorktown), *Crooker (gunner). Everything rational. Went
off to our respective vessels at about 4 or half past highly
satisfied. In the evening saw in the direction of Cape
Mount a signal fire for some slaver to approach. We sus-
pected a certain gentleman in that point of the Compass.*

20 December 1844

*The day commences and ends in the same way as yester-
day, taking in provisions and water to last for four months.*

*I have no time to descant upon anything now even
should the Devil make his appearance and command me
to turn to and write a hasty description of his person,
which he might wish to publish to the world immediately.
To such request under present circumstances I should say*

him nay, though long enduring sulphurious flames should be my portion.

The navy had recently established a storehouse in rented space at Monrovia. The *Yorktown* sent to the storehouse boxes of shoes, bales of clothing, quantities of cordage, and barrels of rice, as well as empty barrels formerly containing bread and whiskey. Loaded aboard from the storehouse were many barrels of bread, flour, beef, and pork, and 118 gallons of whiskey. The bread was part of nearly thirty tons of bread the navy had stored at Monrovia. Some of it needed to be heated in ovens to kill the insects and dry it out.[23] At the same time the ship's cutter was bringing aboard wood, sand, and water. The *Yorktown*'s water was topped off at 12,357 gallons (which at the normal consumption of a bit under 200 gallons per day would have lasted just over two months, not the four months Lawrence mentions above). Lawrence's duties would have included supervising the stowage of these supplies. The *Yorktown* also sent a few items (rice, buttons, and butter) to the *Truxtun*.[24]

21 December 1844

No cessation in labor no stop no stay like the impetuous blows of a skillful boxer on the person of a green one.

22 December 1844

Sunday work still, but a view of the end of it in perspective. A vessel has just hove in sight close under the land. Now commence the races among the Kroomen, for employment on board of her—Lord, but it is amusing to see them paddle, Gods! The canoes fly over the waves from the powerful

*exertions of these naked negroes, "Go[to] it my kiddies, you
are nasty men, and I hope the hindmost may lose," as the
woman said when she looked at the naked men through
her fingers under pretence of hiding them from her view,
when they were running a race.*

23 December 1844

*Dawns with agreeable weather—after breakfast attacked
the remainder of the work to be reduced and at 11 got
everything cleared away and got in order.*

AT SEA

Sailing southeast along the coast the *Yorktown* passes the Liberian
settlement of Grand Bassa, later renamed Buchanan in honor of
the former governor of Liberia, Thomas Buchanan.

24 December 1844

*Light airs and pleasant, the land which we keep in view
(being under way) is very low and seems very barren but
the abundance of Palm and Cocoa nut trees that tower
above all the rest of the Forest serve to lessen the general
monotony of the landscape. Saddle and Tobacco mounts
are two excellent landmarks about twenty and twenty-five
miles to the Southward and Eastward of Mesurado. Sunny
weather though not extremely hot. The town of Grand
Bassa in sight; it is settled by colonization emigrants, and a
considerable [number of] residents have made this place
their abode, for trading purposes. As far as we can judge*

from a view through the glass this must be quite a hand-
some town for an African one. It not being considered nec-
essary to come here, we stood on for about two and a half
hours longer when we let go our anchor in a quarter less
twelve fathoms at a distance of about two and a half miles
from the shore abreast of a place called Newcess. It is sup-
posed that in the course of our passage to Cape Palmas we
will come to anchor about ten times (a distance of not
more than one hundred miles from where we started the
last place). Now really upon reflection, this is no very
unpleasant cruise to a man of curiosity. Thus far I have
been highly pleased with it. Upon perusal of some of the
back pages of this journal I notice that I have given vent to
some of the most lugubrious passages concerning Africa
that ever could have been uttered by the grossest and most
tortured dyspeptic hypochondriac: I think at the time of my
writing it I must have been subjected to one of those spells
of mental depression that are altogether unaccountable in
their visitations to the mind. My opinion is now, enjoying
as I do a perfectly lucid state of mind, that there is very lit-
tle difference between (in point of insalubrity) this climate
and that of the West Indies.

Here Passed Midshipman Colby was invalided off the ship to take passage home on the *Truxtun*.[25] He probably contracted his illness prior to the cruise, but the symptoms are now severe enough to prevent him from his duties, and his departure reduces the ship's officer complement.

The *Yorktown* celebrates Christmas by "splicing the main brace"—giving an extra ration of spirits to all hands.

25 December 1844

Christmas day, fine weather; the main brace was spliced today in commemoration of it: this was very kind in the Captain and First Lieutenant. The fact is in respect to these two gents, they are officers of the old school (navy) strict in matters of duty, unrelenting almost where neglect of it is shown, but a consistent levity (indicating generous nature) is the certain reward of those whose interest is enlisted in the duties assigned him. Sometimes a flash of anger, harsh and cutting, will be darted from them leaving for a few moments a very unpleasant feeling to say the least, but when these clouds, as it were, of passion roll away a serene aspect is left again.

This day the Captain paid me the compliment of asking me to dinner, which meets with due appreciation from me. By the way, one Krooman John Brown returned aboard of us today, having been absent some time to witness the going out of his father, whose lamp of life was some time flickering in the socket. Brown's head was shaved in token of mourning in accordance with the custom of the tribe. This custom somewhat resembles that which was practiced by the ancient barbarians the Jews.

26 December 1844 (Sea Time)

At about 3 P.M. in company with Messrs Hambleton (purser), Neville (master), Williams (assistant surgeon), Edwards (passed midshipman) I went into the cabin to dine where we were met by the Captain with all that ease and affability of manner which is only to be acquired

*through long intercourse with the polished world. After
being seated we commenced upon a genteel and excellent
dinner and soon was opened a strain of conversation of the
most agreeable description that I had enjoyed perhaps ever.
In the relation of any anecdote that was given, graceful and
dignified ease of manner as well as of language marked the
styles of each and every member present. At times a relaxation to the ceremonious style that was at first observed
was so far indulged in as to admit of the recital of some
incident tinged with just sufficient smut to give it
piquancy, but no more. All these qualities served to render
the whole tenor of the conversation highly amusing and to
those of less experience than the elder portion of the company, very instructing. We were dispersed at about half
past 4 by the sound of the drum beating to quarters, previously to which, however, the ship had been got under
weigh; we stood on our course without any further occurrence during the rest of the day.*[26]

SESTROS RIVER

27 December 1844

*Wind and weather the same—running along at the rate of
six knots per hour. At 9:30 P.M. in the evening we came to
in nineteen fathoms water abreast of a place called Snow
[Sinoe/Sinou] River, a great slave mart. The river Sestros
[Sesters] is not far from here; at 7 next morning, we hove
up and again came to abreast of this last mentioned
place—another slave mart. The number of these slave*

*depots on the coast between the Isle Sherbro and Gaboon is
really incredible when we consider how well it is scoured by
vessels of war of the American, English and French nations.
What makes the thing more astonishing is that from Sierra
Leone to Cape Palmas all these slave factories are kept by
Kroomen. Galinas, Cape Mount, Snow River, Sestros River
are a few of the most celebrated, where slaves are always to
be found by purchasers ready penned up, and not the least
attempt at concealment made at these places of the
accursed transactions that these people are guilty of. The
fact is as long as these institutions are allowed ashore so
long will the slave trade exist. The English, French and
Americans and all other nations included in the slave trade
prevention alliance carry out the principle observed
amongst civilized nations, viz. that the domains of one
country shall be held sacred from the footsteps of an armed
force from any other country in times of peace with the
intention of interfering with its internal institutions. This
of course is and ought to be certainly a consecrated international principle amongst enlightened governments, but
here where there is no general government, where the
inhabitants are unintellectual savages, the whole territory
divided and subdivided into thousands of Chieftainships
all eagerly engaged in the pursuit of war amongst each
other with the incentive only of making captives to supply
the slave market, thereby indulging the vile cupidity, peculiar to savage races, [it] reduces this noble principle to a
gross burlesque, at the same time serving as a shield for
rank villainy. To observe this law on this coast, indeed, is
next in point of folly to what establishing international
codes between nations of men and herds of wild horses*

would be. The truth is, it has been thought by many people acquainted with the nature of policies practiced by Great Britain (by whom it was first proposed to put the above mentioned law in force) that it was only a false pretence of hers, to disseminate the notion amongst nations of her excessively scrupulous and almost sublimated delicacy in infringing upon other nations' rights even though a nation might be utterly savage. But her object really is lest that the landing at these various slave marts, [which] might be the means of breaking them up and dispersing the prisoners intended for sale, should actually break up the trade and thereby destroy a station at present the most lucrative to the British government and officers of any other on earth.

28 December 1844

Clear, pleasant wholesome weather. The scenery along here is quite tame in its character. Dangerous reefs of rocks show their rugged head[s] above the water at short intervals along the shore at the distance of about two miles from strand. The location where they are submersed is indicated by the heavy breakers that show themselves every now and then. At 2:30 called all hands, and came to anchor. At 2:15 [3:15?] all to rights, nine fathoms water very rocky bottom and sand. The town of Sinou, American negro settlement, established by the New Orleans colonization society,[27] is in view, very snugly situated in a small indenture which can hardly be entitled to the name of a cove even.

The houses seem of excellent fabrication, being of clapboards and stone. At 9:30 heavy weather. At 11 clear and pleasant. At 5 A.M. this morning all hands were called and the ship got under way—running along the land, the character [of which] remains the same, being very low, very densely wooded, in some part extending down to the very water's edge. At about 10:30 the native town of Settra Krou hove in sight, nothing remarkable in its appearance. The American Brig Echo *at anchor there. This is a place of considerable trade, for Palm Oil, Ivory, some Gold dust etc.; we will probably make a stop here for a brief space.*

SETTRA KROO

29 December 1844

Fine weather and pleasant. At 1:30 came to anchor in a quarter less thirteen fathoms water. The only intelligence at this place is that of the case of a missionary's wife, being here in a state of desolation, her husband having died some time since and left her with considerable money. On surveying the coast in this vicinity, rocks of little less than a hideous aspect show their black, jagged heads, in terrific contrast with the white breakers, that dash themselves in vast resistless bodies against them.

The missionary's widow is Catherine Sawyer, the only white resident of Settra Kroo, whose husband died the previous year and who earlier had lost her only child.[28] When Horatio Bridge visited Settra Kroo he noted that it seemed to have more palm trees than anywhere else on the coast, and that the native houses, built of bamboo with thatched roofs as was customary all along the western coast of Africa, were here often of two stories with a porch around the upper story and a ladder leading up to that level's entrance.[29] The ship's log for 29 December notes, "boarded American brig *Echo* from King William's Town, bound to Monrovia." Lawrence often does not bother to mention when parties from the *Yorktown* board another vessel, which they frequently do as part of the ship's antislavery patrol or for other reasons.

Contact with the unfortunate Mrs. Sawyer stimulates Lawrence to voice his very strong opinion of missionaries and their work.

30 December 1844

Fine weather, the Brig Echo *got under way today at daylight for Mesurado. At 9 A.M., a boat was ashore with a number of us officers who went on a sort of exploring expedition, though few novelties I must confess met our view. At 3 returned on board pretty well tired of our rambles. Tomorrow the Captain is to go ashore to be present at a palaver, which is to comprehend the discussion and satisfactory explanation of certain alleged outrages practiced towards a beggarly missionary settled out here. How wrong our government does to extend its protection to these pitiful scoundrels who alienate themselves from their native land, with the sole object of enriching themselves under the pretext of disseminating the scriptures, instructing and enlightening savages—who they are as indifferent to as I myself am. Oh that, that accursed of all volumes, the fruitful source of so many evils, could be annihilated from the earth and from the encumbrances of men's minds, that it might serve no longer as the cloak for schemes of villainy of the most vile and hateful character that ever entered the imagination of man. Let a burning desire of a lustful*

nature spring up in some miscreant's mind, towards
another's wife, daughter or sister, he makes his approaches
under the garb of a religion monger to achieve the aim of
his desire.

Let him be prompted by a feeling of revenge to an act
of murder and he pleads the inspiration of the holy spirit
as his prompter to free the world of a vile sinner, as he
terms the victim of his hate. Let avarice be the prevailing
passion of some sneaky rascal without the trait of hardi-
hood to make him a thief, and he sneaks to a foreign land
of savages in the shape of a holy missionary to practice pec-
ulation without his hypocrisy and rascality being detected.
Oh! That I could open the understandings of the various
mulcted beings throughout the earth and demonstrate to
them the real character of this class of vampires and drones
that come like the visitations of locusts into their countries.

But why need I inveigh against this numerous class of
rascally vagabonds? Alas! I am powerless! Had I the sweep-
ing quality of a two-edge sword in my tongue, how soon
would I cut off this horde of human vipers—then indeed
might I talk.

31 December 1844

This day commenced unusually hot and continued so
through the night. About 9 A.M. the largest shark and at
the same time the most voracious I ever saw, came under
the stern and began mumbling a half barrel that had been
thrown overboard a few minutes before; after striving sev-
eral times to swallow it whole and not succeeding, he
receded at the distance of about fifteen feet and then shot

ahead, coming in contact with the barrel, knocking the head out completely. An effort was made to capture him with a harpoon, which was thrown into him, but he parted a deep-sea lead line that was attached to the harpoon, and he went away fluking harpoon and all like a dog with a hot rat-tale file stuck in his body.

After this small incident (for want of better amusement) several of us went ashore again, which visit repaid us in novelties for the long row which had to be performed. We found that it was the Sunday which the natives observe here every full moon. In the first place what struck our attention was that of a native judiciary court in full session. The case was that of the trial of a man under charge of the crime of murder, and the consequence was he had to undergo a certain ordeal by which his innocence or guilt was to be established. The nature of the ordeal was this, the accused after entering his plea of "not guilty" was obliged to swallow a quantity of bark from a tree indigenous to the soil, called "Sassy Wood," which is of a poisonous nature and produces violent symptoms of insanity, which are soon terminated, however, by death or by the bark being vomited from the stomach. In which case he is adjudged "not guilty" of the crime of which he may stand accused. Of course in the former case he is supposed to have died a guilty man. All depends in this mode of procedure on the constitution of the prisoner for his escape. Some possess such peculiarity in that respect as to almost immediately eject this bark, in which case the most vehement rejoicings are given way to by the surrounding multitude, who always assemble to witness the operation of these trials, and the exonerated individual is feasted, and celebrated to

an almost indefinite extent. This ordination is also used to
prove whether a man is guilty of sorcery or necromancy, in
case one should suffer from such an alienation. These peo-
ple fully believe in the existence of such supernatural pow-
ers. The case that we witnessed was that of one under
charge of murder and who fortunately escaped under the
"Sassy Ordeal" used, cascading up his dose very soon after
having taken it. This custom much resembles that which
was practiced in the seventeenth century in England,
France, Germany and in fact, all Europe. The two customs
exactly coincide, a remarkable coincidence certainly.

After this scene we witnessed many processions only
observed on their Sundays, composed in some cases alto-
gether of females, who were decked to the very utmost
extent of their powers. The habiliments and decorations as
far as I can describe them consisted of a clout of striped
muslin or one or two pieces of cotton figured kerchiefering,
bound around the middle to hide from view the private
parts, but allowing the dugs to be exposed without the least
reserve, some of which by the bye in the younger portion
resemble in size and form, well sized sugar loaves. The legs
and thighs are covered with all kinds of burnished rings of
copper, Iron, and Brass, some with bells attached. Their
bodies they color with clay all over, in narrow stripes up
and down, in such a manner as to give themselves the
appearance, at a distance, of being covered with wildcat
skins. Many further embellish themselves by using chalk
upon their persons, in such modes as in encircling their
eyes with it, [or] marking their faces transversely with the
clay marks above described. This heightens the general
adornments of their persons to a diabolical degree, as may

be imagined. Few head ornaments are used amongst these people. It occurred to me that under the above described aspect these women must come as near in appearance to tame devils as anything I can think of. Another article here seems to be in great demand too: umbrellas, which they cover when spread with various gewgaws. And thus bedecked these dusky belles of the wilderness walk along in an affectedly slow and mincing strut, indicating the strong spirit of vanity and coquetry with which they are filled. This fact goes far to prove that this trait is natural to the female sex, for here we must see human nature in the "raw" (to use a harsh term). The gait used by these black damsels differs (so help me God) but little from that made use of by our own fashionable girls in America; this comparison is intended as no insult to our more than heavenly angels (the only objects worthy of adoration that I acknowledge being lovely woman; she is my idol, I confess; to her I sacrifice and bow down with the blindest devotion, if handsome, whether chaste or voluptuous). I mean the comparison to go no further. I must mention as a matter of course the foregoing account only refers to the young women of this dark community (it is useless to describe their features; negresses are the same in all countries).

But the elderly women are the most execrable looking wretches that ever infested the earth; nothing of the grotesque in the same line have I seen represented on the stage to equal them. To mention their shrivelled skins, emaciated bodies, scrawny limbs, with bosoms pendant like ladies' empty evening bags made of flank leather of calves hide, their lips, grinning jaws, large open nostrils, and bald heads, can serve to give but a faint idea of their ugliness, for the peculiar and naturally awkward air which seems to pervade their movements and actions of every kind are not to be described.

The men hereabouts differ in no respects from the description given of them some pages back. After making several small purchases of fruits and vegetables and sauntering around the town, we stopped to see the King, who is a middle-aged man with nothing remarkable about his conformation, except that he is slimmer than usual for negroes. A new beaver hat was the only article of dress that rendered his attire different from any of the rest that surrounded him. He was just upon the eve of opening a palaver with our Captain the import of which was mentioned a few clauses back.

Just as we were going to embark in our boat, our notice was attracted by the appearance of two men confined in chains to the supporters of a house. The poor devils were emaciated and pale (that is, as far as a negro can be) probably from scanty supplies of food allowed them by their captors. Upon inquiring as to the case of these men we found them to be prisoners of war, or perhaps (not being able fully to comprehend the broken English explanation that we received) really two aspiring, but rebellious Kroomen who had raised up a party for the purpose of erecting independent chieftainships. I asked what would probably be the fate of these characters; I was answered that they would soon be released and allowed to return to their native district without any further infliction of punishment. This is another proof of the natural good and kind disposition of the African. How different and how superior to that most detestable of all races of savages, the

North American Indian, whose strongest characteristic is that of the most exquisitely cruel vindictiveness towards his enemies and the most subtle treachery towards his benefactors as well as the most unassuageable avarice and covetousness towards those who may have bestowed upon him any boon.

The shore at this place was magnificently adorned by several palm trees in full blossom, which are of the most exquisite vermilion color. After all these occurrences we went on board. About 3 o'clock the Captain finished the palaver that had been commenced yesterday, and returned on board of ship accompanied by the King or Chief of the tribe about S[ettra] Krou. He came with several bushmen of the very wildest kind. From the part of the country whence they came required a journey of twenty-five days. These perhaps were representatives. The aspect of these people was very mild; the whole of their hair was plaited in very small plaits in the most beautifully fine manner. Allowing that these people travelled at the mean rate of twenty miles a day, this distance from which they came must have been about five hundred miles. Nothing further this day.

3

January 1845

Getting under way from Settra Kroo and heading further south along the Liberian coast early on 1 January, the *Yorktown* celebrated the New Year by calling all hands at 6 that evening to splice the main brace. As the cheerfully singing crew down their extra ration of spirits, Lawrence, writing in his cabin, finds the occasion to be introspective.

AT SEA

1 January 1845

Commences pleasantly—we got under way at an early hour, heading for Cape Palmas. Spliced the main brace— nothing transpired all this day.

And now as the sombre shades of night set in, my mind reverts to home. If only in commemoration of the jovial day, I would fain indulge in merriment, but the lack of companions with a congeniality of soul precludes it. Oh how does my heart yearn at the reflection of my numerous, dear and truest friends this night congregated, perhaps (as has been the custom for years) at my own house, with hearts overflowing with all the pleasurable feeling that good souls alone can experience and enjoy—and I far away from these jubilees amongst senseless savages.

But hope seems to whisper, "never mind, Jack, one year from this will find you returned to the bosom of your friends and family, amongst whom you will find many changes for the better, and your arrival will give rise to more rejoicing than what is at present felt.["] Poets when they typify Hope by the image of a lovely woman use certainly a sublime metaphor, but they should further define her as being a lovely woman in the married state, viz: as a wife.

For in our hours of pensiveness, with no certainty to guide our reflections as to the welfare of those nearest and dearest to us, does not hope come with her placid presence to urge soothing counsel to our anxious minds, like an affectionate wife over the pillow of her husband, sick perhaps from an harassed mind? The ship is filled with the glorious choral music of our bold fellows, bless them! They know no care, they scarcely know a future! Why should they? For, for the most part they are alone in the world; they know and practice but little guile, for they have no advantages to reap from the practice of it. They feel but little fear, for they have never tasted sufficiently of luxury for it to enervate their minds, and they see no easier prospect in life before them, and therefore feel not the terrors that men do in different stations in life from the near approach of mortal danger, who have lived and live only for the pleasures of life. And yet not withstanding the few ties they have to bind them to life and society they are not as might be supposed a set of ruffians caring only for the gratification of the passions for the moment, never mind though it be at the cost of broken hearts, and lacerated feelings—no! Alas! They themselves are too confiding, too often the duped. Listen to the general tenor of their songs: they are generally all ballads of a pensive and melancholy character; those portraying the sorrows of a betrayed maiden, or a cruelly treated orphan, will enlist their attention much quicker than either a humorous, or libidinous one, which goes far to show the naturally humane disposition of poor Jack. But to spend much time in vindicating the character of the sailor would be useless, for it already stands eminently for frankness, liberality, and boldness.

This morning the atmosphere wore a lurid aspect, that scarce admitted the rays of sun thro' it, but still no rain came. Dozens of canoes board us here in this part of the coast, some offering fish for barter, for which they take Tobacco, bright colored stuffs, Ribbon, needles, etc.; and Red Snappers, Hake, Parrotfish, Flying fish, are the descriptions that they offer. Others apply for employment (being Kroomen) always producing recommendatory letters from previous employers. Some assert further to strengthen applications that they have been to England, which is very often a fact.

2 January 1845

A Brig in sight—heading straight for Cape Palmas, Lat. 42°6′ N Long. 8°32′ W.

CAPE PALMAS

Cape Palmas is the site of the capital of Maryland in Liberia, which (though later merged into Liberia) was then a separate colony occupying the region immediately south of Liberia proper. Maryland in Liberia had been founded by and was under the sponsorship of the Maryland State Colonization Society. Something fewer than a thousand colonists dwell there, along with a large settlement of Grebo tribesmen.[1] One of the vessels the *Yorktown* encounters at Cape Palmas is full of red-coated British troops.

3 *January* 1845

Pleasant sea breezes. Cape Palmas in view. At 3:30 clewed up and came to with the Larboard anchor in thirteen and a half fathoms water veered to forty-five fathoms. Found two American vessels at anchor here: The Tellus *schooner; the other the Barque* Adario *of New York, Captain Brown. We were boarded in a few minutes after we came to, by the captain of this craft and one of Johnny Bull's boiled lobsters—she is full of them and [they] are going to Cape Coast Castle. After partaking of some wine, these gents returned on board their own vessel accompanied by three of our officers who returned in two or three hours after in a very queer state. And now to notice the town and adjacent country: the promontory on which it is situated is one of not very great elevation; it is a small peninsula that makes out into the sea, joined to the mainland by a very narrow isthmus, equal in width to one fourth of the widest part of the peninsula. On this last feature is pitched the town, which is composed of very nice two story houses of American pine boards. There is nothing remarkable about*

Kroo Town, near Cape Palmas
J. Leighton Wilson, *Western Africa: Its History, Condition,
and Prospects*, New York: Harper Brothers, 1856.

its general appearance though there is a very nice light-house erected here. Beyond the portion of the town just described are situated two large Kroo hamlets, I suppose consisting of 250 houses, the bodies of which are of split bamboo plaited and plastered with mud, and thatched with dry palm leaves, and beyond these again recommences the American portion of Cape town where farms extend seven miles.

The coves which are formed on each side of this Cape are perfectly useless from the shallowness of the water, which will not admit of the entrance of any vessel larger than an oared boat: the base of this cape is surrounded by dark frowning rocks of the most inhospitable aspect.

This town and the adjacent country belong to one of the several individual colonization societies organized in the U.S. America. I was under the impression that it belonged to the English.

4 January 1845

This day I went ashore, to take a more minute view of matters than I could from the ship, so that when I landed I walked directly into the midst of the first Krootown, where the usual superabundant display of all descriptions and degrees of naked thighs, distended stomachs and prominent buttocks of both sexes met my view. After sauntering through this village for half an hour—noticing the various processes of preparing food practiced by these black folks, such as in separating the rice grain from its husk, which was done by mixing up a quantity of it with coarse gravel, and then putting the whole into a rude mortar made of a piece of hard wood and subjecting it to very heavy punching, with a piece of hard wood pointed at one end—regular Mortar and Pestle fashion after the manner practiced by apothecaries when pulverizing any of their drugs. After this the grain and sand are separated by a sort of slight of hand toss given it in a shallow basket; this is done for the most part by the children. The occupation of rice cleaning seems to be exclusively one belonging to the women and children, much on the same plan as the dairy is the peculiar province of women in civilized countries. After noticing these things, I proceeded to the emigrant portion of this settlement, and was much gratified with the sight of the cultivation carried on here on the American plan; rows of Indian corn, hills of sweet potatoes, cabbages and various other esculents were to be seen flourishing in the thriftiest state imaginable. Nice farm sheds, outhouses, horses and different kinds of beasts of burdens roving about served to give the settlement the appearance of an American one. Besides, neat hedges and rail fences bounded the different farms. It being Sunday all the people were to be seen either going to Church or in their houses singing psalms and spiritual songs or reading the scriptures, with all the blind fervor that we find so usual amongst settlers of new countries, especially when situated in the vicinity of races of savages. I got into conversation with several of these good people in their churchward course who gave me various information as to modes used in the cultivation of the several imported species of vegetables so as to procure success in their trials and experiments—for the difference of climate is very often an obstacle to the production of many domestic vegetables used in these species. The census they gave me is about seven hundred.

After spending a little more time amongst the Kroo lads and lasses, checking myself when amongst the latter when I found my eyes wandering in the direction of their queer and peculiar parts, I departed on board of the ship. There is one fact forcing itself upon my mind daily; that is that it is an undeniable truth that this station is becoming more and more irksome every day; the novelty that we first felt is wearing off fast from the monotony and repetition of the scenes and character of the savages.

5 January 1845

Pleasant breezes and clear. An affair involving much of the ludicrous "came off" today as sportsmen say. The circum-stances were these: a very dandified aspiring, and usually fastidious Frenchman, in shape of a steward on board here, like most of his nation very amorous in his propensities, came to the determination to satisfy his inclination for sex-ual intercourse, which for a long time now he had post-poned, thereby rather adding strength to his passion. So to carry out his project he resorted to the stratagem of pre-tending to go ashore for the purpose of buying fruits for the mess. He engaged one of the Kroomen on board here to act as guide and pilot in this affair, relying upon his knowledge of the marks and deeps of this kind of navigation, more than he could upon his own of course. So that in very little time he was suited to his taste of couchmate for the night. The personal appearance of this soft creature certainly did some credit to this gent's taste; for in the first place her

stature was of a very desirable medium for a female, being
equal to 5 ft 10 in, her complexion only deep brown not
pot black, with features to be sure not altogether what we
look for in beautiful females of our own color, her nose for
instance, being so flat as to be nearly level with the face,
with nostrils, that resembled the cavities for eyes in a dead
skull, lips certainly more than pouting, being like two egg
plants hanging together. Her person was exceedingly enticing, consisting of gracefully falling shoulders; admirable
bust adorned with the most languidly pendent dugs that
could never be imagined without being seen, equalling in
length good 18 inches; stomach and hips ample both, the
one amply distended, the other amply expanded; with fine
prominent buttocks, that at once indicated the intention of
nature to form this woman for a mother, the extreme dorsal prominence evidently being adapted for the purposes of
carrying her offspring upon. The limbs of this being differed so little from the rest of females in this point as to
merit no particular notice. The odors arising from her were
about equal also to the general run of the race in that
respect. All these characteristics being considered can it be
wondered that the feelings of a man, especially one of a
warm nature, could remain unmoved at the sight of her;
all her natural charms exposed to view too! He rushed to
her arms to quench his molten lead-like desires like a man
half famished with thirst to a cool limpid stream of water!
And here he luxuriated in an enervating sweat bath of
pleasure all the live long night—but mark the sequel!
These luscious pleasures could not be enjoyed as one might
naturally suppose without an equivalent recompense. But
this sated voluptuary, wherein avarice and lust are counter

balanced, arose at break of day and would have departed without allusion to the pay due the female party or anything else regarding the late nocturnal transaction, so that she and her protecting friends followed up the gentleman to the shore and forbade his departure to the ship until he had settled the just claims due this wild courtesan of the forest. Thus continued matters till late in the day when intelligence of the circumstance came off to the ship, where means were taken to procure his release, which was effected by paying the price stipulated between the two parties. As may be imagined, the steward denied all the assertions made by the negroes. When released and arrived on board of ship, he looked intensely sheepish.

6 January 1845

Wind and weather the same. This day the governor of this place came on board with his secretary. The old gentleman's appearance was really very prepossessing. His countenance is certainly very benevolent. He is a bright mulatto. He and his secretary in coming off to the ship, suffered some (as the black gentlemen at Monrovia said) from "Nausea Marina" or seasickness. After partaking of dinner with the Captain, the two departed for the shore. We were now filled up with water—hoisted in Launch and first cutter.

The governor of Maryland in Liberia, appointed by the Maryland Colonization Society in 1836, is John B. Russwurm, who attended Bowdoin College in Maine and edited a Negro newspaper in New York before emigrating to Africa. During this visit to Cape Palmas four men were flogged for drunkenness and one Krooman for smuggling liquor aboard the *Yorktown*. The wayward steward seems to have escaped punishment beyond ridicule, though perhaps he is the same officers' steward mentioned in the log entry for 29 January as being discharged from the navy at Quitta.

AT SEA (OFF GOLD COAST)

7 January 1845

Got under way, stood along the coast for about three hours when we came to in seventeen fathoms water abreast of a place called "Half Cavally." The ground current increases here to the rapidity of two knots per hour. Nothing within the last twenty-four hours. We hove up after laying here twenty-four hours. The current increasing to two and a quarter knots, we were setting towards the shore so came to again—twelve fathoms water.

8 January 1845

After remaining at anchor for some hours with Topsails and Topgallant sails set, a breeze sprung up and we hove up anchor, stood to the Southward and Eastward. We are now in the Gulf of Guinea sailing at the rate of four and a half knots per hour, the current giving us two and a half knots of this speed.

BEREBEE, IVORY COAST

Proceeding to the Ivory Coast, the *Yorktown* comes to the towns of Grand Berebee and Little Berebee. At Little Berebee a year earlier Commodore Perry had taken strong action against locals who had murdered the crew of and then plundered the American trading schooner *Mary Carver*. The accepted practice was to negotiate with the local ruler, who would either hand over the malefactors or punish them himself. Perry, accompanied by Liberia's Governor Roberts, had attempted a palaver with the king, Ben Krako. The meeting had erupted into a melee in which Perry wound up tussling with the king, who was then stabbed by Captain Mayo. The landing party drove off the two hundred natives and burned the village, while the ship bombarded the surrounding woods. Perry, in a blood-soaked uniform, and Mayo, with a powder-burned face (from a shot someone had aimed at Krako), took Krako aboard the *Macedonian* where the king died of his wounds. Two days later Perry landed further down the coast and marched a dozen miles along the shore, setting ablaze houses and villages as he went. When Perry then proceeded to Grand Berebee, he was received with white flags and expressions of amity. The local king signed a treaty, and Perry restored to him five prisoners taken months earlier.[2]

9 January 1845

Commences with quite exciting weather in comparison to what we have had for the last twenty or thirty days past. We had quite an agreeable squall, so heavy as to require us to reduce sail to doublereefed topsails. It was agreeable without any exaggeration, for the atmosphere was rendered delightfully cool by it. At about 1 P.M. we were opposite the town of Barrabee in Lat. 4°26´ N Long. 6°52´ W, at which place it had been the intention of the Captain to stop, but was dissuaded from it by the accounts given of the anchorage—being of rocky bottom, strong currents etc.—by our Kroomen. This is a place rendered memorable to a small degree by its having been visited with the wrath and chastisements of the American Government through the agency of Commodore Perry, for the commission of the inhabitants of certain outrages upon a trading vessel bearing our flag. The Kroomen show a good deal of fear at the idea of approaching this place lest they should be recognized as being of the number of participators in the above mentioned chastisement, for they were on board of some vessel of the squadron at the time of the demolition of this town. At 1:30 P.M. wore ship to the Southward and Westward, on which course we stood for about two hours, then tacked to Southward and Eastward. At this period great quantities of negroes (regular Congo and Ashantee bushmen) came off with various vegetables for the purposes of barter. A kind of wild Watermelon, Squashes, and the infallible Plantain were amongst the descriptions of fruit. Miniature canoes were offered us. The articles demanded in exchange were bottles, Tobacco, Ribbons etc. No conversation could be maintained between these people and our Kroomen, the languages of the two being totally different.

10 January 1845

Wind and weather the same, a few poverty ridden Bushmen came off to sell what intrinsically amounted to nothing; these were the events of the day.

11 *January 1845*

*Light winds and calms alternating each other is the state of
the weather—scenery, low and sandy—no further evolu-
tion of events.*

12 *January 1845*

*No deviation from yesterday, in any respect, until 5 P.M.
when the town of Lahou was discernable. The Barque*
Madonna, *Captain Lawland, was at anchor off this place.
No news; for Gabon in a few days. We came to within four
miles of this place at about 7 o'clock in evening—Got
under weigh six next morning. Just before getting under
way there came on board of us six bushmen from the above
town, who I should judge must have been of aristocratic
character, from the novel mode in which their heads were
dressed, which was by having the hair separated into
squares of the size of a die and plaited in the most exquisitely ingenious manner although difficult to explain; it
must have cost much straining of eyes.*

Captain Richard E. Lawlin is a well-known legitimate trader
who has for years been carrying goods (rum, gunpowder, tobacco,
and various manufactured items) from the United States to Africa,
then trading his way up and down the coast. In addition to the
Madonna he also owned the brig *Atalanta,* which was engaged in
the same business and sailed under another captain. In December
1844 that captain (apparently without Lawlin's knowledge) capit-
ulated to the enticements of the slave trade, at least indirectly. He
was conducting his usual trade at Cape Mount (Canot's neighbor-
hood) and with Spanish slavers headquartered just north of there

at Gallinas (Canot serving as interpreter and middleman). The slavers, whose barracoons were bursting with thousands of slaves awaiting shipment, offered fourteen thousand dollars for the *Atalanta,* perhaps four or five times her ordinary value. Her skipper turned the ship and her American flag over to Canot, who in turn gave the ship to the slavers. On Christmas Eve she sailed for Cuba with seven hundred slaves aboard. The British naval patrol, having previously been assured of Captain Lawlin's good reputation and the *Atalanta*'s innocence, let her pass without question. When they later learned the truth, the British were furious.

AT SEA (OFF GOLD AND IVORY COAST)

14 January 1845

Calms and light airs composed the weather; the day was a complete blank as to incidents—a barque supposed to be the Madonna *abeam of us.*

15 January 1845

Weather the same. To reduce the tedium of the evening the Drum and Fife were got up and operated upon. The Kroomen then gave specimens of their style of dancing, such as war dances. These exhibitions exactly resemble those in the same line of the North American Indians; they consist of representations of ambuscades, surprisals of an enemy onslaught and other characteristics of savage warfare. These displays were tolerably diverting at first, but the great drawback to them was the rank and offensive odors

*that were exhaled from these negroes, which rose like a sac-
rifice of incense and filled the air for fifty feet in diameter.
The idea occurred to me during this performance that if a
manager of one of our theatres could but get hold of a lot
of these fellows, what flaming play bills would be the consequence, until their novelty had ceased. "Unprecedented
Attraction," ten wild, fierce, untamable and untractable
Bushmen Kroomen will this evening appear in all their full
national costumes, and dance several of their most astonishing and latest invented war dances. The performance of
these singular and most rare savages will be opened by the
renowned Chief of this tribe Blubberlip Higharse (deriving
his nomenclature from the remarkable prominence of the
portions of his person that his name embodies) in an
almost classical delineation of the mode practiced by them
of skinning a dead monkey! To be followed by the next in
rank Josey Bignavel in the act of dragging a canoe out of
the water high and dry. Fatima Swagdugs will then have
the honor of appearing before, for the first time, the first
white public and give her favorite representation of the
manner made use of by these extraordinary people of
imparting nourishment to their offspring (that the female
portion of the audience may not be shocked by the novelty
of this tableau, which is not at all at variance with decency,
the manager has thought proper to cursorily describe this
part of the entertainment) which consists in the woman
throwing her fountain of nutriment; her bosoms, over
either shoulder; the child being lashed to the back applies
its mouth to the milky depository, from its dorsal location.
The manager having so hastily closed this engagement
regrets that he had not time to procure a colored child in*

time to have it trained for this interesting scene, and was consequently under the necessity of making use of a half grown calf in a sack for that purpose. Knothead Flatchops, Crooked Shins Smellstrong, and Jim Splayfoot will then go through a series of war dances. And also some of those in vogue used at some of the various festivals celebrated by them, such as at the completion of the sweet potato harvest, fish scaling and gutting assemblages, these and many other entertainments will be given by this uncommon and rare set of beings, which have to be left out on account of their being so numerous. The public are respectfully informed that these African novelties are only engaged for the limited period of three nights.

NB—each ticket purchaser will be furnished at the box office with a small bottle of Cologne water. This would be I think something of the style of Tom Hamblin, Mitchell or some of the numerous managers about New York did an opportunity like this occur. No circumstances out of the ordinary routine have marked this day, to render it more noticeable than any of the preceding ones.

16 *January 1845*

Calm—as the deathbed of a dying saint—that is, after he has settled his earthly affairs in a manner satisfactory to his affectionate relations. Great exercising of Studding Sails today Lat. 4°50′ N Long. 2°36′ W. At 3 P.M. this day we were opposite Axim, where we were in expectation of stopping but the Captain altered his mind, and so stood on with the wind right aft. A grand error has been detected in the English charts that we use. The Harmattan is laid down as blowing from the East during the months of January to March; it has not as yet made its presence known. Westerly winds have prevailed so far.

DIX'S COVE, GOLD COAST

17 *January 1845*

Pleasant mild weather. Last evening we let go our anchor off Cape Three Points in twenty-two and a half fathoms veered to forty-five fathoms chain (mud for bottom). This morning at 5 A.M. hove up and made sail; in four hours came to abreast of Dix's Cove in twelve fathoms water veered to forty-five chain.

Dixcove is the *Yorktown*'s first stop on the Gold Coast, in what is modern-day Ghana. As in much of western coastal Africa in the 1840s, the European presence on the Gold Coast consisted of various fortified trading settlements along the coast, on bits of territory either rented or purchased from native rulers.

This is an English station; a very neat and apparently formidable fort is erected upon an eminence here which commands the whole cove here and a distance of two miles outside. With this fort we exchanged a salute of twenty-one guns.[3] A Bremen brig is here at anchor. Tomorrow God willing and First Lieutenant consenting, I shall go ashore and reconnoitre.

[18 January 1845]

This morning as anticipated I went ashore. The Fort here was the first object to attract my notice, which proves to be of very slim construction and only intended probably to make a formidable show. The number of guns mounted are thirteen, their calibre—I should guess 12-pound long guns. Its site is upon an elevation of about sixty feet, giving it over the roadstead a tolerable command. The little cove that makes in on the West side is perfectly choked up with rocks so much so as to render it useless as a harbor for merchant vessels. The style of habitations of the natives at this place is certainly very tolerable, the walls being of a very tenacious clay and about 18 inches thick and whitewashed with a lime which is a facture from coral rock. The roofs are well thatched, with dry palm leaves, the flooring and timbers of African oak and cottonwood, which tree[s] attain an enormous size. One I noticed that was no less in circumference than thirty feet, making it about ten in diameter. The Governor's house here (a white Englishman) is a very commodious one, but as may be supposed very plain. He has isolated himself in this solitude for eleven years, but even now is not exempt from attacks of the country fever; two victims to it fell today on board of the Bremen brig lying here. Two cases (the first) occurred today in this ship. Symptoms: violent headache, and derangement, nausea, pains in back and chills alternated by intense fever.

One of the greatest concerns of the African Squadron was the health of the men, and the main threat was African fever. Although a variety of febrile diseases awaited the visitor to the West African coast, the most common seems to have been malaria. Not having yet identified the true cause, medical science of Lawrence's day suspected "bad airs," especially those of the evening and night. As it happened, the sanitary precautions taken by the U.S. Navy, especially the rule against anyone spending a night ashore in Africa, were quite effective. The British policy on the other hand, was one of "seasoning," that is, to let everyone go ashore with the understanding that those who survived would likely be able to function (though perhaps suffer fever from time to time). The British attrition rate was at times rather high. So, too, was that of colonists living in Liberia: of 4,454 who had emigrated there from America prior to the time of the September 1843 census, 874 (20 percent) are listed as having "died of the African fever."

While ashore this day I had an opportunity of viewing the mode made use of by the natives of washing for gold— tedious enough it is too—an occupation principally attended to by women. Quantities of the mould from the gold vicinity are carried down to the shore in calabashes, and wooden bowls, and washed away by a certain knack till nothing is left but the gold in the bottom of the calabashes, which even from five or six bushels is extremely small, equal to about three or four pennyweights. The Fetish men and women here are quite a dignified set of beings amongst this tribe; the men wear their beards in a style similar to what was made use of in Shakespeare's time. This caste of people are a kind of religious drone, who are, like most of those of a similar profession in all countries, a prerogatived set. But at the same time the impositions and deception that they would practice are generally disregarded, and not accredited. Animals are in many instances raised to the dignity of Fetish. A five foot long alligator that I saw was in the enjoyment of this denomination.[4] *How they classify or determine upon what animals to bestow this honour I have never been able to find out. After sauntering about in various directions and finding nothing very different from what I had perceived at the other places where I had gone ashore, I jumped in the boat and came on board.*

AT SEA

20 *January 1845*

This day at an early hour got under way and shaped our course for Cape Three Points, where we arrived at 7 o'clock in the evening.

ELMINA

[21 *January 1845*]

Next morning—at 5 hove up and got under way again and stood on until abreast of the Dutch settlement Elmina, before which we are riding at anchor. Several French and Bremen vessels at anchor. Our anchoring is seventeen fathoms—thirty fathoms chain. The fortifications that tower high upon the crowns of the hills around here would seem to stamp this town as being well fortified at first view, at a distance, but this impression is effaced by a close inspec-

tion, when it will be perceived that the walls of the two long white castles could hardly survive the assault of one broadside from a Sloop of war, so that it is to be presumed that they were erected for the purpose of commanding respect and inspiring terror by formidable appearances only.

This place is very old; it was first settled in 1497 by some commercial company of Holland. This was the period that Columbus was in the very zenith of his glory. By this time the Spaniards had exterminated the inhabitants of San Salvador, assassinated Guanahani their chief, and [were] in progress of colonizing Hispaniola through their favorite means of extirpation. The houses of this town are built generally of stone. The residences of the white dutch and mulattoes are excellent but those of the negroes like all the rest upon this continent are of mud and palm leaves.

The history of European trade and coastal settlement on the Gold Coast is long and complex. At the time of Lawrence's visit a variety of coastal trading forts were held by the Dutch and English. Though Elmina is rather grand in appearance and fortified with some ninety guns, it does not impress Lawrence as being much of a stronghold. It was actually founded by the Portuguese as a base for their gold trade (as reflected in its name, "The Mine"), and later became an important slave port. With the suppression of that trade by the European powers some decades prior to Lawrence's visit, it again serves to protect legitimate commerce.

An instance of as much assurance occurred here this evening as I have witnessed in some time. A Brazilian Slaver—three mast schooner rigged—with colors set came within a quarter mile's distance of us without the least attempt at concealment of her real character. As she passed along down by Cape Coast Castle, however, she was brought to by their guns, and a boat sent from there on board of her. Her shipping documents were examined. Everything was so arranged as to allow of no clue for her capture as being a vessel engaged in an illegal pursuit of commerce.

So that although strongly suspected, she was allowed to resume her course. During the rest of the time nothing else transpired. This place by the way belonged to a private Commercial company, until within about two years since when it was purchased by the Crown.

CAPE COAST CASTLE
———————

22 *January 1845*

Commences with delightful weather. This day we got up our anchor and dropped down to Cape Coast Castle, which yields a very imposing appearance. The Castle that stands upon the brow of a ledge of rocks that overhangs the sea is very large and, being kept in a good white washed state all the time, looks quite splendid. This is covered by another, but much smaller fortification directly back of it to the distance of one mile on a very high hill. On the left again upon another elevation is another small battery, where resides the governor. Back of this place some fifteen or twenty miles commences the territory of the powerful tribe of Ashantees. This place has gained some celebrity from being the burial place of the promising poetess L. E.

*Landon, the wife of Governor McLean [Maclean]. It is
asserted that she committed suicide by taking an overdose
of prussic acid which she had been in a habit of taking in a
qualified form for relief from a certain disease with which
she was afflicted. It is further said she was prompted to this
act, by the unparalleled licentiousness of her husband,
among the native women, and in various other excesses.
But nevertheless his mourning, and sorrow, were of the
most intense nature, on account of her death. Her tomb
here erected is plain, with a significant Latin inscription
upon it.[5] Governor McLean was succeeded by Governor
Hill, a commander in the British navy. Within the last
twenty-four hours we have been honored by many and
sundry visits from her British majesty's military officers—
God! What imbibing or potating powers they possess—
these on board were cussed poor specimens of her majesty's
witty officers—deplorable punning the species of wit
attempted by them—infamous songs, the style of their
music—uproarious laughter their merriment.*

The "promising poetess" Lawrence speaks of, Mrs. Maclean, was
Letitia Elizabeth Landon (1802–1838), a rather famous and successful poet, reviewer, and novelist who wrote under the initials
"L. E. L." Only two months after arriving in Cape Coast Castle as
the bride of Gov. George Maclean, she died from an overdose of
prussic acid, as Lawrence says, though apparently accidentally,
despite rumors of suicide or poisoning by her husband's discarded
mistress. Visitors often sought her grave, which was located with
those of British officers within the castle parade ground. Assistant
Surgeon Williams, accompanying Lawrence, carefully copies her
Latin tomb inscription into his diary.

Not everyone serving on the *Yorktown* is so interested in local

Cape Coast Castle
William Fox, *A Brief History of the Wesleyan Missions on the Western Coast of Africa,* London: Aylott and Jones, 1851.

literary connections. Passed Midshipman Neville, for one, becomes overly involved in socializing with some of the British officers ashore. He misses the boat for the ordered 4 P.M. return to the ship, instead taking a local boat that deposits him, raucously accompanied by two festive British officers, aboard the *Yorktown*.[6]

AT SEA

23 *January 1845*

> *We hove up anchor and got under way amidst a very feeble and lame entertainment given by one of our officers to several red coated gentlemen—and what with the loud commands of the First Lieutenant, the noisy thumping of the Capstan pawls, and the rustling sound of the men's feet overhead, this convivial party took the hint, rose up "en masse," and took up their line of march over the gangway. Forced marches they were too, for quantities of liquors yet remained on hand, powerful magnets for most of the Bull family. To some of this party, however, the time of departure must have been one of deliverance from a very unpleasant state of feeling arising from seasickness—they suffered like inexperienced cats. After this evacuation we were impelled by a fresh breeze towards Accra, where we came to at 11 o'clock A.M.*

ACCRA, GOLD COAST

In Accra Lawrence meets and is entertained by James Bannerman, the son of a Scotsman and an African woman who was educated in

England. Bannerman's business draws gold and ivory from far in the interior.[7]

24 January 1845

At 12 went ashore—landing very bad on account of the surf—but as soon as we did get ashore, we proceeded to the house of one Mr. Bannerman who is a very large dealer in gold, and the possessor of great wealth, and enjoys a state of luxury equal to anything to be met with in the West India isles. After endeavoring to make purchases of articles in which he dealt, though not succeeding in which, all his articles having been bespoke long since, we were invited to partake of an elegant collation accompanied with Wines, Ale, Porter, Brandy, Gin, Rum etc. The company consisted of Captain's clerk (Porter), Assistant Surgeon (Williams), Master's mate (Lawrence), Gunner (Crooker), Midshipman (Carter), one Captain Daily supercargo and Mr. Bannerman and son. Captain D. informed us that he had been in the trade for thirty years, and of course perfectly conversant with every thing pertaining to this country. After a variety of conversation, we rose and commenced upon a ramble, which included a survey of the English fort here; twenty guns of twelve pounds calibre is its force. We then got something more to eat and drink at the house of (Public) one Robert Wm Wallace Bruce—and then went on board.

25 *January* 1845

*This day was only remarkable from the insignificant act of
going on board of the Providence barque* Roderick Dhu, *to
buy stores,[8] on board of which when we arrived we found
the Captain and second mate in the cabin making out
accounts for sundry articles sold. The former was in a state
of convalescence from an attack of the country fever. He
handed out in well approved taste and hospitality a big
bottle of limpid Gin, of which we took tolerable sized
draughts—made our purchases, and after listening to some
of his tedious brags, and aggravated exaggerations respecting his peculiar powers, sagacity etc., we left this strangely
contrasted couple in point of figures—the Captain being of
hoggish model, the mate that of an upright guana[9]—for
our ship. I may mention that he showed us large quantities
of Gold dust, that they had accumulated by barter.*

AT SEA

26 *January* 1845

*On this day we got under way and stood towards Quitta—
a delightful Westerly wind favored us all the night and day.
At about 10 A.M. two vessels hove in sight, which proved to
be, the one an English brig of war in pursuit of the other,
(a Felucca) lateen rigged slaver. This chase lasted for about
six hours, when we lost sight of them.*

QUITTA, GOLD COAST

27 January 1845

At anchor before Quitta [Keta], which is situated upon very low land, but the town is altogether hidden from being surrounded with trees. There is nothing to indicate the presence of a settlement but a partially visible old dilapidated fort surmounted by Danish colors. Ducks and Chickens at this place are $2 per dozen, sometimes as low as $1 per dozen; hogs of 70 and 100 weight $1.00, sometimes 75 cents. The land that bounds this bay is extremely low. Cape St. Paul's very much resembles Sandy Hook [New York].

28 January 1845

Delightful Westerly breezes refreshing us. It is said, but with how much veracity I know not, that this place was colonized by the Danes in 1600 odd. The races of negroes hereabouts are remarkably mild, and are acquainted with the art of husbandry to a rude extent. Anchorage five and a half fathoms—good holding bottom.

30 January 1845

Nothing occurred through this day—until about 8:30 in the evening, the British brig Cygnet *hove into sight as suddenly as a spiritual apparition from the depth of the Ocean. She proved to be the brig in chase of the slaver*

Encounter with a slave felucca
Illustrated London News, 12 April 1845.

felucca that we witnessed two days before. The latter
escaped, but not until she had been lightened by throwing
overboard all the lumber that possibly could be spared,
besides staving her bulwarks.

31 January 1845

These facts we learned from the First Lieutenant of the
Cygnet, *who boarded us and took a glass with the*
Captain. They are of opinion that they know her cruising
grounds, and expect yet to catch her. On the day that we
first saw her she was hove to, waiting to receive her slaves,
which were coming off in large canoes capable of contain-
ing forty persons. As soon as these parties saw us the
Felucca made all sail, the canoes returned to the shore.
Nothing more happened this day.

4

***

February 1845

The British had for years maintained a squadron in Africa rather larger than the American one, though by the Webster-Ashburton Treaty of 1842 they were obligated, like the United States, simply to provide ships totaling eighty guns. At this time they have twenty-six ships patrolling West Africa to the Americans' five. The War of 1812 is well remembered (on the *Yorktown* Captain Bell and Purser Hambleton are both veterans of the Lake Erie campaign) and the issue of British impressments of American seamen that was so important to that conflict became a significant motive in creating the American African Squadron. Additionally, the possibility of war over Mexico or Oregon hovers in the air. However, the two African squadrons cooperate in suppressing the slave trade as much as their national interests permit, and their officers generally maintain a mutual cordiality.

BIGHT OF BENIN

1 February 1845

Clear and pleasant—at 5 in the morning, left this place and stood for Whydah, a native town, of some note as a

*slave mart. Which when we came up with, on seeing two
brigs of War (English) at anchor, the Captain concluded to
stand on, taking it for granted not many slavers were there-
abouts. The superiority of the races of negroes in this Bight
in a physical point of view, makes it more frequented by
slavers than any other port of Africa.*

Having passed the coasts of modern Togo and Benin, the
Yorktown comes to the Lagos River, in what later becomes modern
Nigeria.

2 February 1845

*Weather the same. Nothing occurred until 3 P.M., when we
hove to at the mouth of the River Lagos, where six vessels of
different rig, and nations, were at anchor. An English brig
of war mounting twelve twelve-pound carronades amongst
others; she is called the* Star. *The Captain, a very handsome frank young man of thirty-two or thirty-three years
age, came on board of us. Some of his statements, as to the
number of captures etc. that he had made seemed rather
inclined to the marvellous, though still we could not disbe-
lieve them on account of any counter information. He said
that within three weeks he had captured three slavers, one
of which was the three-masted schooner we saw brought to
by the guns of Cape Coast Castle. After he left the ship, we
filled away, for Prince's [Prince; Principe] Island.*

Lawrence's pen slips here. The *Star,* a ship about half the size of
the *Yorktown,* had six gunports. As her class did carry 12-pound
carronades, Lawrence probably means to say "six twelve-pound
carronades." The "others" might have been a pair of long guns.

AT SEA

3 February 1845

Wind and weather the same. A large portion of the ship's company today were seized with violent symptoms of Cholera Morbus—induced by eating Cocoanuts and Pine Apples.

4 February 1845

Wind and weather same—former ahead; Lat. 4°28´ [N] Long. 5°07´ East; latter part squally—sickness on the increase: Fifteen on the list.

5 February 1845

Strong Westerly breezes, very refreshing; this wind we did not anticipate enjoying, being so near the line—the sick are revived by it.

6 February 1845

The same wind, now and then accompanied by a slight squall more threatening in appearance than any thing else—the scuds fly across the sky continually, so as to give the firmament the aspect of that of high latitudes.

7 February 1845

The same wind and weather. The sea for the last two nights has been most brilliant from the great quantity of phosphorescent matter, with which it is impregnated in this latitude (2°19′ N).

The combing of a large sea would illuminate every sail upon the ship, from Flying Jib and Spanker to Royals to such a degree as to allow of every seam being distinguished.

8 February 1845

The same steady Northward and Westerly wind prevails that has been blowing for the last three weeks—its freshness is quite astonishing to people not accustomed to cruise in these latitudes and Longitudes: their minds generally being impressed with the idea that the most insufferable heat must be encountered.

9 February 1845

Still beating towards Prince's Island—everything same—sickness on the decrease.

PRINCE'S ISLAND

10 February 1845

This day we made Prince's Island at 1:30. At 5 P.M., close in by the land—which to describe I am altogether at a loss for language. I must say that I feel my utter inability to give any idea through the medium of words of the sublime character of the scenery of this island—it is of a most fantastic nature to be sure. Mountains as might be supposed compose the island, but these so fantastically modified in their forms are they, as to render this aspect of the island totally different from most volcanic formed ones that I have ever seen, of which this is one—in some instances stupendous masses of stone, solid and apparently of the hardest limestone, shooting up perpendicularly to a height of 1800 feet like a vast meteoric stone scantily covered with verdure. Others again rise up as is usual from a gradual base, but suddenly assume abruptness to perpendicularity, and end in a vast globe like form resembling at a distance a colossal likeness of a negro's head. Table mountains are still another variety. And all these features are rendered more striking by their being of (as before mentioned) rock, probably limestone, with here and there trees sticking tenaciously to their rude surfaces. Their tops are continually covered with clouds that lazily float around sometimes, clearing away so far as to leave them unobscured for a space of half an hour, when they return again and envelope the heads of these vast elevations so completely as to hide them from view. Their vapors are the sources (never failing) of rivulets clear and cool as crystal. Here and there among the mountain thickets are to be discerned the variformed habitations of the inhabitants.

11 February 1845

Who shall depict by words the glories of this island? He

that could give Niagara or the Alps their full measure of
glory, as did Byron, might succeed, but few less than he.
The former to be sure he never had an opportunity of see-
ing.

What a paradise could wealth, taste, and enterprise
reduce this island to—here might luxury reign to an extent
equal to what the haughty Montezuma maintained in
Mexico. It is a land where a poet's genius would soar to the
loftiest regions of sublimity, through the inspiration that
the magnificent landscape would impart. At present it is
lost, to the sensible world—none inhabit it, but a few
degenerate Portuguese and obtuse negroes, whose notions
extend no further than the gathering a few Plantains or
digging a few Yams to satisfy the cravings of hungers.

12 February 1845

I can enlarge upon nothing here excepting the noble aspect
of the island. Today after a very heavy shower attended
with thunder and lightning had passed away, the dense
mists that almost incessantly enshroud the mountains here,
were withdrawn, and a vast peak was perceived whose
head shoots up to the very highest regions of ether. So sud-
den was this spectacle presented to our view, being totally
ignorant of its existence from the above reasons, we could
scarcely believe but that it had sprung from the bowels of
the neighboring mountains during the previous night.

13 February 1845

Nothing today to remark upon. Population, negroes—

Habitations—huts—Means of subsistence for population, spontaneous products of the earth—Costume of clothing, clout round the middle—State of intellect, one degree above that of beasts—Personal appearance, large orang utangs—nothing more.

15 February 1845

This day I went ashore for the sake of a fresh water wash, and a nearer view of the scenery; cascades flowing down with frothy impetuosity of a length of seventy or eighty feet were met at frequent intervals during our perambulations; chasms of awful profundity were other features, that diversify the splendors of this island.

AT SEA

16 February 1845

The boats having been hoisted in, and everything got ready, the anchor at 1:15 was hove up, and the ship got under way. When we got on the Southern side of the island, the gorgeousness of the landscape was greatly increased—such wildness in scenery I do not think can be equalled by any part of the world unless it be on the Northwest coast of North America or in the Himalaya mountains.

17 February 1845

We left this romantic island and shaped our course for Gaboon River.

18 February 1845

Pleasant breezes in our favor—from the Southward and Westward.

As happens often, shortly after the *Yorktown* leaves port Bell metes out punishment, flogging three men for drunkenness. Passed Midshipman Neville, too, has been intemperate, but as an officer he cannot be flogged. Bell places Neville under arrest; he cannot set foot on the poop or quarterdeck (and therefore cannot stand watch), and may not go ashore without the captain's permission.

20 February 1845

The Capes on each side of Gaboon now visible. At 5 P.M. we neared the land say to the distance of seven or eight miles, when the ship was put away, the weather braces checked in and we stood into the mouth of this large river, took in all sail but Spanker with which we rounded to and let go our Larboard anchor in five and a half fathoms and veered to thirty-five fathoms chain. The bottom is very rocky, very uneven, and strong currents exist here. There is nothing remarkable in the appearance of the land thus far.

GABOON RIVER

The next day the *Yorktown* takes aboard a local pilot to proceed up the Gaboon [Gabon] River. Commodore Perry had specifically directed Captain Bell to communicate with the missionaries there, and to make "every inquiry in regards to the difficulties that have occurred there between the French and natives."[1] The American Presbyterian missionaries had established themselves on the northern bank of the river in 1842. The French meantime had been increasing their presence, having established Fort Aumale in 1843, and having settled some Roman Catholic missionaries the following year, as well as obtaining a questionable treaty from King Glass in which he accepted French sovereignty over the area. At the time of the *Yorktown*'s visit neither Great Britain nor the United States recognized the French claims. In any case it was Captain Bell's job to ensure the welfare of American citizens.

21 February 1845

At 2 P.M. this day we hove up anchor and proceeded up the river to the distance of eight or ten miles. Various small native towns were perceptible on each side of us, one called Quindah, another Glasstown. There is also a French station here, maintained by ten soldiers and one officer! Two French merchant vessels are at anchor here, and one American barque Captain Lawlands (Madonna). Nothing thus far remarkable.

22 February 1845

[In honor of Washington's birthday the Yorktown *hoists American ensigns at the fore, main, and mizzen, and at*

noon fires a salute of twenty-one guns.] *Weather sultry, but
as a matter of course, relief comes with great punctuality at
about noon in the shape of a sea breeze. We have blockaded
a slaver in this river, although we could not do anything
with her if she is under a foreign flag; she is a three masted
schooner. This noble river is navigable for ships of twelve
and fifteen feet draught to the distance of sixty miles, and
above that in boats of five or six feet draft to the distance of
a hundred miles further. A tide of seven or eight feet rise
and fall exists in this river; at about half tide the current of
this river runs about three miles per hour.*

*The country to a large circuit here is fetish in its reli-
gious character. On board of the* Madonna *[with] Captain
Lawland today, we saw some of the fetish gods. Nothing
worth mentioning now will occur until we arrive at St.
Paul's or Benguela.*

*The term "fetish" is like many words in other lan-
guages, not translatable. However, as near as we can come
to its meaning, it seems to signify anything that is sacred.
Anything of a rare or extraordinary nature is always considered as fetish; for example, some time ago was captured
in the vicinity of this (King Glass' town) an exquisitely
white parrot, a description of plumage very rare amongst
this class of bird, and consequently considered by the
natives hereabouts, as being worthy of the elevation of
"Fetish."*

*This day was quite fraught with incidents in itself,
being commemorable with America from the fact of being
the birth day of our saviour George Washington, but then
it was rendered more especially important with us on
board here by being the day on which Royalty honored our*

Mission residence, Gaboon
Wilson, *Western Africa.*

*ship, ay real and legitimate Regality! Although of a most
sombre character that is an undeniable fact! King and
courtiers all black as the doom of the unrighteous. But to
discuss this affair under a grave aspect; it was a scene as
rich in the burlesque line as I have ever witnessed, much
more so (as all was perfectly natural, no constraint on the
part of the actors to attempt to heighten the ludicrous
character of the farce) than anything could have been in a
preconcerted affair of the kind. To give a little system to
this relation it will be as well to mention that two or three
kings govern certain districts contiguous to each other here,
and our ship arriving here, it was proposed amongst each
other to pay her a visit, so that the selection of the day for
that purpose happened to fall upon this day, and at 11
o'clock they arrived. King Glass was the first to make his
appearance; which was rendered somewhat dignified by the
dress of a French post-captain's uniform, which he wore.[2]
But with this exception, the rest were as to dress, made of
shreds and patches of finery picked up from all quarters
apparently; some with blue cloth caps with gilt bands, otherwise naked with the exception of handkerchiefs twisted
round the lower parts of the body; others with beaver hats,
some too small, others again too large, with women's old
dirty frocks. Cocked hats, old boots and naked bodies were
still another costume; the women, much in the same style
as the men. And thus was royalty in these regions represented. Taking it all in all I consider that it was perhaps
more ridiculous in its nature than any similar display that
I ever witnessed in Hayti.*

*So after being slightly entertained by the Captain in
the cabin, they were shown around the ship, a salute in*

*honor of the day was fired in their presence and it was then
mildly proposed for them to leave the ship, which they did
in very good order.*

*The missionary that accompanied them stayed on
board and partook of dinner with our Captain. This man
has been in this part of the world tutoring in his vocation
for eight years. His appearance differs in no respect from
the generality of the genus to which he belongs: large harsh
features compose his countenance; a long and shapeless
body, the character of his symmetry; whining drawling
accents his style of utterance. At about 2 o'clock several of
us went ashore, for the purpose of a little relaxation.
Nothing new or different from what we had seen in other
parts presented itself in the character or manners of the
natives of these parts. We proceeded to the house of the
above mentioned missionary to observe the style of his living, which we found as a matter of course very humble,
abstemious etc.; about on a par with what the monks etc.
indulged in during the supreme reign of Catholicism in the
dark ages; just about as severe and self-denying. From
there we addressed ourselves to the negro girls as far as
harmless frolicking went, and mild draughts of French
Brandy and water. Being satisfied in these matters we went
off on board. These were about the events of the day, worth
relating at all events.*

The Rev. J. Leighton Wilson is a South Carolinian in his mid-
thirties. Though Lawrence has little use for missionaries in general,
his special antipathy to Wilson may be at least partly due to having
read unfair attacks on him in newspapers in the American North.
Wilson was painted as a hypocrite who preached abolition while
owning slaves. He found himself in this anomalous—not to say

embarrassing—position by virtue of having inherited two slaves. Furthermore, Wilson's wife, as part of her own substantial inheritance, had become owner of thirty more. Mrs. Wilson had freed hers and helped them emigrate to Liberia. Mr. Wilson, though, had trouble emancipating himself from his two, who had been inclined to remain in South Carolina rather than accept his offer of freedom and emigration. Belying Lawrence's low opinion of him, Wilson became a major figure in the Presbyterian world mission organization, published serious studies of African languages, and was later recognized as the first non-African to discover the gorilla (in 1846). The missionary Albert Bushnell (1818–1879) is described by Bridge, upon whose ship Bushnell had traveled, as "respected by us all, as a pious, unpretending, sensible and amiable man." Before departing, the *Yorktown* gave the missionaries a storm ensign (a small U.S. flag), perhaps in anticipation of difficulties to come.[3]

23 February 1845

Being Sunday we were favored by Mr. Wilson (missionary) in a religious discourse; about on a par with the generality of these things, the best of which to me are intolerably annoying. To be compelled to listen to one of these exhortations, sermons or what not, is sure to produce the most intense resentment in me towards the utterance of them.[4]

24 February 1845

Weather delightful. No occurrences, but the interchange of visits between Captain Lawland and missionary and wife and our Captain and officers.

The *Yorktown's* log notes that on 25 February the marines were sent ashore to drill. Though they may have done so on other occasions as well, this is the only instance where such drilling is recorded. Perhaps, given the earlier political concerns with the French, Bell intended it as a mild show of force. Throughout the *Yorktown's* voyage, while Lawrence and the other officers were able to come and go frequently, the enlisted went ashore only to perform specific work like loading water and stores. Crew liberty was granted only once during the entire cruise of twenty months.

25 February 1845

The weather of this day being agreeable, for the shadow of recreation I went ashore. Perambulating the riverside for the distance of several miles, picking up what trifling little articles in the way of shells etc. that might fall in my way, we (for I had a companion) crossed a creek, conversed with negro men and women in mutilated French, ransacked one or two negro villages in quest of novelty. Called upon missionary Bushnell, whom I take for a naturally well meaning man, but doubtless falling a prey to a consuming fanaticism, almost as ravaging to his frame as an inextinguishable fever. His hollow eyes, prominent features, weak toned voice, and sad expression all betoken the zealot soon about to fall a victim to a visionary scheme of religious life. He hospitably set before us some light food, of which we partook with most birdlike appetites, having but a short time previously taken a hearty dinner of savory salt beef accompanied by a faithful glass of grog. After consuming half an hour here we retraced our steps, but my mind while returning was filled with musings of a peculiar nature. I

had seen a beautiful mulatto girl at the celestial-medita-
tions-deluged man's house. I had slyly squeezed her hand,
she grinned, thereby showing rows of glittering ivory, she
quickly hove a wanton glance upon me, she reciprocated
my squeeze—I—was—ravished! Was not this sufficient
food for musing? verbum sap. suf.! ! mum![5]

26 February 1845

There being no enjoyment ashore equal to what the glorious breeze aboard affords, I could not summon sufficient
force of mind to go ashore, although solicited so to do.
Nothing occurred, though.

27 February 1845

Nothing of more importance than preparation for going to
sea.

Again with the help of a pilot, the *Yorktown* goes downriver.

AT SEA
———

28 February 1845

Weather the same; at an early hour of this day we went to
sea. In company with the Madonna, we are now bound for
St. Paul's.

5

March 1845

The *Yorktown*'s desired course is to follow the southeastward curve of the African coast to St. Paul, but prevailing winds and currents make this intention difficult to carry out. On 1 March the *Yorktown* crosses the equator, though without any of the traditional crossing-the-line hijinks involving King Neptune.

AT SEA

1 March 1845

Everything the same, wind variable but generally from the Southward and Westward—our latitude was this day 15´ South.

2 March 1845

Everything today might be summed up in the words ditto ditto—wind from the same quarter, ship's sailing the same, temperature the same, mood of the people fore and aft the same—Lat. 28´15˝ South Long. 8°07´ East.

4 *March* 1845

Still celestial weather, for the which we praise God fervently, so we do! On this day in the land under the jurisdiction of Uncle Sam what infernal orgies are celebrating amongst the democrats on the occasion of Joe Polk taking possession of the Presidential chair.

5 *March* 1845

Presented the same monotonous scenes, and to make matters worse, provisions are growing so scarce and are so fast deteriorating, that, we begin to look upon each other with longing eyes, especially upon the Kroomen who possess such fine large hams.

6 *March* 1845

Monotony, never varying monotony! is upon us like a dense impenetrable mist—where we can perceive nothing but it, and nothing else. Albacores without number are wantonly jumping out of the water to the height of six and seven feet.

7 *March* 1845

No better than yesterday, by heavens. The sameness that we are suffering from now is growing alarming—we find it actually affecting our speech, and our habits. We do though experience fine weather; we do though also experience good appetites; we do also experience contentment. We are in hopes of getting a slant of wind, and we are also in hopes of getting soon into port—and we are further in hopes of getting some more provisions, and then we would not care if we were to be three months more this side of the line. But as it is we would not care to be beating at the small rate of gain, that we have for the last eight days. I like a little more change in my diet than beef one day and pork the next, with weevilly and maggotty bread.

9 March 1845

Can't say any change is perceptible. We've concluded to haul in closer to the land. No other wind prevails here-abouts, for ten months in the year but the Southwesterly.

10 March 1845

Fine pleasant weather, by no means as hot as might reasonably be expected. To avoid the strong Southwesterly winds that blow for ten months in the year on this side of the line we altered our course.

11 March 1845

Matters the same; our lives might be styled indolent monotony.

12 March 1845

*At 2 o'clock of this day we made land, and sailed along it
for some distance when we found a current of such strength
as to breast us off from the land so that we were out of
sight of it in the morning.*

14 March 1845

*The only remarkable incident of this day was the prodi-
gious quantity of various kinds of fish that surrounded us.
The graceful and gorgeously tinted Dolphin pursued with
swift and fatal certainty the hapless Flying fish close under
the bow of our ship; the jovial Bonita would indulge in all
the fantastical antics that ever were conceived of by fish;
even the piratical shark was seen, cutting not concentric,
but eccentric, circles in all directions. Still from all these
countless quantities we were only able to harpoon three
(dolphin). As to baited hooks, the[y] were beneath notice.*

To supplement the usual salt meat rations allotted, the navy
encouraged its crews to fish to the extent of supplying hooks and
lines and even nets. The "gorgeously tinted" dolphin Lawrence
speaks of is the dolphin fish, not the mammal.

15 March 1845

*Wind and weather the same, and no diminution in bevies
of fish, but lord! How cautious they are! In fact that one
circumstance proves them as worthless members of the piscatorial tribe—away vile, scaly trash! I hate ye.*

16 March 1845

The wind and weather the same, this day commenced rather propitiously with us in a campaign against the finny tribe of the deep; a shark, dolphin and albacore were the amount of prisoners captured. The shark made an all glorious repast for us today. Being about half grown, he was no stronger in flavor than the odors from one of those sweet young virgins just verging upon that peculiar age (seventeen) when the contemplation of the opposite sex fill their minds and systems with such agreeable sensations. The fact is (now that I am upon the subject I may as well cursorily remark) that if physiologists were to bestow a little investigation upon the matter I make no doubt, but a strong affinity would be discovered, in a constitutional point of view between fish and women. The synonymous smell (though an odd term to apply in the case) that pervades both these species leads me to this observation. Would the nature of this book admit of it I should certainly give it a thorough discussion. There is something in witnessing the dying of a Dolphin that certainly touches one's sympathies, whether from the exquisitely beautiful properties that he possesses, etc. etc.

17 March 1845

Still delightful head breezes; and no fish in view. Our latitude was this day 5°05′ South. Ambriz, our next port of destination, is in 7° odd minutes, but when we may arrive god he knows; the rate of our ship's sailing and the perversity of the winds put it beyond calculation.

18 March 1845

Wind and weather same. Caught an admirable dolphin, feasted upon him egregiously, relished him amazingly etc. etc.

19 March 1845

All of a piece with the 18th—Oh monotony thy name is coast of Africa.

The *Yorktown* is now cruising along the coast of what will become modern Angola. She stops first at Ambriz, some sixty miles north of St. Paul's de Loando (modern Luanda), then at St. Paul's, then at St. Philip de Benguela (modern Benguela), the last being the southernmost point in her cruise.

AMBRIZ

22 March 1845

Wind and weather proving favorable we this day made the land, which proved to be that adjacent to the town of Ambriz; at 4:25 of this day we came to anchor nearly opposite to the bluff that forms the small bay on which, though completely hidden by the said bluff, is situated the town, which is not perceptible a quarter of a mile off, that is from the sea. It is said to be one of considerable size (Portuguese). Three fortifications of as many nations are erected on the bluff above mentioned; they are American,

English and Sardinian. From one of two American vessels
we got the confirmation of Mr. Polk being elected President
of the United States of America. Also that near the city of
St. Paul's de Loando (sixty miles south of this place) an
American slaver was captured by an English man of war.
The slaver proved a magnificent prize, containing 480
slaves and $30,000 in cash.

As the British were not permitted to seize ships legitimately flying the U.S. flag, Lawrence presumably means here that it was an
American vessel being sailed under another flag.

Both the British and U.S. governments gave prize money for
captured ships. In the case Lawrence alludes to, the crew of the
capturing warship would divide a bonanza: thirty thousand dollars
in cash plus the auction value of the ship and its fittings plus five
pounds sterling per rescued slave. Similarly, an American crew that
captured a slaver would receive half the value of the ship and its fittings plus twenty-five dollars for each slave rescued. The British
took captured ships and their slaves to Sierra Leone for legal proceedings and disposition. Less conveniently, U.S. law required a
captured American ship to be taken back to its American home
port for adjudication; any slaves aboard American ships were taken
to Liberia.

23 March 1845

Weather the same. Upon "casting about" a little, I find that
I labored under a mistake, while penning the last day's
journal, in regard to the location of the town as well as
respects the three enclosures, which I made no doubt of
being forts from the circumstances of their displaying colors
from Flag staves. The town of Ambriz so far from being of

any importance is about on a footing with any of the rest of the negro villages that abound on the coast all along. It is moreover situated six miles up the river which commences here. The sheds taken for forts are Palm and Peanut oil depots. Thus all that can be said upon the matter, is uttered. We leave tomorrow for St. Paul's.

24 March 1845

Very pleasant—and very tedious—the two merchantmen are soon to depart from here and with them, my letters.

AT SEA

25 March 1845

Nice weather; we got under way about 5 in the morning— but the little wind that gave us a start deserted us in two hours, and we were carried astern by a strong current which runs here to the Northward at the rate of three knots per hour. Shoals of Porpoises today were sporting around most elegantly, some of their leaps were equal to seven feet high by nine long—and thus ended the day.

27 March 1845

This day commences nicely; light airs and calm the order of the weather. Towards the close of the day a British Brig of war hove in sight, called the Ferret, *Commander Oak*

[Oake]. This vessel has been for four years on the coast; within some seven or eight months she has captured from four to five slavers. This we learnt from her first lieutenant who boarded us; thirty-four of her men had died of the liver complaint within a comparatively short space of time.

28 March 1845

About 6 P.M. of this day we made the city of St. Paul's at the distance of twenty miles. A strong Southeasterly current sets into this bay of nearly a knot's force. The fact is between about 6° South Latitude and 14° South Latitude no regularity governs the currents, there is no calculating upon them. The ground current from the Southward creates so many counter ones so that one is completely misled if any dependence is placed upon the dead reckoning. After running along up the Bay of Loando (upon which this city is located) until half past 9 the Captain, being unacquainted with the ground, let go of the larboard anchor in thirty-two fathoms water and veering out fifty fathoms chain and remained until about 5 next morning, when we stood towards the city, which from the lightness of the breezes [we] did not come to anchor (within three miles distance) until 4 P.M. of 29th.

ST. PAUL'S DE LOANDO

St. Paul's de Loando is the rendezvous (base of operations) of the Portuguese African Squadron.

29 March 1845

*Upon observation with the glass, I found this to be a beau-
tifully commodious harbor, completely defended from
heavy weather on three sides—excellent holding ground—
with fourteen fathoms water within one and a half miles of
the shore. The appearance of the land seems sterile to the
very last degree; Gnarled, stunted trees and scrubby shrubs
seem the only description of vegetation for miles around. A
tongue of land makes out to the distance of half or three-
quarters of a mile into the sea on the Southwest side of this
bay, forming the Southern bounds of the bay. Some seventeen vessels of various rig and nations lie at anchor here.
All Portuguese, three or four of them men of war of the
same nation, one a frigate, another a first class sloop, two
brigs—two slavers are also at anchor here under range of a
fort's guns. They were seized somewhere on the coast by
one of the vessels of war at anchor here—upon what
grounds though I cannot conceive, for it is well understood
by most nations that slavery is an institution strongly
upheld (although not [word uncertain] very often) and the
slave trade connived at by the Portuguese. But for one to
keep pace with the policies and treaties of nations of such
characters as Portugal or Spain would be like placing
implicit confidence and trust in the manners and the coy
entreaties in a city prostitute of fifteen years experience. We
were boarded by a boat from one of the Portuguese men-
of-war and certain civilities usual on these occasions were
tendered us.*

*The town is said to contain three thousand white
inhabitants. As far as the distance will admit I should pro-*

nounce this to be a very well built place. Healthy, too, I
should further think, from the height of the surrounding
country (a great deal of which is table land, the upper stra-
tum of which is red ochre) ending perpendicularly at the
Bay shore. At about 11 o'clock today we gave the authorities a salute of twenty-one guns, which was answered by
the same number.

30 March 1845

Upon going ashore this day, I caught a little insight into
matters. But not landing at the town, being on a fishing
expedition, my view of affairs was limited merely to the
outskirts of this large town, including a survey of the fort
bearing South (due) from the entrance of the harbor.
Which last is on the self same principle of all the fortifications on the coast erected by the various nations, more for
appearance sake than with any expectation of their being
serviceable in holding out a very long defence for the town.
The land hereabouts as before observed is extremely barren; no trees are observable in any direction but the hardy
and lonesome looking cocoanut, and prickly pear, which
last here attains a height of sixty and seventy feet, and is by
the bye in most cases a certain index of the sterility of the
soil in which it is found. A serio-ludicrous accident happened today to one of our boats, which capsized, with its
crew and stern sheets full of three valuable officers, namely,
viz the Sailing Master, two Falstaff sized personages in the
shape of the Doctor and Purser. No injury to any of the
party, however, followed; a little gold lace tarnished the
consequence, nothing more though.

31 March 1845

Sunday—and this day broke in indescribable, nay gorgeous, splendor. The temperature of the weather was delightfully cool, notwithstanding the perfect calm that pervaded the scene. The surface of this admirable bay was so free from the least motion, or even vibration, that it served as a vast mirror wherein were reflected not only all the adjacent country but also all the craft lying in the harbor, and the light that was diffused over everything was of such a peculiar mellowness, that the whole scene resembled some of those specimens of paintings that we sometimes are fortunate enough to meet with by some of those old choice masters of the Italian school. At the hour of 9 A.M. we went to visit this place. When we arrived to the quay we found erected a very convenient stone landing place. It is right abreast of the Custom house, which is quite a respectable building in appearance, answering perfectly well all the purposes to which it is put: and in regard to the whole town it must be acknowledged that considering that this place is in Africa, it is remarkably well built. The houses are pretty much all two storied, and of stone and mortar, rough cast fashion. But it is a most trying place for one to walk much, on account of the dry sandy streets, so that every step that is taken the sand overruns the tops of your shoes. At the Southern extremity of this city upon a hill is erected a fort that was once strong, but now pretty thoroughly dilapidated through the force of time and neglect. Its situation, however, being so eligible, renders it somewhat formidable for vessels as bad as it is if inclined to hostilities, as ships' guns could not be sufficiently elevated to *do any damage to it. The personal appearance of the white inhabitants here as may be supposed, from being so inactive and entirely dependent upon slaves for everything, even locomotion itself, being carried about sedan chair fashion, is despicably insignificant. The men resemble emaciated women, suffering under the affliction of the vestige of Jaundice. Their naturally tawny complexion is heightened by their residence in this country. From want of exertion, they lose half the natural muscular power and their systems seem a composition of flaccid flesh, without sinews or nerves to support it so that it assumes the consistency of aged fish, or jelly. The women, excepting the complexion, which is just like that of the men, are not amiss, features generally good. This place was first settled by the Portuguese as far back as early in 1400 odd. Originally, it was used by the government as a place of banishment for malefactors. But after a series of years, it became purged as it were, and improved with each succeeding generation in its moral character so that now I presume its inhabitants stand in that respect on a footing with the best of Portuguese places; which at best, I think I have understood through certain authors, only stand about number four or six on the standard of honor, honesty and what constitute morals. When I first came ashore here and got in conversation with an intelligent gentleman by the name of Carpa, I by him was informed that all the negroes that I saw were slaves held by the whites. I was astonished—the number of whites equal about 2000, that of the negro slaves 5000, and yet though in their own country, with this superiority of numbers and muscular strength and powers of endurance all in their favor, with a vast expanse of country to escape*

to at the distance of only a few miles from the scenes of
their labors and life of drudgery, they are the most abject,
willing and obedient creatures that the most effeminate
tyrant could ever desire in vassals. I have no doubt that
their intellects are too much enfeebled from their degraded
state to comprehend the meaning of the word freedom, or
liberty. For it is here, once a slave, always a slave, no time
to look forward to what will bring emancipation with it.
They are for the most part (but of course, as in all slave
countries, there are many degrees in the character of slaves)
a slim, emaciated, downcast looking set of creatures. Their
habitations are of bamboo and grass frames, filled in with
red clay. I was further informed that a chain of forts or
barricades are extended from eight or ten miles south of
this city to the same distance on the north, ending at both
ends at the sea shore and running back into the country to
a distance of twenty miles from the coast so that it is next
to impossible for anybody to escape into the wilds beyond,
without at least giving a feasible reason to the guards stationed at intervals along this barrier what their business
there is, so that for slaves at least every hope is shut out of
escape. I should think a space of 200 square miles must be
embraced between these bounds and the seacoast belonging
to the Portuguese. They have a regular coin at this place—
current I believe only on the African coast that is among
the Portuguese possessions. Although it strikes the stranger
[at] first as being odd to see the African under the above
mentioned forlorn circumstances subjected to such a thorough and hopeless state of thraldom, but upon a little consideration it is a subject of no more wonder than, that the
Spaniards as well as the Portuguese should have succeeded

so effectually in reducing one might say all South America
to a state very similar to those under present discussion.

Were one to pass his opinion upon the health of this
place without previously knowing its character in that
respect, he would doubtless be led to pronounce that its
peculiar situation and the general local features of the
country must insure for it a salubrious climate. For in the
first place but little vegetation growing here, no unwhole-
some malaria can have existence from (always attendant
upon alluvial soils) one powerful source of infection, the
air of a district. Secondly, the powerful sea breezes that
blow in here must serve to qualify and dispel at the same
time any atmosphere of an unhealthy nature arising from
any other cause. Again the land around about here is very
high "tableland," and quite free from anything (as above
mentioned) in the shape of verdure excepting a thin
growth of grass and scrubby brush, with now and then a
prickly pear tree; yet it is said that there is much sickness
experienced here by all that are not indigenous—notwithstanding these facts.

6

April 1845

An assignment to the African station was spoken of as the most debilitating in the U.S. Navy, for both men and ships. The tropical waters encouraged organisms that damaged timber, and the African mainland exposed crews to disease and the discomfiting precautions taken to avoid it. Any ship that spent months away from home would find its bottom fouling, its spars weakening, and the crew's food supply a cause for watchfulness.

The U.S. Navy's daily ration for each seaman called for a pound of either salt beef or salt pork, some dried fruit, a portion of butter, and either rice, beans, bread, or biscuit. The seagoing diet also included cheese; pickles; cranberries; tea, coffee, or cocoa; and, of course, the daily four ounces of spirits. Extracting the six- or eight-pound chunks of meat from the barrels, the ship's cooks would boil it and skim off the fat for use in greasing the masts and other parts of the ship. Bread six months or a year old was sometimes baked to dry it out and kill the weevils. Tons of bread and flour too far gone for such rehabilitation were sent overboard; so, too, butter, beef, and raisins. In harbors or along the coast, bumboat merchants offered fresh produce as well as souvenirs, and the ship purchased fresh vegetables and meat whenever practical. (Often the meat arrived in the form of one or more bullocks that were then slaughtered on the beach or aboard ship.) The chickens and turkeys in cages on deck would likely have been kept for special occasions. The crew caught fish whenever possible, and in fact fishing seems to have been one of Lawrence's duties.

ST. PAUL'S DE LOANDO

1 April 1845

At the hour of 5 A.M. today we took the seine to go a fishing. The place abounds with fish of many varieties—amongst those that we took in profusion were, sea mullet, drumfish, large porpoises, red snappers, herring, the delicious and delicate sardine. This evening arrived one of the prettiest crafts I have seen for a long time: a Portuguese barque-of-war. The Portuguese thereby make quite a show in the navy line, by a display of a parcel of old hulks refitted, built and whatnot, that have been bought in from the English and French governments—and with these they make a show amongst their wretchedly enfeebled and dilapidated colonies in the East Indies and Africa—now and then seizing or pretending to seize some vessel which they may suspect is a slaver. This is never done, however, unless it is considered to be a perfectly safe and prudent act, incurring no danger of defeat. The object that prompts such proceedings is, a sycophantic effort to gain the approbation of France or England, for zealous endeavors to suppress slave trade. Poor insignificant Portugal, how despicable you are! Ye are but a nation of jaundiced foxes, too much enfeebled to even bark, but still with all the baser passions alive within ye in as full glow as in a tiger, but without the force to give them action!

2 April 1845

As usual in these peculiar (or rather this) latitude, the day commenced with its accustomed splendor. I feel my mind so strongly imbued with the singular deliciousness of the weather that I am inclined to expatiate upon it every time I assume the pen to trace the few desultory ideas that from time to time stray across my mind. The principal feature of the climate is the remarkable regularity which marks the arrival of the Sea breeze. The time of its setting in is generally about 11 o'clock, after which hour it increases in strength and coolness, until about 2 P.M., after which time it blows steadily and the same temperature is maintained till it ceases in the evening. But it is really so fresh at this period as to be actually chilly for one to go to sleep in. Fish and meat that are exposed to its influence remain sweet and unspoiled for thirty or forty hours. Why this part of the African coast should be so gloriously favored in this particular respect I am totally at a loss to account for—lying only in 8°48′ South. During the existence of this breeze the thermometer ranges upon the average of 74° Fahrenheit. An occurrence worth relating took place today—went a fishing and caught a trifle of fish.

3 April 1845

Went this morning a fishing again—few ensnared though. It is said that on board of a Portuguese sloop of war at anchor here, there are thirty-four cases of African fever. These have occurred doubtless from exposure to night airs, bad provisions and general neglect of the officers in arranging the comfort of the men.

4 April 1845

Weather pleasant: today we fired a handsome salute of twenty-one guns in compliment to the queen of Portugal, whose birthday it is. What her age is I cannot say—being a donna though I think she must be somewhat youthful, that being a title I believe only applied to single ladies. Donna Maria I further believe is her name. The Spaniards and Portuguese have sunk so far in the scale of national dignity that one scarcely feels interested enough in them to ascertain the names of the kings or leading people at all.

5 April 1845

Towards the close of the day I took the seine and some men to haul it—and met with the most glorious success. Fish of six and seven pounds were taken in such abundance as to allow of an equal distribution of them throughout the ship's company. Our previous ill success and subsequent good fortune gave a religious turn to my mind. The fishing scrape of Christ and his apostles in the Sea of Galilee rose up in my recollection, although our appurtenances would hardly admit of a comparison with those of the poor beggarly lousy vagabonds above mentioned. The fishermen would be greatly degraded by being compared (although the most of them were black Kroomen) with such ragged rascals as Paul, Judas, Peter, Stephen, and the rest of them. How to be deplored is it by mankind of the present day, that the whole despicable crew, their cowardly, lazy, knave of a preceptor, had not all fallen into the sea and all been drowned, and thus have hindered so much, of awful calamity, and misery to the whole human race since his

*time and that he has been the cause of. But the vile Jews
ever since they were a nation, have always been the source
of countless troubles to the rest of mankind; I wish them
extermination from my heart.*

6 *April* 1845

*Every thing the same; more success in the fishing line as
much as on the previous day.*

7 *April* 1845

*Arrived a French surveying ship, from Benguela.
Preparations for sea, hogging the ship's bottom, a very good
measure; she proves to have a very foul stomach externally.
This Bay abounds so in fish that the crew supply themselves from along side in abundance with hook and line.*

"Hogging" involved cleaning the ship's bottom by looping a line
under the bottom from one side to the other, with a clumped-up
piece of old canvas (the "hog") attached. The line could then be
pulled back and forth along the length of the hull, scrubbing it
clean of marine growth.

AT SEA
___

8 *April* 1845

*This day we hoisted in the boats; at 2 P.M. got under way
and found the ship's sailing excellent, owing to her trim,
and having her bottom cleaned.*

9 *April* 1845

Fine glorious weather—not very fair wind though—wind looks like hauling in our favor.

10 *April* 1845

Matters remain the same I may say in every respect—and consequently as Lear says, "nothing can of nothing come."

11 *April* 1845

Nothing new but a fine fair interesting wind—with which I think, if it lasts, we may see Benguela in two days from the present.

12 *April* 1845

Fine fair breeze and plenty of it. Caught a beautiful Albacore. Spent half an hour of admiration upon him, fed fowl of his entrails [apparently Lawrence feeds the fish guts to the onboard poultry], withdrew them from his body— prepared him for cooking; he was cooked and devoured.

14 *April* 1845

No change perceptible—perhaps the bread might be said to have grown one quarter per cent more maggoty than on the preceding.

16 *April* 1845

Things the same, excepting that we made the land which in this latitude is extremely lofty, a chain of no inconsiderable mountains seem to run along the coast hereabouts. This in me is mere surmise though, as to their being a chain. St. Philip de Benguela in sight though. Wind failing us though, we were obliged to let go an anchor. Caught two splendid Albacores with a rag bait. This is the sum total of the substance of the day.

ST. PHILIP DE BENGUELA

17 *April* 1845

At about half past 4 of this day came to anchor before St. Philip de Benguela. A very large bay makes in here, but not much protection is afforded to any shipping that might be in it in case of violent weather. The town is situated upon the shore apparently. This site upon which it is built seems an interval amongst scenery of a very lofty description. From the distance that we lay from the shore, it is impossible to discern anything distinctly even through the glass. Quite a phenomenon was observed in the water of this bay, which consisted of stupendous quantities of what are commonly termed "stinging galls." It is said the place abounds with fish of all descriptions.

At an early hour today, I made a trial with the seine, and certainly the rumors in regard to the abundance of fish were verified to the utmost; the miraculous draught of fishes was but a ladies' reticule full in comparison.

The appearance of the country here is as desolate as though it had been but lately visited by the devastations of locusts; from the descriptions that I have met with at different times of the scenery of the Highlands of Scotland, I should think a great similarity might be traced in this respect between the two countries. The hills and mountain[s] here are lofty but instead of the refreshing adornment of verdure that the eye seem[s] to seek for and expect, nothing but dull russet and grey are presented, which give rise in the mind to a series of ideas, of reflective and even a pensive and even melancholy character.

We find arising in our minds questions as to the present state of matters here? What is the character of the white inhabitants? Under what circumstances was a colony first planted in this country? What was the extent of this place, during the height of its prosperity?

The solution of these last questions would be a little difficult, I presume. The utter ignorance of the present inhabitants here would not allow of it but to a very small degree. This much, however, is known: that the Portuguese colonized this place and St. Paul's some 350 or 400 years since and that they became very large and flourishing cities where luxury and the arts flourished to a great extent, but when America was discovered this colony seems to have been almost bodily transplanted to that country. This movement was caused by the thirst of gold, that have ever characterized the enterprise of the Portuguese and Spaniards. From that time these places languished by degrees, till nothing is left of them now but tracts of arid land, scattered over with ruins of various structures, dwellings, fortifications and even palaces, for doubtless grandeur once reigned here.

The present white inhabitants are a mean debilitated race of stingless torpid scorpions, who hold in subjection a set of being[s] in the human form even inferior to themselves, and these are a race of half starved and spirit broken slaves, natives of the country. These beings are compelled to perform labors that usually fall to the lot of animals. While in the discharge of any various tasks, they are kept chained, which is to prevent their escape into the back country. This place, unlike St. Paul's having no barriers, it is found necessary to use the above means to prevent their escape. As may be supposed they are terribly cruelly used—alas the poor African!

18 April 1845

It is a matter of little less than a marvel that this coast hereabouts should so abound in fish of every known description—Herring of every species, Mackerel, Shad, salt water Mullet and Trout, Bonitos, Porpoises, Sharks, Skates, Dogfish, Trevallys, Red snappers, Devil fish, Perch, Cavalhos etc. are some of the varieties that almost at every hauling of the seine you are sure to find in it.

19 April 1845

Today prompted by some little curiosity, I concluded to go ashore, just to see if any thing of an interesting nature might be met with here; but when I landed I found things much as I expected to find them: a collection of miserable ruins each side of avenues formed what might be consid-

ered streets. The habitable dwellings from their dilapidated appearance are scarcely distinguishable from the deserted ruins. Here and there little collections of depressed, emaciated negro slaves, lying or standing about in different directions, seemed the only population of the place until you entered some of their desolate habitations just described, when you might perceive a lanky unbleached wax colored human guana approaching you, with certain motions of his body, a certain movement of the features, that at first you would suppose to have been elicited by the power of the Voltaic battery, but which is to be interpreted as a salute of politeness. He then in a kind of faint manner through the force of signs as well as language, conveys to you the idea that he wishes you to come in and accept his hospitality, which consists generally of a glass of water (possibly discolored with a few drops of bad red wine) and a seat on a rickety chair. But to dwell on such unpalatable subjects as the Portuguese is too disgusting, I therefore desist.

20 *April* 1845

After packing down a lot of fish in salt etc. I calmly awaited the order for all hands up anchor, which was issued at about 5 o'clock and in the course of twenty minutes the ship was heading, under royals and studding sails, North going about two knots per hour.

Captain Bell has taken the *Yorktown* as far south as his orders have directed and now, in accordance with those same orders, the ship heads back north to Monrovia to resupply.

AT SEA

21 April 1845

The day commenced very propitiously—wind all right etc.
I feel very much gratified at the idea of having finished in
all probability our southward cruise. We will soon, it is to
be hoped, reach Cape Palmas and there be regaled with the
sight of genuine white faces of our own countrymen.

22, 23, 24 April 1845

Being so similar in every respect that they do not deserve
individuality—all fine days—wind in our favor.

25 April 1845

I have opened the book and therefore must say something,
but so help me god! I know not upon what subject to begin
upon. The wind and weather the both fair and beautiful—
I am run out.

26 April 1845

Staggering under Studding sails at the rate of 9.4 per Hour,
rather pretty than otherwise; Long. 1°16′ East Lat. 4° odd
minutes. People in state of perplexity, when not able to
conceive a few ideas, are given to rubbing and scratching
their heads to bring about that object. This mode I have

tried for the last five minutes, but I feel the birth of no ideas notwithstanding. The fact is under such circumstances, proving so unfruitful, I shall desist for tonight.

29 April 1845

Just the same—wind fair and pleasant; we have before us the prospect of change, dolesome to think, to rainy weather intermingled with thunder, lightning and tornadoes for all this precious nice weather.

This day the ship's whiskey gave out; a calamity unlooked for but borne with steadiness by the ship's company.

The U.S. Navy allowed each man a daily ration of one gill (four ounces) of spirits, which was customarily mixed with three parts water to make grog. (At the time the navy typically bought sixty-five thousand gallons of whiskey per year.)

30 April 1845

The wind fair and fresh; studding sails both sides, within two hundred miles of Cape Palmas; nothing new.

7

May 1845

The *Yorktown* finds it slow going back north to Cape Palmas, constantly changing the sails or anchoring against adverse winds. It takes twelve days to cover thirty miles. In the meantime, as the ship is often very close to the coast, the ship's log repeatedly records the arrival of fresh meat and vegetables brought off in Kroo canoes or in the *Yorktown*'s own boats. Individuals or messes barter, trading old clothes and empty bottles for vegetables and fruit, as the natives have no interest in money.[1] Distilled spirits are obtained ashore or from various trading vessels encountered, though such spirits are in the form of rum instead of the whiskey customarily imbibed in the American navy.

AT SEA

1 May 1845

Commences with agreeable weather which continued until about 5 P.M. when a squall came out from ahead—took in all sail to topsails, which were clewed down and reef tackles hauled out.

2 May 1845

We have now got fairly into the influence of squally weather. At half past 4 A.M. today we made the land but it proved to be some twenty miles below Cape Palmas, our place of destination, and with all our efforts we could not approach any nearer on account of the baffling winds and strong current. So far from advancing we found ourselves going astern at a most tantalizing rate—so much so that at night fall we lost the land entirely. The morning dawned— but no land. These infernal little squalls so incessantly infest the coast that no prospect of getting in for a week or month for that matter is presented to us. These are a few of the pleasures of the sea.

3 May 1845

A dead calm—another darned delectable feature in the beautiful varieties of the climate hereabouts.

4 May 1845

When the matter is considered of our being forced out of our design of coming to anchor abreast of Cape Palmas four days ago—the place in view, within ten miles then to be hindered by such gentle though irresistible means as light baffling winds and small currents of two knots per hour, it may be considered as a tantalizer of as deplorable a nature as ever Tantalus himself suffered.

5 *May* 1845

*Sunday, a propitious breeze sprung up and sent us along at
the rate of four knots per hour for the length of six or seven
hours, but it was thought prudent to let go anchor and
remain till morning when we hove up and stood along the
land, and in the course of the day we perceived the towns
of Barrabee, and Little Barrabee. Bent the Stream cable to
the Stream anchor, but came to anchor in the evening with
the bower on account of squally appearances both sea and
Landward, a little significant of tornadoes.*

A local ruler, King George of Grand Bassam, comes out to the
Yorktown in his canoe, more as a trader than for reasons of state.

6 *May* 1845

*Every thing still favoring us, such as small breezes giving us
an impulse of two knots per hour to creep along the shore
with. Creeping continued at the same rate. At 10 o'clock
wind died away and to prevent the current from exerting
too strong a persuasive influence in favor of a down-the-
coast progress, the Stream anchor was let go. In this state
we had been for about half an hour when no less a personage came off to us than a "King"! In Regal robes too! Of
the Guelph family too! George 1st of the Kingdom of Grand
Bassa. His splendid robes were composed of a worn out
English sergeant's uniform and a piece of striped calico for
breeches and a foxy beaver hat. The droll old burlesque, or
parody on royalty, stumbled up on the poop, commenced
chaffering for some old clothes in return for some vegeta-*

bles and fruits that he brought with him. He disposed of his articles and cleared out. Got under way and beat towards the Cape.

7 May 1845

Beating in vain towards Cape Palmas. It would seem as if we were under the power of some enchantment similar to that imposed upon the Flying Dutchman of Cape Good Hope. We gain n'ere an inch upon any of our various tacks; the wind right in our teeth and the current crowding us to leeward, like a fat wife crowding her slim husband over the bed side of a narrow truckle bed. Finding we made no progress, we concluded to come to again—which we did, with Stream anchor. A mysterious, but at the same time very melancholy, matter took place today: a marine of a pensive disposition committed suicide by drowning himself it is supposed. No previous hint of his intention had been given by himself—he complained in the night that he could not sleep nor had not for a long time past. He went on deck (it is presumed) and jumped in the Ocean.

8 May 1845

Squally unpleasant weather; wind and current both ahead. This day was despatched a boat from the ship for our point of destination, Cape Palmas; she arrived hither towards the close of the day bringing but little intelligence I am sorry to say. The heavy surges that are perceptible ashore are of a truly terrific aspect; they dash against the rocks that lie scattered along at frequent intervals, with such a force that they form vast white masses of eighty feet in height—portions flying off in the shape of dense clouds of vapors. One is reminded by the tremendous heavings just described of the downfall of many glorious edifices of Persian marble, through the agency of an earthquake.

9 May 1845

Unpleasant squally weather; all circumstances bearing upon our sailing being so averse that we continued at anchor until this morning, when we hove up and made three or four miles, but soon on account of the wind failing us, we had to come to with Kedges. This day in looking through some papers from the States dated March, I was much pleased with meeting with an extra message of Mr. Tyler's on the subject of the slave trade, through Mr. Wise (the Brazilian minister). I notice some valuable information is set before our Congress as well as before the people of the United States in general which I feel well satisfied was not generally well known in regard to the duplex and hypocritical conduct of Great Britain on the subject of the slave trade. These exposures are valuable to the Americans as they will know what courses to pursue in these matters, when England is connected with them in any manner hereafter.

The *Yorktown's* anchor set would have included two anchors in the "bows," of which by tradition the starboard was called the "best bower" and the larboard (or port) one the "least bower"; a stream anchor carried at the stern, intended especially for anchoring in rivers and other confined locations; and a pair of kedge anchors, which in essence were backup anchors to the others. At times, as here, the kedges, being smaller and easier to handle than the bowers, might be employed for a temporary anchorage. As Lawrence has noted various times earlier, the stream anchor might also be used when the heavier bowers were deemed unnecessary.

10 May 1845

Commenced with delightful breezes, but all a-lulled.[2] However, we hove up and strove to beat the ship a little nearer to the Cape, but it proved of no avail and we had again to come to several miles to leeward of w[h]ere we started. Canoes loaded with fruits and vegetables are alongside continually.

In addition to whatever the crew members may have traded for individually to vary their official diet, the ship's log notes that the second cutter and canoes bring aboard some rice and cassava, purchased from the local missionary.

11 May 1845

Every thing remains the same, continual efforts to advance a little are made, but they avail nothing.

12 May 1845

This day we took advantage of brief land breeze[s] and were enabled to make about five to seven miles. The breeze failed, the current pressed us astern, ship kept her feather's edge to it as long [as] she could, and when she could stem it no longer turned broadside to it and ran to leeward like the devil in chase of a runaway sinner. We checked this simple flight by letting go our larboard bower and a sufficiency of chain.

13 May 1845

The day set in pleasantly, and with it were ushered propitious catspaws of wind, that sent us along at a very tolerable rate considering the contrary current. We made the lighthouse at the distance of about fifteen miles today.

14 May 1845

Still progressing at the same moderate rate. Nearing the Cape fast—came to anchor—made sail next morning, hove up, made sail, wind failed, let go stream anchor, hove up, stood towards the Cape.

CAPE PALMAS

15 May 1845

At 4 o'clock of this day we came to abreast of the town. Sent Kroomen for water, purser went on board of an English Brig, for some rum to match the water—upon trial found they would not mix—had to drink the rum raw—

"Raw rum toddy Oh! Is good for the body Oh." We learnt that thirty-two emigrants had arrived at this place since we were last here, all in good state of health.

For four days we have to be rolled about abreast of this place and then we proceed to Monrovia.

Fifteen gallons of rum slaked the *Yorktown*'s thirst on this day, and another 18 gallons the next day.

The *Yorktown* also needs to replenish her very low water supply. Over four days she takes aboard about 6,000 gallons, bringing the total to 11,136—about a thousand short of her capacity. Like everything else off the African coast, the water is brought out by the ship's cutters and by Kroo canoes. Such coastal visits enable a brief improvement in the crew's diet; during this stay at Cape Palmas a bullock and a load of fresh vegetables come aboard each day. As the normal meat ration for the crew was 132 pounds per day, and the typical bullock weighed 200 to 300 pounds, those aboard may have experienced some increase in quantity as well as quality at such times as this. Within a day after getting under way again, though, the crew is back to salt pork and beans.

It is now the rainy season, with rain nearly every day, at about the same time every day, as regular as clockwork. As Captain Bell described it, "the rain would come in torrents for several hours without a moment's intermission, after which the sun would come out in all its intensity, unaccompanied by a breath of air; at such times the vessel would smoke like a furnace."[3] Lawrence takes it in good humor.

16 May 1845

Commenced pleasantly. Towards evening things wore a threatening aspect; however, nothing serious grew out of it. Rain came in as an afterpiece, thick mists as the second act, sunshiny weather the happy conclusion. Taking in water at the rate 2700 gals per day, discharging it through many sources at the rate of 200 gals per day, the income of this fluid will probably cease by Saturday night.

17 May 1845

As predicted in the foregoing day's Journal, no more water was taken in. Clearing the first part of the evening, and we got under way with a promising wind, which though proved false by 10 P.M. and obliged us to let go anchor.

AT SEA
———

18 May 1845

Hove up in the morning (wind favoring) and proceeded on our course. If things continue thus we may see Monrovia in four days.

19 May 1845

A pleasant breeze—varied by blandly drenching rains; quite voluptuous they render us.

20 May 1845

Still pleasant and favoring breezes, for the which "Thank God say I!"

MONROVIA, CAPE MESURADO

21 May 1845

*Here we are at anchor, and fairly inundated with all kinds
of intelligence from the land of the free. If there was any
brandy on board ship, I should say I was cocked but there
being none, I must necessarily ascribe my excitement to the
news just received, all good too. Hell fire and brimstone,
three cheers and hot flip for 15 barkeepers!—here darn
you! take this 25 cents to pay for it and keep the change.*

One can only guess what news so delights Lawrence. It could
have to do with national politics, perhaps the passage of legislation
to annex Texas. On the other hand it could be something more
local, or information he received about friends or family.

22 May 1845

*This day was ushered in by transcendently beautiful
weather—and abundance of labor—which consisted of
disposing of Bread, Beef, Pork, Flour, Beans, and Whiskey
in a proper manner in the bowels of the ship; nothing more
to say upon that subject. At this place we got rid of our old
gang of Kroomen and shipped a new lot. I have strained
my memory to produce something more that may have
occurred during the day but nothing more will come, so I
desist.*

The *Yorktown* is now able to replenish her supplies from the
navy storehouse maintained at Monrovia. In addition to many

View of Monrovia
J. W. Lugenbeel, *Sketches of Liberia*, Washington, D.C.:
C. Alexander, 1850.

barrels of beef, pork, bread, flour, and rice, she also takes aboard eleven barrels of whiskey and thirteen bales of clothing for the crew.

23 May 1845

The day has set in in a most tearful manner! Rain unqualified and unaccompanied by either thunder or lightning came down in the most relentless manner all night through—saved the water as far as we could, which amounted to sundry vessels full.

24 May 1845

When morning came we naturally and rationally expected a slight cessation of hostilities in the pluvial warfare, but nary a bit as Pati says;[4] however, a little moisture is not bad, after all.

Today during the rain, I was amusing myself with a Liberia paper (printed weekly), and amongst other clauses I notice one wherein was set forth the mean, contemptible and cowardly abuse that was practiced towards a Captain and crew of a schooner of one of these Liberia people by an English Brig called the Lilly. *This brig has been on the coast for a good number of years and during the time that she has been out here, her specimens of insolence and oppression where resistance would have been in vain from weakness, have been very numerous, and in the present case a rapacious spirit so far urged the Commander and officers as to incite them to board, seize and actually to rob the above mentioned schooner under pretence that she was*

*a suspicious vessel, likely to be engaged in the slave trade.
Every suspicion of this kind was satisfactorily reversed by
the mate (the Captain at the time happening to be ashore),
but notwithstanding, every thing was insufficient for these
wolves in sheep's clothing, so they lugged her away to Sierra
Leone.*

*I hope that love may never hold so firm a place in my
heart, as hate for these English robbers does at present in
my heart—may bewildering and bloody anarchy soon
overwhelm them is all I vent myself in.*

25 May 1845

*Weather cloudy, rainy and otherwise unpleasant, although
intervals of clear weather favored us some notwithstanding.
Today the melancholy intelligence reached us of the occurrence of seventeen deaths on board of the USS* Preble
*(Captain Freelon), two of whom were officers, the rest
shipped men. It was predicted when she left New York that
she would be an unfortunate ship on account of the lax
manner of carrying on duty and enforcing discipline on
board of her. The night set in rainy; nothing more can be
said respecting this day.*

The *Yorktown* continues to load various supplies (rice, sugar,
cocoa, shoes) from the navy storehouse in Monrovia, and offloads
knocked-down barrels and other unneeded items.

26 May 1845

Weather precisely like that of yesterday—rainy season, why should matters in that respect differ? Two sober coopers went ashore today on duty, two drunken coopers returned on board tonight.

Extremes produce their opposites generally. Hoisted in boats, got ready for sea; at night ready for sea. Winds we propitiate thee—O! Aeolus, we supplicate from thee favoring breezes: we will sacrifice unto the[e] two roasting pigs, two dozen fried oysters, Beef steak and Turtle Soup with brandy and ice water to match if thou grantest this favor. If thou feelest otherwise inclined, blow ahead and be damned, for we will make the best of the matter by beating to Porto Praya.

AT SEA

27 *May* 1845

Wind from the Southward and Westward—rain squalls of great frequency; made a tolerable run this day, nearing Cape Mount fast.

Today the drunken coopers and some other men who misbehaved pay the price. At 11:30 A.M. all hands are called to quarters to witness their punishments: E. E. Wilder gets twelve lashes for insolence and neglect of duty; Peter Shannon and John Witham get seven lashes each for drunkenness on duty; and Charles Speedy gets eight lashes for general misconduct.[5]

28 *May* 1845

There came a puff of wind rather too strong which parted the rotten foot rope of our Main Topsail, and split up our topsail to the third reef band; it looked like a big bellied man with his belly ripped up to the navel. It was sent down, a new one bent in its place, and from it we took the hint that the fore Topsail would be all the better for a short respite. Consequently, it was also unbent and sent down and a new one sent up in its place. Cape Mount we are now abreast of. A man of war of some nation (J Bull we think) is laying at the anchorage firing guns, but for what purpose they best know. And [a] brig is also at anchor there. Villainously squally in appearance, the weather is. Struck aback wind ahead, calm.

The British ship is signaling with a flaghoist at the fore and guns fired at intervals, but to whom it is signaling is not recorded in the ship's log.

29 *May* 1845

The calm continued till 12 meridian when a beneficent breeze took us along sweetly. Caught a gaudy albacore— soon reduced him to sizeable hunks ready for cooking. The names of our new Kroomen sound so oddly that I cannot avoid putting them down; they are as follows: Yellow Will, Jno [John] Jesus, Pea Soup, Bottle Beer, Sea Breeze, Jack Neverfear, Jack Razor, Jack Buntline and Jack Smoke. We are going to make a decent day's work of it; I am gratified thereby.

30 May 1845

Commences nicely—fine wind, laying our course. Long. 13°34′ West Lat. 7°32′ North. The day came in and went out as calmly, as noiselessly and insignificantly as the most modest, retiring, and unassuming man in the world could desire to creep out of life. Like unto nothing was done, nothing was said, that was worth recording; so I leave the day thus.

31 May 1845

Commenced sultry, Lat. 7°32′ N Long. 13°59′45″W. Shoals of various fish were noticed today carrying on great sprays. We managed to detach from some of the parties two nice tender young sharks, which we soon made into a rich dish of fried fish. A breeze is setting in—it has set in delightful—nearing Porto Praya fast.

8

June 1845

The *Yorktown* is now on her way back to Port Praya on the Cape Verde island of St. Iago, the rendezvous for the U.S. African Squadron. Port Praya offered a comfortable harbor, safety from the African fever, and convenient availability of supplies. However, the port's distant location was also an operational liability since the weeks it took to transit to and from the part of the African coast assigned to the African Squadron greatly diminished the time the squadron could actually patrol it. Though everyone concerned recognized the problem, the rendezvous location was not changed until the late 1850s.

AT SEA

1 June 1845

Sets in beautifully! No rain, fresh Northwester wind—which proves not very fair for us to be sure, but then, what's the use of being particular? Plenty of provision; what difference if she should not get in for two weeks yet? Towards evening we half caught a good sized Porpoise, that is we struck him through with the harpoon, but he got

off when he was up out of water as high as the Bowsprit;
ship going through the water prettily.

2 June 1845

This day opened with very nice but calm weather. At 4,
however, a breeze sprung up from the Northward and
Eastward, which allowed of our laying our course. Latitude
this day was 9°28 North Long. 14°31´ West. Distance from
Porto Praya about 640 miles N by W or nearly a course of
NW. What a vague kind of task it is that I thus impose
upon myself, in writing every evening as I do a certain
portion which nearly amounts to nothing? But system is
everything; that is why I keep it up.

5 June 1845

A slight puff of wind carried us a few miles in the right
direction. The day however closed with a heavy squall,
right from astern. We reduced sail to double reefed fore and
main topsail, furled mizzen topsail, hauled down Jib,
hoisted fore Topmast staysail, hoisted Fore Topsail, but not
the main.

6 June 1845

This squall lasted about one hour when all was nearly
calm again. What should produce such a variety of cur-
rents hereabouts is truly surprising. Lat. 10°30´ Long.
17°02´ Westerly.

7 *June 1845*

Wind nearly directly ahead—light at that—only 10´ dif-
ference in our latitude from that of yesterday.

    It would be somewhat desirable to get in now, as our
stock of provisions has grown so small that no variety is
offered. This is about the order of our courses: breakfast—
maggoty bread, and tea; Dinner half-spoilt salt beef the
same bread, and [uncertain word]; supper—ditto bread,
and aforesaid tea. Dinners three times a week varied by
pork and beans.

8 *June 1845*

Wind more in our favor, fine delightful, nay enchanting
weather! With a seraph (unship her wings) the whiskey we
have, a set of preventer clews to my hammock, and stretch-
ers for both ends—so as to accommodate two (myself and
seraph) I would be willing with such weather to live out
here notwithstanding the hard grub four months or even
five longer. Lat. 12°07´ N Long. 17°49´ West.

9 *June 1845*

The same unbroken monotony. One fish caught; poor devil
flapped his tail imploring eloquence—but what would
pathetic eloquence avail in the case of a fat sheep in the
power of hungry wolves? Common sense answers "damned
little"! Ergo, this last effort of poor fishy was thrown away.
By the appearance of the skies, it is strongly opined that the

*wind will in the course of three or four hours haul to the
Eastward, a circumstance that would half ravish our souls
with gladness. Talking of ravishing, it leads to an agreeable
train of ideas, it is a process that many of us flatter ourselves with the anticipation of yielding ourselves up to—
that is, whenever we find any young women equal to the
hardihood that the task requires. Lat.13°33′ N Long.
18°34′ West—distance 300 miles W by N ½ N course.*

10 *June 1845*

*The same wind and weather as that of yesterday. Wind, as
prejudged some hours since, proved somewhat more favorable, but nothing very extravagant in the way of breezes
was granted us. A very formidable current setting to the
southward was discovered during the last twenty-four
hours; its rate of velocity was one and two-thirds miles per
hour.*

11 *June 1845*

*I perceive no change in the state of matters, ni wind, ni
weather, we are fairly in the trades (Northeast).*

12 *June 1845*

*Bowling along at a most joyful rate; joyful for it promiseth
a speedy deliverance from the scanty allowance of
damnable fare which is at present our lot, but then an alle-
viation is presented to us in this matter and that is, that we
are accumulating vast amounts of credits for patriotism—*

we are serving country, we are patriotic martyrs, no two ways about it!

13 *June 1845*

Accursed is our fate! Great Jesus what have we done that thou shouldst thus baffle us in our course? How have we offended thee that thou shouldst have prevailed on your father, to have increased the Northeasterly currents, to have altered the variation, and put our chronometers out of kilter, and thereby completely thrown us out of all reckoning! We have duly read your Scriptures for you, been particular on every muster day to have the Bible and prayer books placed on the chest lids and what could we more?

I was led to this series of religious exclamations this day when we made the land about thirty miles to windward instead of to leeward. I felt my heart sink like a stone in a stagnant pool, I felt the bile agitated within me, but all to no purpose though, I must confess. I knew the unweatherly qualities of the ship, and at once feel the chill of despair shoot through when I considered the improbability, the impossibility, the uncertainty of our ever beating up to windward, which was the course of our port. We stood off all night, lost all view of the land by the morning, stood to the Eastward by Northward the rest of the day.

14 *June 1845*

The wind (from Northward) freshened very much after twelve. It is determined to get a good offing before we attempt to run in, on account of the tremendous current setting from Northward and Eastward throwing us off from our course one point at least. Towards morning the sea grew so heavy that to keep her from pitching, the Flying Jib boom was got inboard and Topsails single reefed—and thus remained matters. In the course of the night, she was several times tacked so that she might be got as far to windward as possible, and thus things remained till 10 o'clock when the land was made, which proved the Island St. Iago. Soon after were discovered at anchor an English steamer (the Penelope *flagship, Commodore Jones) and American Sloop* Preble. *Two letters were very welcome which I got here.*

(A current of sixty odd miles was discovered at the expiration of the twenty-four hours, astonishing—god bless us!)

PORTO PRAYA, ST. IAGO, CAPE VERDE

15 June 1845

Went ashore, immediately made an onslaught on fresh provisions, a little claret wine to temper the former; distorted a quantity of French into English construction in presence of a Frenchman, who kept his temper very well at hearing his native tongue thus scored and tortured, and answered my queries and questions in apparent good nature. Fisted a bottle of brandy, for a poor friend in a state of mental depression and came on board.

16 *June 1845*

As usual commenced with the agreeable task of breaking
the hold out, and opening upon a series of work, which
from a queer notion of the First Lieutenant he always
insists on being taken hold of backwards. Went ashore some
several times on sand expeditions. Mutual exchanges of
visits took place this day, between the Preble's as well as
the Penelope's officers.

17 *June 1845*

Confusion has seized upon the ship! and meek tranquility
fled! Like unto a town in a state of siege, according to the
ancient mode of warfare, heterogeneous masses of all sizes
and materials are unsparingly heaped up[on] us. Now
through the undefended hatches are hurled ponderous
boxes of Sugar, and woe to the luckless being who may be
under the smashing influence. Ever and anon lubricating
and at [the] same time insidiously alluring butter barrels
were projected with beplastering effect. Strategy of the
craftiest kind was used: Kegs of raisins, with all their
attractive sweetness, were hauled out as a bait to attract
the men and then were pitched with certain aim amongst
us, and he thanked God who escaped these snares. Nay
cheese, wrought from the quiet cow's udder, was brought in
as harassing munitions of war. Thus were matters waged
between the Spar deckers and Berth deckers until 8 P.M.
when the night set in and put a cessation to hostilities. The
day dawned, when soon action was the order of the day.

> *Berthdeckers soon swept the deck and cleared it of every*
> *encumbrance, burying deep in the bowels of ship the*
> *damnable weapons and articles of offence and assault*
> *above enumerated, and barring this all was insipidity.*
> *Visits exchanged between the officers of the various ships.*
> Truxtun *arrived from Palmas (Canary Isle) and ordered*
> *by the commodore to take a cruise of three months longer*
> *down the coast as far as Gaboon River. The* Penelope *has*
> *just got under way.*

As elsewhere, Lawrence here has stretched his wings as a writer, exuberantly describing the action of provisioning ship. Part of the crew on the upper (spar) deck are lowering or tossing supplies of all sorts down to the men on the lower (berth) deck, who in turn send it all down into the hold to be stowed. A certain amount of physical raillery would be normal, and an occasional container of something tasty might "accidentally" break open to be unofficially shared about in the course of the work.

20 June 1845

> *Great preparation going on for the reception of company*
> *on board of ship. Stowing cargo and filling up with water,*
> *great confusion still.*

The log does not indicate who the "company" might be. The replenishment Lawrence has been describing includes boxes of cheese and sugar, barrels of butter, beef, flour, and beans; bolts of duck and canvas, and 980 yards of dungaree fabric; a thousand pounds of tobacco; kegs of pickles and raisins; dried fruit, vinegar, and molasses.

AT SEA

21 *June 1845*

Great hurry and bustle in getting ready for sea—unmooring ship—hastening off provisions for the messes—singing out here—hailing there—so help me God there's no peace to be met with. At 8:20 in the evening hove up Larboard anchor, set the Jib, Topsails and Spanker and cast to the Southward and Westward. Soon hauled up. Ship close hauled (six points) with courses, single reefed Topsails, Topgallants, Jib and Spanker. Went large nine knots per hour. At daylight discovered Land and a barque. The land was that of the Island of Fogo, the southernmost of the Cape de Verde group, remarkable for its lofty peak, being about 8100 feet above the level of the sea. Its form is that of a section of a cone, something like the Peak of Teneriffe without the apex of that mountain. It is a volcano, although at present in a tranquil state. Its crater must be of great extent from all appearances that the distance of eight or nine miles allows of.

22 *June 1845*

The Northward and Easterly trade wind blows with almost the strength of a common Northwesterly breeze on the Coast of America; toward evening we find it necessary to single reef topsail almost regularly. We have now cleared the most southwesterly of the de Verde group, which is called Brava.

23 June 1845

*The Trade Wind I have generally noticed hauls and veers
with the sun between North and East, never blowing,
though, from the Westward of North or the Southward of
East. Ship going seven, eight, and nine knots, close hauled,
thought good sailing we opine humbly. At 7:30 kept the
ship away to speak a brig, which proved the* Calme *of
Liverpool, last from Lisbon, bound to Tahiti, no news.*

24 June 1845

*Fresh trade breezes, but nothing more to mention. Bent
new courses and Jib—but what is that to the world? Echo
answers, "what sure enough!" Alas nothing; silence follows.
Thus closes the day.*

25 June 1845

*Fresh trade breezes. Nothing observable though, besides the
atmosphere has now become of the most delightfully salubrious temperature. The ship's sailing has been six, seven,
eight knots per hour during the last twenty-four hours.*

26 June 1845

Wind and weather the same. Lat. 21°04´ Long. 28°33´.

27 June 1845

Wind still fresh. Several times this day the ship went nine and a half knots per hour—upon a wind, up to six points—remarkable sailing.

28 June 1845

Still the trade wind continues—puffing at times with a good deal of freshness—there it goes now! All hands reef Topsails. "Man the Topgallant clewlines and weather braces," "let go the halyards," let go the bowlines, haul in weather braces, clew up topgallant sails, haul in the weather topsail braces, let go the halyards, haul out the reef tackles, lay aloft topmen, trice up the booms, lay out take one reef in the topsails; down booms and lay down, let go and overhaul the reef tackles—hoist away the topsails; sheet home and hoist away the top gallant sails—haul in the lee braces—haul well the bow lines! I can go no further. A rumor that grates harshly on my heart says we revisit again the accursed of all lands, Africa.

30 June 1845

Being now upon the edge of the trades, the weather is extremely squally, at one time dying away almost calm, in half an hour or in less time after breezing up so strongly as to require one and perhaps two reefs in the topsails. Ten knots again upon a wind with Topgallant Sails and single reefed Topsails, bowlines hauled taut. Lord God! We defy the world to beat it.

9

July 1845

The *Yorktown* may be making good speed through the water, but perhaps because of the prevailing winds she takes a rather indirect route back to the African continent. She will travel a thousand miles north to the Azores before heading south and east to go another thousand miles to her destination at Funchal, Madeira.

AT SEA

1 July 1854

Fine clear weather, the sky serenely beautiful. At 3 P.M. of this day the wind hauled in our favor so far as to allow of our heading East; eight days out to this date.

2 July 1845

A continuance of the same beautiful and invigorating weather; no incident occurred out of the usual routine of matters. This day Lat. 31° 44′20″ North Long. 34° 07[′] West; Madeira bearing nearly East by North.

3 *July* 1845

Weather the same; wind ahead—but that is a circumstance perfectly endurable, as the weather is delightful.

JULY THE FOURTH

[Here Lawrence celebrates the national holiday in capital letters.[1]]

This glorious day even in such an insignificant place as this book, when discussed deserves a separate page by itself. It dawned upon us with all the magnificence that the important circumstances (to Americans) connected with it deserve. And I doubt not but that we enjoyed ourselves one and all to an amount equal to any body in the States in as rational a manner. We eat and drank to a moderate extent, which former consisted of an immense turkey, Potatoes etc., our beverage pure whiskey and water. After this a supper; after that a series of miscellaneous reflections and conversations upon the revolution of the U.S.; then rationally turned in.

6 *July* 1845

Ditto Ditto Lat. 33°31′ Long. 32°28′45″.

7 *July* 1845

Wind fair for us for the last twenty-four hours. Ran 210 miles, at times the ship going large eleven knots per hour.

8 *July* 1845

No variation in the weather, which is clear and pleasant but the wind is ahead.

12 *July* 1845

Wind and weather the same as on the preceding days. At 8 A.M. this day we made a sail which at 9 A.M. proved to be the packet ship Gaston *of New York, from Marseilles for New York. This proved a fortunate circumstance, for by her we got some intelligence in regard to the relations of [our] country and those [of] Great Britain, Mexico and France. The various considerations and discussion of the above countries seem all tinged with a determinate and hostile shade. At 10:30 both of us filled away and stood on our courses.*

At the time the United States was in the process of admitting Florida and Iowa to the Union, as well as Texas. Annexation of Texas was a complicated issue, however, because it would both upset the balance of free and slave states and antagonize Mexico. Texas nevertheless wanted to join the Union. A war between the United States and Mexico seemed likely, with Britain or France possibly allying with Mexico. At the same time the Americans and British were negotiating the Oregon question, which involved the location of the northern boundary of the American territory and had been the inspiration for recently inaugurated James Polk's campaign slogan, "Fifty-four forty or fight!" Fighting seemed a possible outcome, though the final settlement was achieved without it and placed the boundary far south of Polk's proposed line, at the forty-ninth parallel.

13 July 1845

Wind scarce and ahead, alternated by calms. All things otherwise the same.

16 July 1845

In regard to wind and weather no change. At daylight a ship was discerned, which proved to be a whaler. In the course of the morning she lowered her boats and gave chase to a shoal of black fish, capturing a quantity; they returned. At 9 A.M. we lowered a boat and sent on board and ascertained her name to be the Jas Murray *of New Bedford, three weeks out and bound for New Zealand and Northwest coast America. She furnished us with a number of interesting papers. At half past nine we were somewhat astonished at discovering land which proved the Island of Pico, one of the Azores or Western isles, distant about eighty miles. At 10:30 the boat returned from the ship* Murray. *Much Oregon excitement stirs up the nations, we perceive.*

Wind very light from the Southward and Westward. We observed today in various points of the compass the different islands composing the Azores group, viz. St. Michael's, St. Mary's, Pico etc. Twenty-five days from Porto Praya this day.[2]

17 July 1845

A pleasant wind from the Southward and Westward. We passed so close to the island of St. Mary today as to be able

*to distinguish individuals, and consequently we had a full
view of the Town and various buildings upon the Southeast
point of the isle. The whole face of the land displays the
most beautiful state of cultivation that earth is capable of
being brought to. The town too, is cleanly in the extreme in
appearance and composed of for the most part two and
three story houses, painted white with red tiled tops.
Vegetables such as Potatoes and onions seem in great abundance in the fields. Extensive fields also of various grains
cover the face of the island. The base of the Island as it
were is of level and plains land, but back from the sea,
mountains spring up with sudden abruptness to a great
height, probably three and four thousand feet above level of
the sea. The principal exports from these isles are Onions,
Oranges, and Barilla.*

20 July 1845

*Fine fair and fresh breezes. Early in the morning of this
day the Island Madeira was discovered at the distance of at
least seventy-five miles.*

FUNCHAL ROADS

The *Yorktown* heads in to Funchal on the island of Madeira, past a
group of islets called the Deserters. Meanwhile, on the other side
of the Atlantic in the harbor of Rio de Janeiro, the barque *Pons,*
which the *Yorktown* had encountered during her previous visit to
Funchal, is preparing to enter a new trade. Captain Graham has
arranged that his first mate will skipper the *Pons* to Africa, taking
as passengers a man named Gallano and a number of Portuguese

seamen. At Cabinda the ship will be transferred to Gallano for thirteen thousand dollars—perhaps twice the normal market value.[3]

21 *July 1845*

*The same pleasant invigorating weather. Towards 2 o'clock
the wind hauled so far to the Southward and Eastward as
to oblige us to give up the intention of weathering the
Brazenhead Point and keep away to the North side of the
island, then through the passage of the Deserters, a passage
by the way generally used. The towns of Espiritu Santo, we
then had an opportunity of seeing. Towards 8 o'clock in the
evening, the ship was hove to, in which condition we
remained till day light next morning, when stood on and
came to anchor before this never-to-be-sufficiently-dwelt-
upon-town of Funchal. The Danish Frigate* Galathea *of 26
guns arrived in some two hours before us. Just previous to
our coming to an anchor we found it necessary to get out
the boats and tow our ship on soundings (thirty-eight to
forty fathoms), in which we were kindly aided by the boats
from the abovementioned man of war. No sooner had we
approached the harbor when we were surrounded as usual
with a fleet of boats, laden with every conceivable species of
provisions: Bread, Fresh mackerel, nicely cooked; Fresh
Eggs also cooked; Ice; milk; ream; and all the varieties of
fruit that this elysium on earth produces: Green Gauges,
luscious plum, purple with gushing richness, delicious
Grapes, Peaches, Cherries, Apricots, Pears, apples, Bananas
etc. were literally speaking flooding the ship in the course of
a very short time. Then came the trades people with further varieties of stock in trade: shoemakers, tailors, hatters,*

toy makers, feather flower makers—each and every one
with his enticing little articles tempting you and insensibly
drawing away your dollars like magnets. Then came the
washerwomen to play their parts—but to dwell on a separate description of each class [of] these people would
require more time and patience than I am willing to
bestow so I here end. Upon revisiting this place, I found no
alterations excepting a new and substantial wharf or pier
is in progress of erection for the accommodation of boats
etc. The old one it seems was washed down by the heavy
swell that was setting in when we left.

22 July 1845

Mild, calm and enchanting weather as usual in this
heaven. Made preparations for going to sea. Visited for the
last time Mr. March's wine establishment and tasted of a
variety of his costly wines and made a moderate purchase
of some; came off to ship.

AT SEA

23 July 1845

Got under way at 11 P.M., and stood to sea—bound for
Palmas Canary Isle—wind may be looked upon as a bless-
ing, being so fair for us (Northeast).

24 July 1845

Wind still gracious from the reason of its being the trade wind (can't help itself being bound for the Grand Canary which lies about South by East from Madeira). At 8 A.M. the adorable Peak Teneriffe was discerned, but soon the Sun's obsequious parasites, the clouds, rose up in the strength of their dense volumes and obscured it from our view. Still so were we not to be baffled; we stood on and glimpses were caught, notwithstanding the vaporous spite, of above mentioned volcanoes. Thus are vanquished all sinister designs in all cases.

PALMAS, GRAND CANARY

At Palmas, Grand Canary, the *Yorktown* meets the *Jamestown*, flagship of Commodore Charles William Skinner, who relieved Commodore Perry on 20 February. The *Jamestown* is a first-rate sloop of twenty guns, half again the size of the third-rate *Yorktown*. Salutes are exchanged appropriate to the respective ranks of Commodore Skinner and Commander Bell.

25 July 1845

The same steady wind continues. The morning light ushered into view the Isle Grand Canary. At 10:30 we came in the roadstead, which is on a par with the rest of the Atlantic isles perfectly destitute of all shelter.

We had the felicity to find the hitherto receding ship Jamestown. *Fired a salute of thirteen guns answered by seven; now has the tug commenced of all kinds of work— let it come.*

The aspect of this town is very favorable to the view at the distance from which we lay. In truth external appearance of most Spanish places is favorable, being generally built of stone and nearly always whitewashed. In the afternoon went for a load of sand.

26 July 1845

Wind from the Northward and Eastward and an enormous swell on, rendering it a very dangerous matter to land at the usual place.

28 July 1845

All things the same in the sea and weather way. Used an opportunity of visiting the Jamestown; *everything on the most approved plan. Had an agreeable conversation with old Mr. Whitten (gunner). In the afternoon went ashore to view the place, the extent of which cannot be less than three and a half or four miles in circumference. It has been in past times when Spain was a nation a place possessing good defences. The ruins of a wall which once enclosed it (a very ancient Branch of fortification) are perceptible on one side of the town. Besides it is commanded by a strong castle upon a mountain just overlooking it. The streets are, like Funchal, elegantly paved and kept very clean. The dwellings are for the most part excellent substantial fabrics of stone and mortar, the quality of the stone used for this purpose is of dark grey or lead color, and almost as hard as brimstone. An extensive Cathedral in an unfinished state is built here that must I should guess cover the extent of one and a half acre of ground. It is about two hundred years old. Take it all in all, it may be styled an interesting building, for historical associations that a man is led to reflect upon, but its actual appearance is of such a dark character that it cannot lay much claim to beauty. The style of architecture seems to me to be of such a composite order between the Gothic and Ionic that I should not venture a hint even, as to its purity or beauty of style. Spacious and commodious hotels, theatres, and coffee houses are numerous. The bed of a river is excavated and goes through this town, substantial bridges thrown over it at different intervals. But the river only flows five or six months in the year, I believe, and that is during the rainy season. This place contains 18,000 inhabitants.*

A very curious and novel mode of constructing dwellings is here practiced by the poor people in the suburbs, which consists in excavating a place of any required dimensions on the side of a hill, supporting it inside by means of rude arches, then building the front of it up with masonry of stone and mortar. Great numbers of prostitutes infest this place, a very detrimental circumstance to it. A wet dock it would seem at some past period has been commenced here, but probably for want of funds, was dropped. Its inhabitants are equal to about 18,000. The limited time that I had ashore allowed of but very short views.

29 *July* 1845

The ever present trade wind keeps this place in a most salubrious state of temperature: the swell that sets in here is altogether governed by it, sometimes being so very heavy as to render it necessary to ride at a very long scope of cable, at other times comparatively mild. This day went on shore with the launch to procure a lot of sand, and in so doing had an opportunity of noting the actual capacity of the bay that makes in to the Southward and Westward. It allows of vessels of twenty to twenty-five feet draughts of water to come in in all parts, and on the Southeast boundary is a very high mountain which breaks greatly the natural force of the trade wind, yet strange to say no town or settlement has ever been here built to take advantage as it were of these small traits so favorable to commercial transaction. Verdure hereabouts and in fact as far as I can notice all over the Island seems very scarce. I noticed also the source of a number of people's employment here which consists in gathering kelp or seaweed and is used to make barilla, wherefrom is manufactured the famed Castile Soap.

Here in the Canaries, after nine and a half months at sea, the enlisted crew is at last granted forty-eight hours of liberty ashore. Organized for watchstanding in two sections, port and starboard, they are given liberty accordingly. Here at Palmas will be their only liberty time during the twenty-month cruise, though they do get to go ashore from time to time in working parties.

30 July 1845

Wooding, watering ship. All the Starboard watch on liberty—poor wretches! how dearly they pay for their reckless abandonment to drunkenness and all species of brutality: aching heads and bodies, irremediable nausea, fever for-

bidding actual rest, yet inducing an all pervading sensation of stupidity and an almost insatiable thirst are branches of the consequential suffering that a man has to undergo that gives way to these debauches which in the service is styled liberty.

31 July 1845

With the early day commenced my labors, those of going after liberty men. Drunkenness in all its forms were presented to my disgusted view. Well might it be given to children as an example preventative to their falling into the same habits. As was the case with the Helotes in the time of Spartan renown.

10

August 1845

The crew of the *Yorktown* continues to enjoy their liberty ashore. Palmas often hosts the crews of merchant ships and whalers behaving in a similarly festive manner.

PALMAS, GRAND CANARY

1 August 1845

Wind and weather delightful. Our ship's people were ranging the town, with a looseness and licentiousness equal to what was indulged in by the janisaries of Turkey during the very zenith of their power. Drinking; whoring, with the adjunct of obstreperous mirth; and horse riding and fighting were the chief of their enjoyments. And when the day for returning on board came, to cap the climax, they drank to such a tremendous degree as to reduce themselves to frenzy—beating themselves while in this state against rocks and exhausting their breath and strength with bellowing and meaningless gesticulation. And after when on board came weakness, and a general prostration, sickness, headache, sad depression of spirits and delirium tremens. These are the enjoyments that the sailor looks forward to at the end of a three years cruise with the same pleasing anticipations that a fanatic does towards the period when the world shall be destroyed with fire, and all those not agreeing with him in the articles of his faith; and he be saved and mysteriously elevated to regions where choral music on a large scale be the food and staff of life, with draughts of celestial love instead of brandy and water for beverage. Yes, I say alas, it is for the above mentioned description of revelings that the sailor penuriously hoards his money while on shipboard, that he may in one or two beastly debauches dissipate all, —and then go to his proper station again, which is that of slavery and toil.

2 *August 1845*

The poor fagged out wretches returning on board, by degrees. Nothing new.

3 *August 1845*

Went ashore to look round at it—men enjoying themselves. Where are thy torments Oh! Hell if these be pleasures. Looked through the cathedral—priests practicing chanting—the roof of this edifice is a splendid specimen of groined arching. Much expense has never been incurred though for the purposes of adornment, which I should set down as an index of either the honesty of the priests or the

sense of the people, the one in not extorting the money nec-
essary for it, or the last in not yielding up anything for that
purpose. Lord of Heaven, what a multitude of these Padres
as they are called abound in this place—demure in expres-
sion as one could desire—for illustration see back of book.
[The final leaves of the manuscript having been excised, no
illustration remains.]

4 *August* 1845

Nothing new; all the liberty men on board—ship in an
uproar.

7 *August* 1845

Went ashore for a little recreation—got very little sure
enough—came off with what I got. Walked about ten miles
into the country, observed the exceeding squalid state of
living made use of by the peasants of the island—a few
stones piled up very often without mortar (stone fence
fashion) in the shape of a square serve as the body of a
dwelling and for a roof limbs of trees as rafters covered
with old fragments of mats etc. and then over all a quan-
tity of clay or sand is about the description of habitation
used here by the generality of the Peasants. This is not
always the case, but a large portion of the above mentioned
class of people dwell in no better residences than those just
described. The "fandango" is the national dance with these,
and they are much attached to it; at all the rustic enter-
tainments held amongst the people of these islands it is
almost the only dance.

But it is nearly as dangerous to attend one of these festive meetings as it is to attend an Irish one of the same nature, for the swains always bring with them on these occasions immensely heavy sticks of the quince tree, which they, before using, season in an oven, then besmear with oil and again grease, which process leaves them in as pliant a state as whalebone. The length of these sticks generally equals five feet and should any thing occur to displease one of them or excite their jealousy they will thrash about them with these sticks and with them prostrate friend and foe, wife, sweetheart, daughter or sister, indiscriminately. This of course will lead to a general melee. Amongst the first steps taken at these times is to extinguish the lights, then each one proceeds to his thrashing labors with a will, and before quiet can be established, all must be knocked down senseless. Drank some gin and water, remarkable for its weakness from the copious admixture of water used. Talked with a young man residing here (a Londoner and merchant); gave considerable information upon many subjects relative to the Canary Isles in general; Teneriffe, Fortuventura [Fuerteventura] and Canary in particular.

8 August 1845

Nothing to add—preparations for sea.

10 August 1845

Captain returned on board. Got under way and stood to sea.

Lawrence does not explain that Captain Bell has been ashore since the *Yorktown* arrived on 25 July, when the captain fell and dislocated his elbow and splintered the bone in his arm. The *Yorktown* would have sailed with the *Jamestown* on 4 August, but at the surgeon's advice Commodore Skinner ordered her to linger a few days so her captain could stay ashore and let his bone knit.

At this time, too, the *Yorktown* got a new officer. On 1 August Skinner transferred Lt. William Chandler off the *Jamestown* in order to bring harmony to his flagship, Chandler having been "on several occasions disrespectful and insubordinate" to the *Jamestown*'s captain and much the same to the commodore himself.[1] Chandler comes to the *Yorktown* disgruntled at having been degraded from first lieutenant of a first-rate sloop to second lieutenant of a third-rate sloop.

AT SEA

11 August 1845

Fine pleasant and favorable breezes (the trades). Heading our course with all Steering sails set. Nothing to notice though, any more than the ship sails remarkably well.

PORTO GRANDE, CAPE VERDE

At Porto Grande, Cape Verde, the *Yorktown* again rendezvoused with the flagship *Jamestown;* the storeship *Southampton* (about the size of the *Yorktown* but having only two guns), recently arrived from Norfolk, Virginia; and the *Preble.* The storeship would remain at Porto Grande to support the needs of the other ships. During this stay at Porto Grande, Lawrence may have been relatively at leisure, but the ship bustled with activity. Though the *Yorktown* had been sailing "remarkably well," she needed considerable refitting before returning to the African coast. Commodore Skinner put all available men from the squadron to work on her, recaulking her hull and repairing her rigging, spars, and other fittings. A topsail yard from the *Jamestown* was whittled down to replace the *Yorktown*'s rotten fore yard. A forge was landed ashore for working some of the larger iron fittings, while the flagship's deck was taken over for sailmaking and light blacksmithing. The *Yorktown*'s first cutter was sent ashore, where carpenters spent two weeks repairing it. The crew painted the hull, the cabins, and the spars and yards. The *Preble,* ready to head back to the United States, gave a chronometer and some other items to the *Yorktown.*[2]

14 *August 1845*

At half past two this day we made the land, which proved to be the Isles St. Vincent, St. Antonio, and in the distance St. Nicholas. In the course of two or three hours we were in the Harbor Porto Grande on the Northwest side of the isle St. Vincent. The aspects of these islands are sterile in the extreme. The strata composing the soil are all visible, and are piled up to a prodigious height. All is dim color with the scenery, without the relief of verdure in any direction. Whether the name that this harbor bears was intended to express its excellence or not, I cannot say, but I should hardly consider it strong enough for that purpose. It is almost entirely land locked, which renders it very smooth, in the first place, and besides there is a great sufficiency of water for vessels of any draught—and good holding ground moreover. The store ship Southampton *and flagship* Jamestown *were at anchor, by the first of which I received*

*an entertaining batch of letters. The form of this bay is
something like a sugar loaf, the plane section of a cone
wide at the entrance and narrow at the opposite extremity;
at its entrance is a large [word unclear] rock, called "bird
island," from it being so covered with "Guana."*

Having received word of the death of former President Andrew
Jackson (on 8 June), all U.S. naval vessels fly their flags at half mast
for a week. The Portuguese governor of the island with great cour-
tesy flies the Portuguese ensign at half mast for the same period,
and fires a salute of twenty-one guns at one-minute intervals.[3]

15 August 1845

*Very fresh breezes but pleasant; in fact a half gale of wind,
but with two anchors down and a good scope of cable on
each, with the sheet chain ready bent, what do we care?
Little enough, as may rationally be supposed; sent aloft the
jeer tackles, got the fore and Main Yards down, commenced
stripping them; Topgallant mast down, Jib boom and
Flying Jib boom down, with all the gear.*

16 August 1845

*Wind today very light. All hands busy at something. By the
way (now that an opportunity is allowed me) this seems
one of the most deplorably desolate regions that ever the
eye of man lit upon. I consider it no better than a mountainous desert; the variety of scenery consists only in the
different colored sands and gravel and different magnitudes
of hills and mountains.*

17 *August 1845*

Wind fresh from Northward and Eastward. Weather pleas-
ant. Upon referring back to the store house of my memory,
the fact appears to view of a famine having been suffered
from, some eleven years ago, throughout nearly all this
group of isles induced by the want of water, by which defi-
ciency vegetation of every species languished and died, and
many of the inhabitants in consequence expired of starva-
tion. Succor was sent from the U.S. and much relief thereby
tendered. I am led principally to notice this fact from the
barren aspect of the landscape. It would not (one would
pronounce) be a surprising circumstance if the visitation of
famine should sweep over these islands frequently, for as
before observed nothing but dull russet-brown appears to
the view in any direction—certainly an index of the steril-
ity of the soil. In the interior the soil is little improved, but
fortunately fish abound in these islands, which somewhat
compensates for the deficiency of vegetable food.

18 *August 1845*

Wind and weather the same with the exception that the
wind blows at times very violently in puffs. At 10 o'clock
this day a court-martial was convened, the cases of Messrs
Marin (Lieutenant) and Neville (Passed Midshipman)
were tried. Ship nearly stripped and getting overhauled.

The secretary of the navy, concerned that the navy's image was
being damaged by too many courts-martial, had told Commodore
Skinner to keep them to a minimum. Hence the commodore could
hardly have been pleased to convene courts-martial on two of

Bell's officers. Indeed, undoubtedly thinking of his own image, Skinner wrote to the secretary and explained that although Bell was a fine captain, he believed matters might not have come to such a head had Bell handled things differently. At ten each morning for the next ten days the *Yorktown* will hoist the jack to the mizzen and fire a gun, and the court will convene.

20 *August 1845*

Strong southerly breezes; court still in session.

21 *August 1845*

The same strong wind, which by the bye it may be observed gives existence to very strong current in the Bay of Porto Grande. In going ashore today with a launch load of bread (condemned) these same wind and current were so strong as to take us nearly on a lee shore, but which by great difficulty we managed to clear.

22 *August 1845*

On this day finished the witnesses on the part of the prosecution. The day was rendered memorable to me from the circumstance of coming within two feet of cutting in two or swamping the Commodore's gig with himself in it. This happened from not keeping a proper lookout ahead. I was subjected to the mortification of not only a reprimand but also a suspension from duty, not altogether unmerited I confess—but what was a suspension from duty considered,

in a penal point of view, to the deepest of all mortification,
that of being considered guilty of lubberly conduct in man-
aging my boat? This I cannot reconcile to my mind.

23 *August 1845*

Weather the same, court-martial still in session, the case of
Mr. Marin concluded, defence finished, how things tend
cannot guess. About 3 o'clock the Commodore sent to know
the name of the officer guilty of such "criminal negligence"
as to run him down? The Captain of this ship sent him my
name adding all the circumstances thereto attached. And
strange to say the Commodore instead of displaying much
anger, only sent back that he would request my restoration
to duty, but desired the heinousness of my offence to be
represented to me, with a view of deterring me from being
instrumental in a similar recurrence of a similar accident.
But no eloquence in the shape of reproof could equal the
stinging mortification that lurked about my heart arising
from reflection on the subject. The manner of Captain Bell
on the occasion, though, so increased my veneration for
him that I found it difficult to refrain from tears when he
addressed me on the subject. How is it that brave and gen-
erous men display such eloquence without the least inten-
tion, very often? I feel that I am a slave in one sense to the
Commodore as well as our Captain as far as obedience to
lawful and righteous orders go, when issued by them, but it
is a thralldom that I flatter myself virtuous men would
boast of.

Capt. Charles H. Bell, USN
Crayon and pastel, L. Buchheister, 1856
National Portrait Gallery, Washington, D.C.

24 *August 1845*

*Sunday. Went ashore. Visited the burial ground appropri-
ated to the American seamen and officers and there met
the melancholy sight of several of the graves of our fellow
citizens and countrymen, both officers and men, Passed
Midshipman Henry amongst others—who could withhold
a sigh? More eloquent, more pathetic than the most finished and studied sentences.*

Passed Midn. William Henry had been aboard the *Yorktown* for
about a month while the *Yorktown* was fitting out in New York, but
Lawrence would not have known him then as Lawrence did not
report aboard until weeks after Henry had been transferred from
the *Yorktown* to the *Preble*. The transfer was fatal, as Henry was one
of that ship's nineteen victims of African fever.

*The female inhabitants of these huts that compose the
hamlet here are remarkably well featured and well made—
quite perniciously enticing—apt to lead one from the path
of rectitude unless very guarded; huts are to be kept clear
of, if one wishes to maintain good resolutions. Voluptuously inclined doubtless, dern 'em!*

The ship's log indicates that on 26 August 1845 one Lt. James A.
Doyle detaches from the *Yorktown* owing to illness. Lt. Richard C.
Cogdell, who has come from Norfolk aboard the *Southampton,*
replaces him. Cogdell has been in the navy for fifteen of his thirty-
three years. He is, however, known to have had a serious problem
with alcohol and is not a likable man. In October 1843 Cdr.
Franklin Buchanan, while in command of the *Vincennes* in
Pensacola, Florida, had requested Cogdell's orders to that ship be
canceled. Buchanan said Cogdell's reputation was such that he had

not the "*slightest confidence* in him as an officer, and his being placed at the Wardroom table as an associate of gentlemen is a matter of regret to them, as well as myself." Told he must either drop the matter or make formal charges, Buchanan responded with the latter, charging drunkenness and "scandalous conduct" and appending a list of some forty witnesses to his written claim.[4] Buchanan had to take the *Vincennes* to sea almost immediately after his submission, however. Apparently for that reason Cogdell, recuperating in the hospital from being on the losing end of a drunken brawl, was not court-martialed. In February 1844, expecting him to be ordered to their ship, the officers of the *Bainbridge* (except the captain) had taken the extraordinary step of writing to their commodore, asking that Cogdell not be sent to their ship as they were "seriously opposed to having for a shipmate a person of his known character and habits."[5] That April Cogdell was court-martialed in Pensacola for drunkenness and absence without leave, and sentenced to dismissal. However, he somehow managed to get a reprieve—likely due to his family's prominence in South Carolina. President Tyler commuted the sentence to six months' suspension from rank and pay. Shortly after his suspension was over Cogdell was on his way to the African Squadron. Captain Bell did not want him, but was given no other choice. On 21 August the *Yorktown* had also transferred Midn. Jonathan H. Carter to the *Preble* in exchange for Midn. H. G. D. Brown.

27 August 1845

> *Mr. Neville's charges today were concluded and the wit-nesses for the defence also were finished. The case will end tomorrow; on the 30th the* Preble *will leave, carrying with her the delinquents, and the proceedings of the court.*

28 August 1845

Wind and weather the same; Messrs Doyle, Marin and Neville were detached and ordered to the Preble. *For the second of these gentlemen and last also I feel so much kindness towards that I regret their leaving the ship vastly. In revisiting the coast again, I shall frequently be reminded of Mr. Marin from the fact of his and myself having been ashore together so often at various places. The circumstance will give rise to many a pensive reflection when it shall rise up in my mind.*

The cases of Acting Master John S. Neville and Lt. Mathias C. Marin were actually quite unrelated matters, though the two were tried by the same court. Serving as the *Yorktown*'s senior passed midshipman and her sailing master, Neville had fifteen years of naval service. His previous cruise, under Bell's command on the *Dolphin* two years earlier, had not been a happy one. Bell had extracted him from the hospital to sail to Africa, and then had been obliged to send him back early for his health. Neville's problems now, however, were irresponsible behavior and alcohol. His drunkenness at Funchal and again at Cape Coast Castle (while in the company of British officers) had been obnoxious. Finally, on 19 February Bell placed Neville under arrest. That Neville apparently remained under arrest and off the watchbill for the six months prior to the trial, during which time his services would have been quite useful, indicates the degree of Bell's displeasure. (Neville's popularity was not enhanced by his pet parrot, which annoyed everyone by soiling the wardroom floor.) The court-martial sentenced him to be dismissed from the service, a sentence later upheld by President Polk.

Marin's case largely involved his inability to get along with Lt. Henry Steele. Like Steele, Marin had bothersome medical problems, his involving his stomach and eyes, so that both men were more irritable than they might otherwise have been. The conditions of an African cruise would not have helped either's condition, though in fact the friction had begun on the other side of the Atlantic. Nor was it Marin's first such dispute; in 1843 he had been court-martialed and suspended from rank for disobedience of orders and treating a superior officer with contempt. While aboard the *Yorktown* on New Year's Day 1845, Marin had taken over Steele's chair at the head of the senior wardroom table. Steele told him to move, was rebuffed, and reported the event to the captain, who ordered Marin to yield place to Steele. Apparently Marin returned to his customary seat at Steele's left, but Steele suspended him from duty and the rancor simmered. As months went by it erupted in a series of petty incidents. Steele overheard Marin referring to him as a "damned son of a bitch" and a "son of a whore." Steele produced his receipt for the extra dollar for the arms on his chair, and said that in any case it was not the chair itself that mattered but the location. At table, though Steele claimed the first helping of food by his seniority, Marin at times would deliberately serve everyone else first. For his part, after speaking "roughly" to Marin about leaving a wet overcoat in the wardroom, Steele for months refused to speak to him at all except in line of duty. Steele also removed a cot Marin had been using to sleep outside. Marin at one point challenged Steele to set aside his office as first lieutenant and slug it out; Steele declined. Perhaps the most insightful moment came when Marin, after calling Steele names, said, "I want to go home." At that point they were over eight months out of New York. Sickness, weariness, a prickly sense of personal pride, and the conditions of the African coast were taking their toll. Though Steele was perhaps irritable, it appears he had not done anything absolutely wrong, and he was the senior officer. Marin was found guilty and sentenced to dismissal. President Polk, perhaps recognizing Marin's illness as a mitigating factor in the situation, changed that sentence to twelve months' suspension. For the *Yorktown* and the African Squadron, though, the net effect of the proceedings was to reduce the officer ranks by two more men.[6]

From his armless seat at the junior ("steerage") wardroom table Lawrence, who both admired Steele and liked Marin, would have seen the goings-on and must have felt lucky not to be involved.

29 August 1845

Wind and weather the same. The only remarkable circumstance that occurred this day was the departure of the Preble. *As she passed the Flagship, three cheers were exchanged between them; she hove up her anchor and made sail in a complete calm but in the course of half or three quarters of an hour a slight breeze sprung up and soon she was borne along at a moderate rate which in the same ratio must have risen the joyous feelings of all on board. What satisfaction must the poor invalids (and they were numerous) have experienced when they thus saw themselves at length in the course of being delivered from so much misery of body and depression of heart! about to be restored to an atmosphere free from the rank malaria which they had been forced to languish in for months. Propitious breezes speed her, say I!*

31 August 1845

Was like unto it. Some went to church on board Jamestown—*so did not I! Finished painting at last.*

11

September 1845

Anxious to be relieved of their African duty before being ordered to begin another tour of the coast, the crew of the *Yorktown* eagerly awaited the arrival of the *Marion*, which they knew had been ordered to join the African Squadron. (The *Marion* will finally arrive in late October, though not as the *Yorktown*'s relief.)

PORTO GRANDE, CAPE VERDE

1 September 1845

Set in no wise differently from what it has for the last ten or fifteen days past. Two gross disappointments today we were all subjected to: two vessels made their appearance at the distance of ten or twelve miles; we of course set them down as the Marion *barque-of-war each time, but alas! they stood across the harbor, dashing our hopes!*

2 September 1845

Weather same. Swayed up and fidded topgallant masts,

getting affairs in order to go to sea on Saturday and to pro-
ceed to Africa, that teeming realm of pestilence. It is to be
feared that we will not escape the deluging season.

The ship's repair effort is nearly finished. A mast of a large sailing ship is not a single pole. The *Yorktown*'s masts were made of
three sections; a fid was a large pin inserted through holes in the
top of one part and the bottom of the other, helping to hold them
together. The crew also performs a variety of mundane chores,
such as taking their hammocks ashore for scrubbing.

3 September 1845

Weather same. Bent sails, and a number [of] insignificant
and uninteresting acts were transacted, that would be
ridiculous to mention.

4 September 1845

The weather of this place, and even of these islands all
together, is a matter not to be enlarged upon, being of such
extreme regularity. During the rainy season it is always
gusty, rainy and unsettled; in the dry, clear, fresh breezes
and salubrious; such are the two seasons in these bland lat-
itudes. Now is the dry season here, consequently no other
than the above varieties are noticeable.

This was a day marked with (in comparison with the
general monotony) a little celebrity, on account of a visit
from the Commodore and captain of Flag ship. An inspec-
tion of the ship, was one of the features of the occasion; a
comfortable and social dinner I suppose another; this in

*the matter is as far as I can go. I left the ship in the midst
of her honors and went to enjoy a sentimental ramble on
the margin of this bay. T'was [a] lonely one but what with
the invigorating Northeast wind, and the exercise that the
yielding sand gave to the body when each step was taken,
that the most pleasant and most agreeable train of
thoughts were induced that could have possibly been
enjoyed under any other circumstances. I found no shells,
though, one object of my perambulations, so I retraced my
steps, and soon returned on board.*

AT SEA
———

5 September 1845

*Preparations for sea—plenty of business for all hands. In
the morning of this day (latter part by sea time)[1] we
crossed our Royal and Topgallant yards, clewed hawse,
unmoored ship and got under way in the course of about
three hours. After the anchor was atrip she was wore
round, on the Starboard Tack and stood out of the harbor,
a sail in sight standing down for the bay apparently. We
now consider ourselves upon the commencement of our last
cruise, may health attend us! The day continued as delightful as it began, and we were favored with a delicious fresh
trade breeze all day.*

The *Yorktown* heads back to Porto Praya on the Cape Verde
island of St. Iago.

7 September 1845

All things the same. At daylight the Isle St. Iago in sight, at 6 A.M. the isle Fogo ditto. Standing along the land, crew mustered, rules and regulations read, nothing more. Several sails in sight.

PORTO PRAYA, ST. IAGO, CAPE VERDE
___

8 September 1845

At about 2 P.M. the wind sprung up with some freshness and we at 4 P.M. made the town Porto Praya. Beating in (wind hauling ahead) at 6 ran in under Topsails, Jib and Flying Jib, and came to in ten fathoms water. Here we are to lie twenty-four hours, when we proceed upon philan- thropic cruising.

AT SEA
___

9 September 1845

Strong Northeast winds, an English whaleship stood in for the harbor today. When within two miles of the town hove the Main Topsail to the Mast, lowered a boat. She then lay off and on until the boat returned, filled away and stood to sea. The town was nearly exhausted this day of provisions to furnish our ship. Turkeys, Chickens, Hogs, Bananas, and

Oranges were in such profusion on board as to pall the appetite with the sight of them. It is a matter worthy of some speculation to the curious to notice the difference in point of fertility between this island (St. Iago) and that of several others of the group. The contrast between this and that of St. Vincent's particularly may be drawn: they lie nearly in the same latitude, the faces of the country of both are very similar to each other, being very mountainous and dry to aridity, they are each exposed to the same winds (Northeast trades), the climate of course of the two is the same, and lastly (as far as a common inspection goes) the soils seem of the same description. Consequently whence arises the great difference in point of fertility in the soils of the two isles? It must be owing to some great geological cause that escapes the notice of the casual and unprofessional observer. The island of St. Vincent is little more than a desert, its vegetable productions are so very limited, but strange to say the Watermelon thrives here prodigiously and attains to great perfection notwithstanding the great scarcity of water. But, St. Iago is really a highly fertile island, more so than any of the rest of the group. Next to it probably comes St. Antonio in this last point of view. As to the islands of St. Mayo, St. Lucia, Branco, Fogo and Brava, I am quite ignorant of and therefore will not venture to assert anything relative to them.

10 September 1845

Going along at the rates of 7, 8, 9 and 10 knots per hour with the trades, towards the close of this day the wind became very faint. At 10 A.M. all hands were called to wit-

ness punishment. Certainly a very unpleasant duty to a man possessing any humanity, but nevertheless a penalty vitally necessary to discipline in case of the violation of any regulation established in a ship. Seafaring people can neither be held in a state of obedience and regularity without the fear of some punishment. For they are no more than wayward children for the most part, without discrimination, prudence or forethought, blind to their own interests, suspicious of the intentions of those benevolently inclined towards them, and implicitly credulous towards those who cater to their appetites, with the design of ultimate peculation. 'Tis true indeed great alacrity may be elicited from sailors in the performance of their duties by the partiality they may cherish for an officer, but still there must be some respect amounting to fear of him before this alacrity can be commanded. But [to] expect to reduce sailors [to] a state of necessary discipline either through the force of love or by the powers of reasoning is nothing more than chimerical nonsense—for sailors, like children, are too fickle to retain any affection long, and too sensual to regard rationality when it would impose restraint upon any immediate indulgence. Thus we are obliged to use severe punishment to prevent frequent recurrences of irregularities. It must under all these circumstances be admitted that severe penalties on board ship are the wisest and most politic manners in the end.

Flogging is a regular practice in the navy at this time. Though Lawrence has not commented on it until now, Captain Bell metes out this corporal punishment not infrequently for various infractions, sometimes to a single sailor but often to two or three at once. Such punishments tended to occur after the ship had left a port,

Flogging
E. Shippen, *Thirty Years at Sea*, Philadelphia: J. B. Lippincott, 1879.

and Porto Praya with its attendant bumboats could offer weary sailors refreshment beyond meat and vegetables even if liberty was not permitted. The punishments recorded in the ship's log for 10 September are as follows:

> Thomas Parson, Captain's Mate—12 of the cat for
>   mutinous conduct; disrated
> George Connor (Foretopman)—9 for drunkenness;
>   disrated to seaman
> Thomas Beesby (Captain of the Main Hold)—11 for
>   neglect of duty; disrated
> John Buck (Marine)—7 for disobedience of orders
> W. Nief—7 for drunkenness
> L. Nichols—9 for drunkenness
> J. Worthy—7 for drunkenness
> C. Robinson—12 for drunkenness
> J. Witham—7 for drunkenness[2]

12 September 1845

Wind and weather the same. Was honored by an invitation to dinner in the cabin. Entertainment genteel, and delicious; the conversation delightfully agreeable—easy, refined, and intellectual—and of course highly entertaining.

13 September 1845

Wind very light, thermometer 84°, nothing observable except calms and light rain.

14 September 1845

Weather the same. The evening set in very beautifully and calmly; the day closed in more gorgeously magnificent manner than I remember of ever having witnessed before. Such indescribably beautiful tints, as well as fantastic forms, as were assumed by the clouds at the declination of great objects of Persian Worship struck the observation even of the thoughtless sailors. At intervals, light blue, light green and silvery white grounds would appear in juxtaposition with deep Orange, Yellow and intense Crimson and carmine colored clouds. This is [a] topic so harped upon by every penny-a-liner, that it is really sickening very often to remark about anything of the kind at all in the most cursory manner, but the rarity of such exhibitions as were this night presented to view were so extraordinary as calculated to leave a strong impression on the mind for a long time to come. But they proved magnificent and unerring indices of rain, and calm weather.

15 September 1845

The day set in a most fitful manner to be sure. Rain, sunshine, and calm followed each other in quick alternation, like the capricious moods of an indulged beauty.

16 September 1845

Wind and weather the same. Nothing to note, barring the appearance of a few friendly sharks and swordfish.

It is a tedious time, with extreme heat and humidity to the point that Lawrence's fellow steerage member, Assistant Surgeon Williams, exclaims, "from the manner in which I have perspired for the last week, I should not be surprised if I became as dry as a piece of smoked beef." Williams expresses a general feeling in wishing that "we had with us Mr. Webster, by whose celebrated treaty we are stuck in for such abominable cruising. His presence with us for a week would relieve all the party, then he might make another such treaty if he chose."[3]

17 September 1845

Noting the changes and incidents of the days hereabouts is vastly important it must be confessed! Made and reduced sail as required, how important! How interesting will this account be in years to come to know that within the space of twenty-four hours, all the Larboard studding sails were set, and all the Starboard taken in, and vice versa! Perhaps ten or fifteen times! Though there is one serious fact now making itself manifest: that is, that a sweet breeze is impelling us towards Monrovia at a most cheering rate.

18 September 1845

During the last twenty-four hours the most delightful breezes have favored us, delightful from two reasons: first, because refreshing; secondly, because fair for us. By the way in noticing these features of the weather, I must not neglect to make the observation that between the latitudes of 10° and 11° N to about 7° odd N and between Longitudes 19° West and 14° odd West very light winds and calms seem to prevail almost always, but one or two degrees either side of the above points the navigator is pretty sure of meeting with winds. The tract of ocean comprehended between the above latitudes and longitudes may be about where the great Northeast and Southeast trades fail, although this is of course mere conjecture. With a very slim basis of probability to rest on, it is in itself a fact that forces itself upon the frequenters of these seas with most irksome force.

19 September 1845

Wind from the Northward and Westward, fresh too, but what renders the weather particularly unpleasant is the frequency and heaviness of the rains, the present time being the latter part of the "rainy season." But towards meridian it usually clears up as it did today. At 10 A.M. land in sight; that contiguous to Galinas river it proved. An hermaphrodite brig rigged steamer was laying off from the river about six or seven miles. Her name was the Hecate, *Captain West (British). Sent a boat on board of us; three months on the station. Finding it would be profitless to come to at Galinas, hauled our wind and stood for Cape Mount. We may now be considered as having entered upon our old cruising ground again. It certainly is a most tedious ordeal to be got through with, but nevertheless as it is as inevitable as fate we must strive to be cheerful in the prosecution of it. Four long months to be endured in this state of exile! It is a theme not to be dwelt upon, lest too many regrets arise and engross the soul.*

20 September 1845

*At 5:30 A.M. of this day we made Cape Mesurado. At 11
A.M. clewed up and came to anchor, sent a boat on shore to
ascertain the news. No letters or intelligence of any kind.*

MONROVIA, CAPE MESURADO

21 September 1845

*Nothing occurred worth mentioning. It seems that the
French have purchased a tract of land on the Northern
bank of Gaboon river, in which is comprehended the town
of King Glass. It would seem that the worldly interests of
Mr. Wilson, the intensely pious missionary situated down
there, have been intruded upon by the transaction and that
he actually made a puny attempt to interrupt it, and that
too at a risk of producing difficulties between our country
and France. The insignificant wretch! Turn the rascal
naked amongst savages say I.*

The "news" from Gaboon relates to the French methods of
establishing sovereignty. A year earlier French officials had gotten
King Glass drunk and induced him to sign what he believed was a
friendly letter to King Louis Philippe. The document was actually
a cession of territory, a document that Glass, even if sober, had
insufficient authority to sign. Now it is learned that in August, a
month before the *Yorktown*'s present visit to Monrovia, a French
warship had enforced that nation's claim over the strong objec-
tions of the natives, by (among other things) cannonading the

vicinity until the Africans ran up a French flag. After a shot hit his church and others landed nearby, Rev. Wilson had run up the American flag (likely the storm ensign the *Yorktown* had given him in February) as a sign of neutrality, though the result was only to further antagonize the French.[4] As before, Lawrence's opinion of Wilson is strongly biased, perhaps by anti-Wilson commentary in northern newspapers.

While anchored off Monrovia the *Yorktown*, as usual, replenishes her water supply.

22 September 1845

Wind light, weather pleasant. Taking in a supply of limpid fluid. A dangerous surf all along shore—bad landing.

23 September 1845

Nothing new, wind and weather unpleasant. Too much rain entirely for comfort; everything in a half slimy state for the incessant humidity.

24 September 1845

Wind and weather the same. Towards evening the Barque Cambria *got under way and stood to sea, but in the course of half an hour she hauled her wind and stood in again and came to about two cables length from us. In the morning the Captain came on board, with a complaint that his mate and three men were in a state of mutiny. Our first Lieutenant was sent on board to inquire into the case, and found that the difficulties arose from the Captain's attempting to force bad provisions upon them with a view of economizing. This was very properly resisted by the mate and crew, hence the charge of mutiny from the Captain, who is probably some dastardly niggard, whose avaricious soul is bent on accumulation, never mind though the most petty gain be obtained at the price of sufferings nay death of scores of his own kind. Alas that the profession should be so disgraced with so many dispositions of a similar kind with the same poor wretch.*

25 September 1845

The Cambria *got to sea during the latter part of this day. An English ship (likely a sloop of war) was seen in the off-ing; an English cutter came to anchor here, likewise an English brig, the* Australian, *bound for England with a load of Palm Oil.*

26 September 1845

Wind and weather light and cloudy. Nothing further occurred than the above mentioned circumstances, until near the close of the day, when a schooner with American colors hove in sight and stood in for the road stead a long way inside of us, then backed her topsail, but seeing that we were watering ship, which she intended also, she wore round, filled away her topsail and stood out toward Cape Mount.

The English ship HBM steam sloop *Hecate* sends a boat to the *Yorktown,* undoubtedly to discuss the suspicious schooner.

She was a topsail schooner, with very taut spars and alto-gether a very dashing looking craft. A boat from this ship was sent to board her with the First Lieutenant in it. She soon returned, with the intelligence that many of her out-fits laid her liable to the suspicion of her being a slaver. She was from New York consigned to the noted Mr. Carnot of ambiguous memory residing at Cape Mount. These cir-cumstances being considered by our Captain as sufficient warrant to follow her we immediately hove up anchors and got to sea heading for Cape Mount. Schooner's name is the Patuxent, *New York, Captain former mate of the* Atalanta *(Jackass brig).*

CAPE MOUNT

27 September 1845

Commences extremely unpleasant. At 6 P.M. a moistening damp shed its favors upon us by way of preparation for the deluge that overwhelmed us in the course of one or two hours after the first mentioned favor. We arrived abreast of Cape Mount about half past nine in the evening (although hardly discernable from the thick mist that pervaded the atmosphere), came to at 11 P.M. In the course of one or two hours after being at anchor certain lights were discovered in a direction that led to suspicions that the embarkation of slaves was going on. Accordingly two boats were lowered, manned and given in charge to the First and Second Lieutenants, who went in quest of the lights to ascertain what they led to, but meeting with such amazing strong

*currents, they were, after four or six hours useless rowing,
swept half way down to the Galinas. At five in the morning
they after much fatigue got on board. When the morning
dawned the suspected schooner, a brig, barque and English
steamer* Hecate *were all in view.*

28 September 1845

*The same continuation of rain. At 1 P.M. hove up anchor
and stood in towards the Cape. When within one or two
miles of the shore let go our anchor and sent a boat on
board of the* Patuxent *schooner in charge of First
Lieutenant. A search commenced on board of her, and
many articles calculated to condemn her were found. The
Captain was ashore and (as was afterwards found out)
was along with Mr. Carnot up the river on a negro pur-
chasing expedition. Still the Captain, wishing to make
assurance doubly sure, has determined to wait for another
day or two.*

29 September 1845

*No wind, but weather ah! Christ how deplorable! At 1 P.M.
we cheerlessly hove up our anchor, and with thoroughly
damped spirits as well as Jackets, made sail to Topsails, Jib
and Fore Sail, and at three quarters of a mile from the suspicious schooner came to anchor. As above related no posi-
tive steps were taken towards securing our prize, or what
subsequently proved our prize, till the morning of this day
(say 8 A.M.). The Captain of the* Patuxent, *Davis, then*

came on board to satisfy the Captain of our ship in regard
to the suspicions entertained against her by him. After various discussions, and examinations of shipping documents
etc., sufficient and cogent reasons were deduced for taking
her as a prize and detaining the Captain and Mate as prisoners, who were by the bye two as bright and intelligent
looking men as I have seen for a long time. I confess that
my sympathy was enlisted in their behalf. But, they are
men arrived at the years of discretion and of course fully
aware of the chances against them in this precarious and, I
must conscientiously add, nefarious game.

The Captain apprises or rather asserts that the prize
cost him nearly $4000, but that I should judge to be an
exaggeration. The mate of her is a man about as well calculated for an enterprise where danger and daring and
action were necessary to the achievement of any object as
any I can now think of or remember ever having seen. He
is all vivacity and perception apparently, with a frame that
indicates the utmost of muscular power to be expected in
the human frame. Of course the utmost plausibility is mustered by these unfortunates in their attempt to establish
their innocence, but alas for them it avails not! Shaw, the
mate, is a Maine man. The mite of prize money that she
will yield will be imperceptible by a less power than that of
a microscopic one, I fear. Mr. Chandler, Second Lieutenant,
is prize master. A crew has been sent on board of her and
soon she will depart for the "land of the brave and the
home of the free," I suppose. The chief grounds for suspicions of her being a slaver were that she had materials for a
slave deck, much rice (to feed the slaves on) and informal-
ity of shipping documents.[5]

29 September 1845 [sic]

Weather clear and calm. At daylight as handsome a brig of war was discovered at anchor with English Colors set as I remember to have ever seen. She is one of the celebrated simonds' models. But as no communication was held between her and our ship I could not find her name out. Captain Chandler took formal possession of his command this day, and sailed for Monrovia. Reports are abroad that the Patsey C. Blount *is out here on a slave expedition. This vessel was formerly a packet between New York and Balise [Belize]. We got under way at 9 A.M. and stood for Cape Mesurado.*[6]

AT SEA

30 September 1845

Wind and weather pleasant as usual, though rain a never failing concomitant in a greater or less degree. The current during these twenty-four hours proved so strong, that even with a three knot breeze we fell to leeward all the time. The currents in the vicinity of the Mount for at least thirty miles in circumference are governed by no uniformity. The causes of their strength and direction I suppose might be traced to local circumstances, but still no calculations can be founded to ascertain those periods or places where these shall be found. In the morning (during the night the wind having slacked off) we found ourselves to the Northward of Galinas River a distance of thirty odd miles from where we

started. *Nor were our prize and a large English [vessel]*
standing in the same direction any more fortunate than we
were; in fact they fell further to leeward than we did. Thus
did the day lapse away in watching our progress, or ret-
rogress as the case might be.

31 September 1845

This day set in with a breeze in our favor, and carried us
along at a rate sufficient to stem the current here to be met
with, and at 3:30 P.M. we found ourselves to the weather
gauge of Cape Mount.[7]

12

The Patuxent

The case of the *Patuxent* provides a particularly clear example of the difficulties the U.S. Navy and the officers of its African Squadron could confront in their efforts to stem the slave trade.

Though she had no slaves aboard at the time she was taken, the circumstantial evidence available to Bell, as he pointed out in his correspondence to the secretary of the navy, decidedly suggested she was intended for operation as a slaver. Indeed, the *Patuxent* met most of the points of suspicion listed in the secretary of the navy's directions to the African Squadron (any one of which would have made her liable for seizure under article nine of the Quintuple Treaty of 1841). In addition Bell believed that Captain Canot, one of the most notorious slavers of the time, actually had purchased her. She had certainly visited his establishment several times and had carried him (under an assumed name) to Sierra Leone and back. When taken the *Patuxent* had eighteen hundred gallons of water aboard, plus casks available to hold more. She also carried nearly nine thousand pounds of rice. Such provisions were the amount needed to sustain several hundred slaves on a voyage from Africa to Brazil or Cuba, but vastly beyond the needs of her crew of ten. Though it was later claimed that the water was serving as ballast and the rice was to be sold along the coast, water was not commonly used as ballast (except in slavers), there was little coastal trade in rice, and at the time of boarding the captain, Nathaniel T. Davis, had declared he had nothing for sale. The stanchions in her hold were removable, and her cargo contained planking that could be laid to make a slave deck. Canot and Davis claimed the planking was intended to sheathe the hull of the small ship Canot was building at New Florence. However, Bell pointed out that the ship had been under construction for four years, so it was suspected Canot kept her unfinished as an excuse for employing blacksmiths and carpenters that could make manacles and slave decks for what was believed to be Canot's real business of slave-trading. (The *Patuxent* had visited Cape Mount four times without offloading the planking.) Her papers, too, were irregular; the crew names on her sailing document did not match her actual crew. Furthermore—and an especially aggravating point— Captain Davis had previously been mate of the *Atalanta,* which under the nose of the two watchful navies had recently taken several hundred slaves to Brazil, a shipment which Bell believed was for Canot's account.[1]

No doubt it was because of her association with Canot, as well as Davis's association with the *Atalanta,* that the *Patuxent* had been closely watched. First the British, then Bell, had followed her at sea, while the Liberian government had sent someone to keep an eye on her from the shore. The ship's movements were suspicious, as though she awaited an opportunity to take on a load of slaves and slip away, and Bell believed that Canot had slaves hidden and waiting at inland barracoons. Clearly the British Navy, Bell, and the Liberians all were convinced that Canot intended to use the ship in his old trade. Indicating the evidence was as strong as they could hope (short of having slaves aboard), Bell stated, "If this vessel is acquitted, it will be useless to keep a force on this station." He added, "If it is necessary, before a vessel can be condemned in our courts, that the slaves must be actually on board, not a seizure can be made, for the flag is changed the moment she has her living cargo, and then our cruisers have no right to touch them."[2] One senses here the voice of frustrated experience, though Bell soon would prove himself dramatically wrong.

On 27 October Bell placed Lieutenant Chandler, his second lieutenant, in charge of the prize vessel. Chandler was ordered to sail her with the *Yorktown* to Cape Mesurado before escorting the *Patuxent* to her home port of New York for legal disposition.

Though Lawrence's first impression had been that she was "very dashing," the *Patuxent* was on closer look an unimpressive prize. A foretopsail schooner of ninety-six tons built in 1833, to those who boarded her the *Patuxent* showed her age, being not particularly well kept. Her cargo of rice and lumber, too, though incriminating, was of modest value.[3] Captain Bell knew that whomever he sent on her prize crew would not return to the *Yorktown,* so he may have taken the opportunity to get rid of some of his less desirable people. While Chandler seems to have been a perfectly able seaman, with twenty-five years of navy service, his intemperate personality made it unlikely that under his command the *Patuxent* would be a happy ship.

Lawrence would record his own opinion of Chandler's second in command, Midn. William Cushman, but Chandler was to describe Cushman as "uncommonly ignorant of his profession" and by his "deportment . . . indifference to the service and incapacity—and want of character, worse than useless to me."[4] In part we may blame the conflict between the two on Chandler's irascibility, but in fact when Cushman later that year became a student at the new Naval School at Annapolis (which later became the U.S. Naval Academy), he rather bore out Chandler's evaluation. He ranked last or almost last in every subject, and failed to graduate.[5] As for the eight enlisted members of the *Patuxent* crew, little can be said except what will be seen of their behavior under Chandler's command.

The *Patuxent*'s masts and spars were sound, though Chandler described her sails as "nearly unserviceable." After the two ships arrived together at Cape Mesurado, the *Yorktown*'s sail maker and carpenter made some repairs to the *Patuxent*'s mainsail and hawse pipe.[6] Captain Bell took off a small bullock and a sheep and had them slaughtered to feed his own crew. That left about six dozen chickens and a couple of small goats, to which were added rations appropriate to feed the prize crew for six weeks (considered ample for the voyage to New York).[7] The *Patuxent*'s four Kroomen were let go ashore, but the six non-African members of her captured crew had to work their way to New York under arrest.

Chandler began his voyage westward on 6 October. It was ill-starred. Two weeks out he discovered the water supply had been overestimated and restricted its use. Two days later he flogged his youngest crewman, giving First Class Boy William Stoughton twelve lashes for disobedience to orders and neglect of duty. Under good conditions the *Patuxent* ought to have made it to New York within a month, but the weather was not favorable. On 10 November the whiskey stores, which had been transferred from the *Yorktown* in leaky breakers, ran out, so the customary daily lifting of spirits was ended.[8] Much worse, the ship was leaking too. By 14 November Chandler decided it was leaking so dangerously he could not make it to New York. Calling all hands, he announced his decision to head for Bermuda. Pumping more and more frequently, they arrived at Bermuda on 19 November.[9]

Chandler needed to justify his failure to make New York, plus the necessity for whatever expenses might be incurred. He contacted the U.S. consul in Bermuda, who arranged for a formal survey of the ship by local experts. That same day, as a crewman pumped constantly to keep the ship afloat in the calm anchorage, the experts certified her to be unseaworthy, with serious leaks and other damage. Chandler could thank his stars he had not needed the ship's boat, as it filled with water as soon as it was hoisted over the side.[10]

In order to get a better look at the leaks, some of which were inaccessible below the waterline and behind the cargo, Chandler had the ship unloaded and careened, no small amount of work on the part of his combined crew of navy men and prisoners. Indeed, their numbers swiftly diminished, for after two rather grueling months at sea the shore enticed. By 21 November Chandler had three of his fourteen men in the local jail and two missing, plus one of the original crew refusing to work. Chandler's own senior enlisted man, Boatswain's Mate Samuel White, had engaged in "disrespectful and riotous conduct." That evening, after Chandler left Cushman in charge, three of the prize crew absconded. One returned "in liquor, and exceedingly mutinous and abusive."[11] Chandler not only had to pay the authorities to round them up (two were not readily found), but also was billed for daily jail fees. The next day he compensated for the loss of work by his delinquent men by engaging four local laborers to help with the offloading. He also rented space near the dock to use as quarters for officers and men, and to store the materials from the ship. The Bermudans had their own pace, though, and Chandler's own men were scarcely better, so the work went slowly. In response to Chandler's report describing his situation, the secretary of the navy directed him to "lose no time unnecessarily" while, however, paying "the strictest regard to economy."[12] The letter bearing this advice crossed in the mail with one from Chandler describing his efforts to do exactly those things, though under difficulties "almost impossible to conceive" (including, by then, having four men in jail).[13]

Patched, recaulked, and tarred, her ballast and cargo loaded back aboard, and with her worn mainsail frugally strengthened by strips from a cut-up topsail, the *Patuxent* was at last ready to sail again on 18 December. On the morning of 20 December she rode a fair breeze westward. The ship's sails and rigging were, even after patching, "forlorn," and though Chandler's jailbirds were back aboard, his cook, one John Brown, remained at large on Bermuda with a ten dollar price on his head. Still, Chandler congratulated himself that soon he would be entering New York Harbor, or at least some American port.[14] By that night, though, the winds turned contrary and the leaking, which the repairs had diminished but not stopped, got steadily worse.[15] The worn sails, too, in the face of what became gale winds, tore quickly. Chandler and his disgruntled crew had little rest, some constantly pumping as the leaking increased to three hundred gallons per hour, while others took down, stitched up, and rebent first one sail and then the other, as the sails tore repeatedly in the gale. Finally calm weather gave respite to the sails, but the leaking continued unabated. There was really only one option. A glum and weary Lieutenant Chandler brought his unseaworthy craft back into Bermuda on Christmas Day.[16]

Once back alongside the wharf, Chandler had a new survey made of the *Patuxent*'s condition, which confirmed he was lucky to have made it back alive. Again he stripped her down, removed the sails and entire contents of the ship, and placed the lumber on the wharf and the rest of the cargo in an adjacent rented warehouse. The ship was hove out and repaired and economically resheathed with boards and tarpaper instead of copper. Of necessity he ordered new sails. It would have been a better investment simply to abandon the hull, but the ship was the tangible evidence in the case against the crew.[17] Chandler financed mounting expenditures upon the credit of the U.S. Navy. He also tapped another source to defray the expenses of the ship's original crew: one hundred dollars cash that Captain Davis had agreed Chandler could hold until their arrival in New York. This time Chandler's men were less troublesome; he had to imprison only one, from Davis's crew.

Finding Midshipman Cushman worse than useless and insolent to boot, Chandler took on a Mr. John Camp, an experienced mate who wanted a ride to New York, as a temporary officer without pay.[18] However, within a few days Mr. Camp had wandered off and returned drunk, which Chandler pointed out was a poor example for the men. After more difficulties he fired Camp.

Though Bell had ordered Chandler not to let any of the original crew set foot ashore until reaching New York, that order obviously had been impossible to enforce in Bermuda. Indeed, while the ship was under repair he had been obliged to hire lodging in a building near the wharf for all hands not in jail. There on the afternoon of 24 January, as he wrote his latest report to the secretary of the navy, Chandler looked out the window to see his intended mail ship, the Portuguese schooner *Humilidade,* leave port for New York. An hour later Thomas Shaw, the *Patuxent*'s mate, came in to hand him a farewell note from the *Patuxent*'s Captain Davis, who to Chandler's distress had chosen to break his solemn word of honor and depart aboard the *Humilidade.* Hastening to a hilltop, Chandler could only watch the ironically named *Humilidade,* already far enough out to sea to make pursuit impossible, sailing away under a fresh wind. All he could do was return to his desk, take out a fresh sheet of paper, and send a description of Davis to the attorney general in New York by the next steamship. Then he was obliged to compose yet another report of misfortune to the secretary of the navy.[19]

At last on 20 February 1846 Chandler extracted one man from jail and issued new winter clothing, shoes, tobacco, and other odds and ends to everyone for the voyage. The next day, again leaving behind his long-absent cook John Brown, he got under way for New York.[20] The weather was rough, but by 1 March he had made it as far as the Gulf Stream east of Cape Hatteras. There the easterly gale winds approached hurricane strength, shifted to southerly, and after about a day eventually subsided leaving, as Chandler put it, "a most awful, ugly sea from Eastward and Southward, besides a chop sea from every other quarter, threatening to deluge at each moment, and bury in the cross, our little vessel."[21] That was only the prelude for what was yet to come. Half a day later the wind picked up again, building intensity until Chandler found himself struggling to survive the most powerful storm he had ever encountered in his twenty-five years in the navy. He tried heaving to, but soon saw part of his lee (starboard) bulwark carried away, plus one of the crew, who somehow managed to struggle back aboard. As the storm raged on most of the rest of the starboard bulwark was ripped away, and another crewman was injured. Chandler decided he might as well try scudding before the wind and steering through the enormous cross-seas. On deck with one man, while the others were battened below, he spent anxious hours hoping to survive. Bone weary, Chandler could do little but watch as a huge sea towered up from astern and avalanched over the ship, sweeping both men away, though each managed to grab something in time to avoid a watery grave. Drenched and bruised they fought their way back to the tiller, to find both compasses gone, plus much of the larboard bulwark, the booby hatch, and assorted fittings. The worst was over, though; Chandler was able to lie to for a day and a half until the gale abated enough for him to sail on to New York. Late on the night of 8 March the battered *Patuxent* worked her way past Sandy Hook against an ebb tide, anchoring off New York in the early light of the next morning. Apologizing for having to write with a sprained hand, Chandler reported his arrival to the secretary of the navy.[22]

Now the wheels of justice could begin to turn, which initially they did with alacrity. Indeed, though Captain Davis had stepped ashore in New York on 10 February Chandler's letter by steamer had trumped Davis's escape by sail and he was arrested the next day. Two legal actions were involved when an alleged slave ship was captured. First, those of her crew who were American citizens could be charged with being engaged in the slave trade. The penalty could be up to two years' imprisonment plus thousands of dollars in fines. (Because under U.S. law the crews of ships caught actually carrying slaves aboard could be charged with piracy and hanged, the common practice was for an American crew to take a ship to the coast of Africa, then sell the ship to a non-American owner whose non-American crew would quickly load a cargo of slaves and head west across the Windward Passage. Often the new captain and crew had crossed the Atlantic as passengers on the ship they were to take over.) Crewmembers who were not American citizens were not prosecuted but might be held as witnesses. (In the case of the *Patuxent* only the captain and mate were Americans.) Additionally, a "libel" (condemnation) action would be taken against the ship itself. If that action succeeded the ship would be sold at auction and the proceeds, after expenses, would be paid to the navy as prize money.

Within two days of Chandler's arrival the *Patuxent* had been turned over to the marshal, and the U.S. attorney had filed suit against the ship. A week later, on 17 March, Chandler was in court experiencing the considerable satisfaction of testifying against Captain Davis and the mate Shaw. Bail was set at four thousand dollars for Davis, who took two weeks to pay it, and twenty-five hundred for Shaw.[23] The following week Davis turned the tables, charging all the officers of the *Yorktown* plus the entire prize crew of the *Patuxent*, down even to the absent cook Brown, with trespass and illegal taking of his goods, claiming damages of fifty thousand dollars. In Chandler's letter reporting this turn of events to the secretary of the navy, the required mode of address sounds unavoidably ironic: "Sir, I have the honor to inform you, that I have been under the necessity, this morning, of giving bail,—to the amount of $5000, to the sheriff of King's County in this state." Daniel Clark, one of Davis's original crewmen, whom Chandler had jailed in Bermuda for wandering off and getting drunk, also brought action against the *Yorktown*, and Chandler had to post an additional thousand dollars bail.[24]

Oddly, Davis seems not to have been informed that the libel action against his ship had already begun. Presumably for this reason, though he had been out of jail for several days when judgment was made in that case on 4 April, neither he nor any representative showed up for trial. A default decree was made and the ship was advertised for sale. Reading the advertisement in the newspaper in the nick of time, Davis successfully filed a petition to stop the sale and try the case.[25] Further, he seems to have somehow gotten his case for "unjust seizure" (against Chandler et al.) to the Supreme Court of New York.[26] Meanwhile, the mate, Shaw, filed a claim for $177 in back wages plus $100 for his sea chest and contents, which he claimed had been washed overboard after Chandler had it placed on deck.[27]

All this legal action by Captain Davis and his crew delayed resolution of the matter. Chandler, who had gone home to his mother in the District of Columbia, returned to New York for another hearing in early May, though he would much rather have been on his way to the Gulf of Mexico, where the anticipated Mexican war was erupting.[28] In late June Davis filed an "action of trouvee" against Chandler for the hundred dollars of Davis's that Chandler had spent in Bermuda. Chandler had to write the district attorney a full explanation of what he had done with the money.[29]

Toward the end of the year Canot himself, the owner of the *Patuxent*'s cargo and the person who had chartered her to carry it, arrived in New York, seeking a new shipment of planking and ship fittings to replace the one now in legal captivity. With this replacement cargo aboard a newly chartered barque he headed back for Africa in late December, before the case closed.[30]

The legal dust did not settle until 19 March 1847. At a hearing on that date the ship was ordered discharged for insufficient evidence. The judge did find, however, that Captain Bell had seized her with probable cause. Then, though officially found "innocent," the ship was sold to cover costs. The schooner herself, when new fourteen years earlier may have been worth the $4,000 Davis had mentioned aboard the *Yorktown,* but she had cost the navy some $3,000 in repairs and other expenses during the voyage home.[31] She went for $675. Her cargo sold for $421.75.[32] After costs and payment of Shaw's back pay (but nothing for his sea chest), what was left went to Davis, who had already signed it all over to lawyers.

Examining the story a century and a half later it is difficult to decide whether the *Patuxent* was guilty or not. In his memoir published some years later Canot shows astonishing candor in describing his career as a slave trader, yet with regard to the episode of the *Patuxent* he draws a picture of complete innocence. Indeed he expresses indignation at the legal finding of "probable cause for seizure," saying this "*jeu-de-mot* deprives the aggrieved party of redress and protects the captors from a just prosecution for damages hastily and inconsiderately inflicted." Of course, since he had earlier promised the British to stop trading in slaves, his posture may simply reflect a wish to retain his image of relative virtue.[33]

13

October 1845

The *Yorktown* beats her way south along the coast to Monrovia in company with her prize. After preparing the *Patuxent* for her Atlantic crossing and watering the ship, Captain Bell will continue south and west along the coast toward Gaboon.

AT SEA

1 October 1845

Beating towards Monrovia was the single transaction of the day. The current that sets to the Northward hereabouts equals one and three quarters knots. Several ineffectual attempts were made to tack, so that at last when close in shore we were obliged to wear. Finding that we drifted two points off our course, at 8 P.M. let go anchor in fifteen fathoms water veered to sixty fathoms chain. In the morning at 5 A.M. hove up and stood towards Mesurado, which at this time was in view.

2 October 1845

Plenty of rain and a half propitious breeze from the Southward and Eastward. Worked up to the distance of one and a half miles from Cape Mesurado when let go anchor in ten fathoms. At daylight hove up and beat towards the Cape. A Bremen brig sort of rather got to windward of us this time, but at 11:30 came to, in eight fathoms.

3 October 1845

This day set in delightfully serene. As the moon quarters tonight it is strongly suspected that the dry season will be ushered in with it. Strong preparations making to get the prize with her nondescript commander off.

4 October 1845

At 4 P.M. of this day the Patuxent *went to sea, sped by three cheers from our ship. As deplorable a midshipman accompanied this expedition as probably ever brought ridicule and contempt upon the service; his name Cushman.*

6 October 1845

Clear sunshiny weather again. It is now observed that the current that flowed with such force towards Cape Mesurado a few days ago has since suddenly changed its direction to that of an exactly opposite one; in index I suppose of a change of season.

Prior to leaving Monrovia the *Yorktown* takes aboard two distressed British merchant seamen whose schooner had been wrecked in the vicinity.

7 October 1845

Weather unpleasant. The first part of this day we got under way and stood down the coast. Nothing occurred.

The Governor of Liberia, J. J. Roberts, visited the ship, though apparently without any special fanfare.

9 October 1845

Sanguine. The devil's Peaks etc. in view.

10 October 1845

We are progressing along the coast at a moderate rate where nothing new is offered to our view. Settra Krou is in sight. A letter was despatched by our kind dispositioned Commander apprising Mr. Connelly of the approach of his wife in a brig late from Boston, whither she had been on a visit.

11 October 1845

At an early hour of this day we arrived at Cape Palmas. Sent a boat on shore; received no news. At 9 A.M. next morning hove up anchor and headed for the village of Taboo. In the course of our passage (say 4 P.M.) we were overtaken by HBM Steamer Hecate, *Captain West, on board of whom we transferred Dan'l Lynch and Jas Rowe, distressed English seamen. No intelligence. Bound for Princes' Island.*

TABOO, IVORY COAST

12 October 1845

Wind continues as it has been for the last two or three days, clear and pleasant. At 5 P.M. came to abreast of Taboo [Tabou], and the "White House," a house somewhat celebrated by us in the course of our last visit to this part of the coast.

The White House is the Tabou mission house, a convenient navigation landmark.

13 October 1845

Weather same. The object of our visit to this town was to settle certain matters, that did not actually amount to difficulties, but more properly perplexities, that had arisen amongst the inhabitants of Taboo and the Kroo people situated in the vicinity of each other. It would seem (to render matters a little intelligible) that at some past period two years ago the inhabitants of several towns in the vicinity of Taboo and for twenty miles to the Eastward, had displayed a piratical disposition towards some of our "nation's vessels" for which Commodore Perry inflicted severe chas-

tisement on them, and forced them into a promise that they would never be again not only not guilty of similar atrocities, but even to act as allies to any vessels under our flag in case of the attempt of any other tribes to molest any of our merchant vessels on their coast. At the time a number of Kroomen were here established as spies upon their conduct and to notice whether they would violate any of the late stipulations there, as we were under the impression that the treaty forbid their locating upon the coast at all. This the Berriby [Berebee] people attempted the other day, when notice of the move immediately was made known.

The Captain of this ship directly summoned all the Kings and headmen on board, which was promptly attended to, the treaty produced and in a very good state of preservation too and it was found that no violation of it had been committed, so that a peace palaver was the consequence—a little undiluted whiskey followed, backed by Biscuit and cheese. These entertainments gave them exalted opinions of our munificence. In the course of the day the White House missionary came on board. At 5 P.M. these proud Kings were obscurely hinted to, nay it was blandly insinuated, that the affairs of their several Kingdoms required their attendance. This remote insinuation was all we ventured upon lest their proud and fiery African hidalgo spirits should leap forth at the affront at the suspicion that we wished their absence, and that we should be overcome by a torrent of confusion that would follow from some biting harangue in the rich Guinea Language, that the above circumstance would prompt to the utterance of. At 5 the ship was cleared of them. In the morning a continuation of the palaver is to take place, or more properly speaking the complement—or supplement of it. Queer court robes are here worn as one might dream of! Damned funny I say!

The larboard bow gun fired a one-shot salute to the departing monarchs.[1]

AT SEA OFF IVORY COAST

14 October 1845

We hove up at 9 A.M. and stood along the coast, at frequent intervals boarded by various potentates. The fact of our Bread, Cheese, and Whiskey entertainment spread far and wide through the country and many visited us from the expectation of deriving the same treatment, but it was found that the fountain of munificence was intermittent in its character, and that before the arrival of many subsequent visitors it had ceased to flow.

BEREBEE, IVORY COAST

15 October 1845

At 5 P.M. we came to anchor abreast of the district subject to the rule of King George of Berriby, where it is anticipated some harangues will take place. The gentlemen of these parts having so little to do, and therefore so much leisure upon their hands, consider time of as little value to

*others and to themselves. Consequently they make their
visits indefinitely long until they are undignifiedly
prompted to take their departure. Today, as it were to miti-
gate the rudeness [of] our conduct in this particular, a couple of bottles of whiskey were bestowed upon the chiefs that
were on board, four in number.*

AT SEA

16 October 1845

*Wind and weather still delightful. We hove up early in the
morning and stood along the coast to the distance of
twenty miles when we came to in the beautiful Bay of St.
Andrews, a bay a little memorable from the visitation of
Commodore Perry (mentioned some seven or eight months
since). At this place came on board various chiefs from the
adjacent country to hold a palaver in obedience to the
summons of our Captain. The talk being concluded, two
Paixhan shells were discharged from a gun with the view to
illustrate to these savages the hazard they would incur by
exciting our wrath. These things being witnessed, and a
present of a gallon of whiskey being made to them (a present commensurate to the regal occasion) they departed in
the enjoyment of all the satisfaction that men passionately
fond of liquor might be expected to be under with the perspective of plentiful liquor and festive entertainment in
view. At 10 A.M. hove up our anchor and made sail to
Royals and flying Jib. Course ESE.*

17 October 1845

The same delightful and favorable wind. Standing along the land; near meridian the harbor of Dix's Cove was in sight.

18 October 1845

Standing on, with a delightful Westerly breeze. In the latter part of the day Dix's Cove was in view but no stop was made.

ELMINA, GOLD COAST

20 October 1845

Fine breezes and that's about all that could be boasted until about 8 P.M. when the town of Elmina hove in sight. It being moon light we stood on until about 9 when it was considered prudent to come to, which was done, in thirteen fathoms water two and a half knots current. In the morning at 5 A.M. hove up and stood in to Elmina roads where we anchored at half past 7 A.M. At 11 A.M. I concluded to take a short turn ashore. I was somewhat surprised after having circumambulated the place to find it of the extent it is.

It is positively very regularly laid out; all the streets are in fact wide avenues sheltered [and] shaded with trees

Elmina
Wilson, *Western Africa.*

each side so as to form complete arbors. The houses to be
sure are composed of but unbaked clay with thatched roofs,
but nevertheless regularity is a trait that enters into the
construction of them. I had an opportunity of experiencing
in two instances the hospitality of some of the better class
of these people. Seeing a house of very superior construc-
tion I was prompted by curiosity to enter. When I had
arrived at the top of the flight of steps leading to the main
entrance, I was intercepted by a collection of negroes seated
on their hams in a circle round one who was weighing gold
dust that the surrounding people had brought in from the
gold districts. Ten dollars per ounce is the price generally
considered amongst them the standard. When we got
through this inspection we proceeded in the house to one of
the principal chambers where we were met by two very
nice halfbreed Dutch girls. The proprietors of the house,
although they could utter no English sound, made us wel-
come and entertained us with Santa Cruz rum and claret.
After a little we took our departure and strolled to [the]
house of a native negro, called "King Joe," who keeps a
house of entertainment etc. We availed ourselves of his pro-
fession or the character of his house and when satisfied
hauled our wind and stood to the Southward and
Westward to the house of Mr. Bartell, where we came to,
purchased or priced some gold trinkets. Partook of some
entertainment he kindly set before us, which when finished
after suitable acknowledgments to the gentlemen we visited
the castle of the town, really quite formidable in its charac-
ter notwithstanding its age (having been built in the year
1482 by the Portuguese from whom it was taken by its
present possessors, the Dutch, in 1642). There is a moat
twenty-five feet wide and about the same depth that meets

the sea at each extremity. These premises being examined
we took a ramble into the outskirts of the Town and closed
the adventures of the day by witnessing a native's funeral.
Something perfectly novel but too tedious to describe
though. A river of four miles extent irrigates the land in the
vicinity of this town.

ACCRA

21 October 1845

Hove up anchor and stood towards Accra, where we
arrived at about 11 A.M. next morning. No news. In the
course of the afternoon a sample of all the produce of
Africa was brought alongside: Birds, Beasts, Jewels, Fruits
and Vegetables. The Captain, being amused by the general
turmoil to which the ship was exposed, besides being
prompted by his own beneficent feelings with a view to
indulge the crew in a rational manner, allowed the pur-
chase of every description of articles that were brought on
board.

22 October 1845

The day opened in the same manner as the last closed; in
fact it was devoted to trade. At 11 A.M. the American brig-
antine General Warren *came to anchor at Accra—Captain*
deceased, mate sick; brought intelligence that the Atalanta
had been taken by the British brig Penguin.

The *Atalanta*, it will be recalled, was the ship on which Davis, captain of the *Patuxent* (now on its way to New York), had just previously been first mate. The *Atalanta* had belonged to Captain Lawlin, who with his other ship *Madonna* had accompanied the *Yorktown* in the vicinity of the Gaboon, selling the naval vessel various supplies from time to time. Lawlin had a solid reputation as a long-time coastal trader with no connection to the slave trade. This reputation, however, was cast in doubt after his skipper of the *Atalanta* sold that vessel to slavers operating out of Gallinas, and the British cruisers there let her slip past them because they thought she belonged to Lawlin. They were later outraged to learn she had carried several hundred slaves to South America. Thus the *Atalanta*'s capture would have been particularly satisfying to the American and British naval officers. (Lawlin subsequently went to great lengths to defend himself, protesting that he had been hundreds of miles distant, at the Gaboon with the *Yorktown*, when the ship was sold, and blaming his skipper for having been dazzled by the astronomical price the slavers had offered.)

At 5 P.M. got under way and stood to the Eastward.
Nothing occurred during the night, ran along the land during the day.

QUITTA, GOLD COAST

24 October 1845

At 3:30 came to before Quitta [Keta, Ghana], the land of cheap poultry and stock in general. As a matter of course, in the course of one or two hours after our arrival our decks were flooded with ducks, chickens, turkeys and so on.

Got a good lot, hove up anchor at 4 and stood to the Eastward.

In addition to the fowls Lawrence mentions, the *Yorktown* also acquired four bullocks for the crew. Within a couple of days, though, they were back on salt rations.

AT SEA
_____

25 October 1845

This day we got under way and as far as the wind would allow of it; laid our course for Prince's Island; West by South on one tack and about Southeast on the other were our courses.

26 October 1845

Matters about the same—Sunday—Sailing at the tardiest rates.

28 October 1845

As above ditto ditto ditto. Lat. 2°40′ North Long. 2°17′ East—a sail in sight.

29 October 1845

Wind and weather same. The sail above noticed at about

2 P.M. *was made out to be a brig, standing about one or two points higher than we, our course being about SSE, she from South by East to South. At 5 P.M. she neared us so that we were enabled to speak her. She proved to be a prize taken by an English steam frigate* Styx *under Brazilian colors. She was in charge of a lieutenant bound for Sierra Leone. Her foremast was fished from the Head to the deck. No further news. The evening closed in with the most threatening appearances; reduced sail to Topsails, Foresail and Jib. At about 7:45 sure enough as had been anticipated, a very heavy squall came out on our lee quarter. Laid square the after yards, put the helm up, laid square the head yards, when she went before it at the rate of twelve knots; clewed down the Topsails, hauled out reef Tackles, and let matters so remain till 8 when the Mizzen Topsail was furled. At 10 all calm again; made small sail. The morning opened clear and pleasant. Nothing further occurred during the day.*

30 October 1845

We seem to have got into the peculiar latitude of thunder, lightning and rain squalls, alternated by very light airs and calms; our progress very slow.

14

November 1845

The *Yorktown* has some difficulty working her way down the coast and then to Prince's Island. While the British squadron already includes some steamers, the American squadron is entirely sails. The squadron commodores would repeatedly urge the inclusion of steamers as more effective in pursuing slavers, and indeed Bell himself and Lieutenant Paine in their report to Secretary of State Webster in 1842 had recommended a steamer be included in the African Squadron. Nevertheless, steamers did not join the squadron until well into the 1850s. In 1845, of the forty-six ships the U.S. Navy had in commission six were steamers. However, the slavers, too, still relied largely upon sail, and it was also possible under the right conditions for a sailing ship to outrun a steamship.

AT SEA

4 November 1845

First part similar to the day previous but towards the latter part, the wind freshened and we soon hove in sight of that fairyland like isle, Prince's.

But unfortunately fell so far to leeward of our port
that we were obliged to stand off and on all night—
Beating, beating, beating, closed the day.

5 *November 1845*

Commences with the same transaction—viz. beating much
and gaining little. Towards sunset, discovered the Steamer
Hecate *getting under way. In the course of fifteen minutes*
she was under a head of steam and standing down to us.
She came alongside of us and the Captain very politely and
kindly volunteered to take us in tow—which of course our
Captain gladly availed himself of—and consequently in a
little time we were getting towed into West Bay at the rate
of six miles per hour. At 10 P.M. we were at anchor and
everything snug; our Captain (per invitation) went on
board of the Steamer, and stayed until 12, when she got
under way and went to sea, a certain index that Captain
West behaved in a very agreeable manner. In the morning
we awoke and found ourselves within a half mile of the
shore. Although this is the second time we have visited this
place, still the sublimity of the landscape strike[s] one with
as much force as when first visited; the various beauties
usher in a multitude of reflections, respecting the resources
of the island for almost any purpose, its wondrous fertility
and to what a garden of Eden it might be reduced after the
expenditure of some years labor.

PRINCE'S ISLAND

---

6 November 1845

*Weather lachrymose in the extreme; watering ship. Took
many delightful fresh and salt water bathes this day.*

7 November 1845

*Everything carried on in the same way as yesterday.
Scrambled along the rocky and rugged path leading to a
negroe's nest dignified by the name of fort. An indolent
Portuguese is head man there; a worn out slatternly looking strumpet he maintains as one of his sources of pleasure.*

8 November 1845

*Watering ship and wooding. Went on a kind of exploring
ramble. Stopped at Larreo's house, a freed man of Madame
Maria Ferrera's, a woman (widow of immense wealth—
owning nearly the whole island and a troop of about three
hundred slaves).*

Dona Maria Ferreira, along with another wealthy widow, did
virtually rule Prince's Island.[1]

9 November 1845

*Went ashore on a wooding expedition; used the same
opportunity to make an exploring expedition. Came
aboard with my mind still further stirred with wonder-
ment at the eccentric and fantastical moods of nature, in
forming this uncultivated paradise.*

11 *November 1845*

Sunday, offered nothing new. Took our ease as of course we should do.

Though Lawrence sees no reason to record it, in reality the ship is quite busy during its time at Prince's Island, including part of Sunday and all of the next day until finally weighing anchor. The crew are painting the ship and blacking the guns; moving the cables, shot, and the two Paixhans guns forward to bring the ship down by the head so the carpenters can repair the rudder; scrubbing the bottom; painting and cleaning the hull; and loading the usual water and sand.

AT SEA

---

12 *November 1845*

During the latter part of this day, we hove up anchor and made sail, and left this beautiful Island.

The *Yorktown* now heads for the mouth of the Gaboon (modern Gabon) River.

13 *November 1845*

Sailing at a very moderate rate, encountering rain and wind squalls, intermingled with thunder and lightning; unpleasant!

14 November 1845

Weather fine, on the look out for land, at 9 P.M. discovered it on the lee bow. At 9:45 let go our larboard anchor in eighteen and a half fathoms. Here we lay until 11 A.M. when an English brig of war was discovered standing down out of the river towards us. After having reconnoitered us at a distance she wore round and stood back again.

GABOON RIVER

15 November 1845

When we immediately called all hands and got ship under way and followed her into the river and when we got just inside of the Capes of the river—she struck! but kept on and grated along the whole length of her keel, touched slightly a second time and then went on without further incident or accident. In fifteen or twenty minutes after this a pilot came on board: we then came to opposite King Glass' town.

Sailing several miles up the wide mouth of the Gaboon River the *Yorktown* passes the small French blockhouse, Fort Aumale. Captain Bell's sympathies are with Mr. Wilson and the local inhabitants, whom the French (after ignoring the *Yorktown*'s storm ensign on Wilson's flagpole) had recently bombarded while asserting their sovereignty over the area. Bell ignores the French flag. The result is a series of uncongenial visits and notes. Salutes are finally exchanged, but the affair becomes one involving international diplomacy, with correspondence up and down the chains of command on both sides of the Atlantic. Eventually it must be settled between U.S. secretary of state James Buchanan and the French ambassador to Washington.[2]

16 *November 1845*

As usual going back and forth from the ship to the shore. During this day a very insolent note sent from the Commander (!) of the Blockhouse recently established on this river, called Fort "Aumale" in honor doubtless of the Duke D'Aumale. The purport of the note was a demand of a national salute from the Captain of this ship. This insolence met with the most appropriate and effective rebuke that could have been used, which consisted in maintaining a disdainful silence in regard to it. The Captain of a small gun Brig called the Malovine *bristled up on the occasion— "à la Porc-Épic"—and refused in the indignation of the moment to take charge of a document containing a complaint of the Blockhouse Commander's conduct to the Commander of the French Naval Forces.*

17 *November 1845*

Weather same; went on shore to a Beef shooting match; nothing more.

18–19 *November 1845*

Nothing occurred. Arrived a French barque of war etc. etc.

19 November 1845 [sic]

Opened clear and pleasant. Got under way at an early hour; passed the French vessels of war without apparent notice from either side. The little Bristol brig Englishman *kept company with us. The Captain, Mr. and Mrs. Wilson (the missionary) remained on board of our ship till 5 P.M. in the evening when they were put on board of the brig and each pursued its separate course. While coming out of the river fell in with steamer* Hecate, *from Congo river; gave us information of slaver there under American colors—made sail for it.*

AT SEA

20 November 1845

Wind from Southward and Westward. At 11 A.M. again fell in with above brig, spoke her and stood on.

25 November 1845

Set in with very heavy squalls from the Southward and Southward and Eastward—furled all sail to topsail, which clewed down and in the course of the day single reefed them and set Topgallant sails—wind fair and foul for us alternately.

15

December 1845

1 December 1845

*Wind South and Westward in light breezes, heading SSE—
at 2:15 discovered a sail standing to the Westward. At
about 3:15 made her out a barque (American built);
showed her our colors. She showed American colors, but
her manner of steering being so wild that suspicion was
awakened in the minds of the officers as to her legal character. Consequently we bore down on her, hailed her, and
received for answer that she was the Brig* Pons,
*Philadelphia, bound to New York—Captain Galiano. A
boat was sent on board of her (her main topsail hove to
the mast) in charge of the First Lieutenant, and when he
got on board Portuguese colors were run up. From the barque the First Lieutenant then informed us that she had no
shipping papers and was a slaver with nine hundred slaves
on board!!! She was immediately taken possession of—her
crew sent on board of us which amounted to forty people
in toto.*

THE CAPTURE OF THE *PONS*

When first spotted by the *Yorktown* the *Pons* tried to edge away, which only made the Americans more suspicious. The captain of the *Pons,* later identified as a Portuguese named Gallano (or Gallino), mistook the *Yorktown* for the British brig *Cygnet,* whose watchfulness had for twenty days delayed loading the slaveship. Gallano hoisted what would have been the protective American colors. Captain Bell responded with American colors, then confused Gallano by switching to the British flag. When Bell hailed and asked what ship, the answer was, "Barque *Pons* of Philadelphia, from Cabinda, bound for New York." Bell then dispatched his first lieutenant, Steele, to board her. Steele recognized the *Pons;* he had been aboard her in the Philadelphia Navy Yard two years earlier when she had been doing some work for the navy, and in November 1844 he had seen her at Madeira.[1] As Steele's boat reached the *Pons* her captain, recognizing U.S. uniforms, hauled down his U.S. flag and hoisted a Portuguese flag. Meanwhile Bell maneuvered the *Yorktown* closer alongside the slaveship. As he did so, and at the moment Steele climbed aboard, Bell observed someone throwing something overboard from the *Pons*'s cabin. (It was a handkerchief tied up with the ship's American papers and other incriminating documents, weighted with two hundred musket balls.)[2] Bell called out to get Steele's attention, but by this time the slaves sensed a possible rescue. The jubilation of nine hundred shouting voices erupted beneath Steele's feet. It was a sound, said Bell, that "could be heard a mile"—and rendered Bell inaudible to the lieutenant.

Confronting the *Pons*'s captain, Steele demanded the ship's papers. "I have none; I have thrown them overboard," responded Gallano. "What is your cargo?" asked Steele, then receiving the reply, "About nine hundred slaves, from Cabinda, bound for Brazil." Since the ship had shown the American flag, had no papers, and had the words "Pons of Philadelphia" painted on her stern, Steele took possession of her as a prize.[3]

In his official report to Secretary of the Navy Bancroft dated 11 December 1845, Bell writes:

> I was so anxious to despatch the vessel in the shortest time for Liberia, in order to land the slaves, and relieve them from their miserable confinement, that it was not in my power to give you a more particular account of this vessel. . . .
>
> The *Pons,* under the command of James Berry, was at anchor at Kabinda for about twenty days before she took on board the slaves, during which time she was closely watched by H.B.M. Brig *Cygnet,* Commander Layton. At about nine o'clock on the morning of the 27th November, the *Cygnet* got under way and stood to sea immediately. Berry gave up the ship to Gallano, who commenced getting on board the water, provisions and slaves; and so expeditious were they in their movements that at eight o'clock that evening the vessel was underway, having embarked nine *hundred* and three slaves. Instead of standing directly to sea, she kept in with the coast during the night. At daylight they were off Kacongo, about twenty-five miles to the north of Kabinda, when they discovered the *Cygnet* in the offing. They immediately furled all their sails and drifted so near the shore, that the negroes lined the beach in hope of a shipwreck. They continued in this situation until meridian; when finding they had not been discovered, they set their lower sails in order to clear the shore, and as the *Cygnet* drew off from the land, they afterwards set their more lofty ones. Two days afterwards we captured her. Her crew consisted of Spaniards, Portuguese, Brazilians and some from other countries, and although continuing under the American flag, with probably American papers, not one American was on board.
>
> As I could not dispatch her the evening of her capture, she kept company with us that night; the next morning I regret-

ted to learn that *eighteen* had died and one jumped overboard. So many dying in so short a time, was accounted for
by the Captain, in the necessity he had of thrusting below all
who were on deck, and closing the hatches, when he first fell
in with us, in order to escape detection.

The vessel has no slave deck, and upwards of *eight hundred and fifty* men piled almost in bulk, on the water casks
below; these were males, about forty or fifty females were
confined in one half of the round house cabin on deck. The
other half of the cabin remaining for the use of the officers.
As the ship appeared to be less than three hundred and fifty
tons, it seemed impossible that one half could have lived to
cross the Atlantic. About two hundred filled up the spar deck
alone, when they were permitted to come up from below,
and yet the captain assured me that it was his intention to
have taken *four hundred more* on board, if he could have
spared the time.

The stench from below was so great that it was impossible to stand, more than a few moments, near the hatchways.
Our men who went below from curiosity were forced up sick
in a few minutes. Then all the hatches were off. What must
have been the sufferings of these poor wretches when the
hatches were closed? I am informed that very often in these
cases, the stronger will strangle the weaker, and this was
probably the reason why so many died or rather were found
dead the morning after the capture. None but an eye witness
can form a conception of the horrors these poor creatures
must endure in their transit across the ocean.

I regret to say that most of this misery is produced by our
own countrymen; they furnish the means of conveyance in
spite of existing enactments, and altho there are strong circumstances against Berry the late master of the *Pons,* sufficient to induce me to detain him if I should meet with him,

yet I fear neither he or his employers can be reached by our present laws. He will no doubt make it appear that the *Pons* was beyond his control when the slaves were brought on board. Yet from the testimony of the men who came over from Rio as passengers, there is no doubt the whole affair was arranged at Rio between Berry and Gallano before the ship sailed. These men state that the first place they anchored was at Onin, near the River Lagos in the Bight of Benin. Here they discharged a portion of their cargo, and received on board a number of hogsheads or pipes filled with water. These were stowed on the ground tier and a tier of casks containing spirits were placed over them. They were then informed that the vessel was going to Kabinda for a load of slaves.

On their arrival at the latter place the spirit was kept on board until a few days before Berry gave up the command, covering up the water casks in order to elude the suspicions of any cruizer. For twenty days did Berry wait in the roadstead of Kabinda protected by the flag of his country, yet closely watched by a foreign man of war who was certain of his intention. But the instant that cruizer is compelled to withdraw for a few hours, he springs at the opportunity of enriching himself and owners, and disgracing the flag which had protected him. As we are short handed I have shipped those men, much to their gratification, who came out as passengers in the *Pons* from Rio to Kabinda, in order that their testimony may be taken should Berry be in the United States on our return and committed for trial. I have landed the balance of the prize crew here, with the exception of one who died of coast fever, a few days after he came on board this Ship.

In my letter of the 30th ultimo I stated that I should send to the United States in the *Pons,* the Captain, Cook and cabin boy. Afterwards I found it necessary to send two others to assist the cook in preparing food for the slaves.[4]

Actually the *Pons* was not 350 tons, as Bell had estimated, but only 197.[5] Eight hundred fifty human beings had been crammed naked below deck into a space of less than 2,000 square feet.

Lawrence's entry continues:

> *The Captain [of the* Pons*] it must be admitted was a man of most dignified appearance—and showed no more agitation than he would have in a probability on the most commonplace occasion. Mr. Cogdell was then sent on board her as prize master, and myself, as his chief mate with twelve men as a crew. Upon boarding this vessel, I felt such a load of misery fall upon my heart that I almost wished myself a wild beast, that I might escape the pain of sympathy that I felt for the sufferings of the wretched slaves (created my fellow beings) confined on board. Of course, they knew some change in their destiny was about to take place, and in their desperate agonies, hope construed it the change about to take place in their favor, and when our boats approached the barque they hailed us with clapping hands and outstretched arms. But who can represent by words the state of the wretches below in the hold? To mention that their tongues were white and dry for want of water, and that their lips were cracked open from same reason, and their bodies covered with loathsome scabs (called the "Cocrau") and that they were under the influence of a burning fever, that almost burnt one's hand to touch them, would give a faint notion of their suffering—and the atmosphere was of a temperature of about 160 to 180 Fahrenheit—and alas how few could we succor from this*

miserable state, how few could we alleviate from their suf-ferings—a!

2 December 1845

Wind light; calms etc. this day. Having got things in order we parted company from the Yorktown *at 4:15. The wind sprung up; we soon lost sight of her. Fed and watered the slaves. In the morning there were twenty-odd dead bodies; these people died of thirst etc. etc.*

Under different circumstances Lawrence would have enjoyed being aboard the *Pons*. An exceptionally well-constructed and beautiful barque designed for fast sailing, she had been built in New Jersey near Philadelphia four years earlier. Ninety-five feet long, with a twenty-three-foot beam and depth of hold of ten feet, she measured 196 and 57/95 tons.[6] She had three masts, a square stern, and a scroll head.[7] Near the foremast was the "caboose" or cookhouse, containing a large brick fireplace with a grate for the large cook pots. Aft of that was the longboat, protected by a roof. Farther aft was the cabin, then a small quarterdeck with a cabin for the pilot.[8]

When Steele and his men boarded her they found 50 female slaves, all naked and most seasick, confined in half of the cabin, the other half having been occupied by the ship's officers. The sight and smell in the cabin were bad enough, but the 850 male slaves were confined below in the hold, with all the hatches battened, except for one about four feet square covered by an open grating that provided their only ventilation. The Americans learned that 7 had died during the three days prior to the *Yorktown's* arrival.

While it was customary among slavers to use lumber to construct a temporary slave deck in the hold, this was not done in the

Pons. Instead, when Lawrence and others of the prize crew went into the hold, the fetid, dark, and boiling-hot space where they had to crouch into about four feet of headroom, they found the slaves lying on mats laid over bags of farina, the grain customarily fed slaves on the Middle Passage. The bags of farina covered over and filled the spaces between barrels full of water that had been put down over the ballast. Shortly after the capture slaves from the hold were permitted up on deck, though there was only room there for about 250.[9]

The navy men quickly opened the hatches to give more air to those below. When they passed down a bucket of water the captives fought each other for it like dogs for a bone. Because Gallano had wanted to avoid attracting attention his crew had cooked no food, and had not fed the slaves at all during their three days aboard prior to the *Pons*'s capture. The Americans broke out farina, cooked it with oil, and fed their starving passengers. The mere task of cooking and distributing farina for almost a thousand people, and doing it with any degree of order, would have been a considerable labor for the small prize crew, who in addition, of course, had to manage the ship.

Aboard the *Yorktown,* once they parted ways with the *Pons,* the officers and men were disgusted at what they had seen and relieved not to have been chosen for the prize crew. They also daydreamed about spending their prize money, for every man aboard would get a share of the prize paid for capturing a slaver. Assistant Surgeon Williams, for example, began to think of buying a horse.[10] The prize crew had more pressing concerns.

3 December 1845

Wind and weather the same. The slaves were a little easier today.

4 December 1845

Wind light from Southward and Westward. At 12 midnight a squall struck us aback. Reduced sail to topsails and kept her before it (South). Toward 8 A.M. wind died away and it fell calm. Ten slaves dead.

5 December 1845

The wind at 5 P.M. today set in fresh and continued so for 24 hours. Fed and watered slaves; twelve or fourteen dead.

7 December 1845

Sunday. On board one week this day. Wind from South-ward and Westward; course W by N—Lat. 57′48″ South Long. 2°29′ West. Up to this date ninety-one slaves have expired—oh for a deliverance from this floating hell; my heart is oppressed with a thousand cares—god deliver us.

The final leaves of Lawrence's journal have, like the opening ones, been cut from the book by hands unknown for reasons unknown. The dramatic cry of despair with which Lawrence's journal now ends is, sadly, even more fitting than he knew at the time.

Lawrence had now been sailing for a week on a ship filled with appalling human misery. Of the two officers and ten men in the prize crew he was the junior officer, assigned under Lt. Richard C. Cogdell. As has been seen, Cogdell was hardly a model officer. Indeed, he was an alcoholic and depressive. Knowing something of his past behavior Bell had objected to getting him, but it was Cogdell or nothing. Assured that Cogdell had reformed, Bell took

to 180 Farenheit – & alas how few coleld we here
cure from this miserable state, how few coleld
we elevate from their suffering – &a.

Wind light – calm &c this day having got things
in order we parted company from the Yorktown
at 4½ 15 the wind sprung up off soon lost sight
of her – fed & watered the slaves – in the morning
there were 20 odd dead bodies – these people died of
thirst &c &c –

3d   Wind & weather the same – the slaves were a
little easier to day

4th   Wind light from s° & w° – at 12 and ½ a squall
struck us aback reduced sail to topsails & kept
her before it (South) toward 8 a.m. wind died
away & it fell calm – 10 slaves dead –

5th   The wind at 5 p.m. today set in fresh &
continued so for 24 hours – fed & watered slaves
12 or 14 dead –

6th   Wind & weather same

7th   Sunday on board one week this day – wind
from s° & w° corner W ½ N – Lat 5½° – 48″ South
Long 2° 29″ West up to this date 91 slaves have
expired – oh for a deliverance from this floating hell
my heart is oppressed with a thousand cares – god deliver
us, &c &c &c &c &c &c &c &c &c &c &c &c &c

him and hoped for the best. At the time of the capture of the *Pons* Cogdell was Bell's second most senior officer after Steele, who was the first lieutenant—and the only other lieutenant. Though he was not someone Bell might regret losing, Cogdell had apparently behaved well enough up to that point, so he was at least a reasonable choice for command of the prize crew. However, not long after parting company with the *Yorktown* Cogdell began drinking heavily and treating his crew abusively. At one point when the *Pons* encountered a squall and the commanding officer should have been on deck, Cogdell was too drunk to leave his berth.[11] That Lawrence does not mention Cogdell's behavior in the last week of his extant journal could be due to caution about writing down (even on supposedly private papers) any derogatory remarks about a superior. More likely it indicates the extent to which any personal problems were overwhelmed by the more universal anguish he felt for the plight of the recaptured slaves. Eventually, though, Lawrence would feel compelled to speak up.

LANDING THE RECAPTURED SLAVES AT MONROVIA

Taking the slaves back to where they had embarked would likely have been the equivalent of again putting them into the hands of those who had sold them in the first place. Most would have wound up back in barracoons waiting to be packed onto the next available slave ship. They could hardly be taken to the United States. As American interests had established Liberia specifically to receive freed slaves from the United States, American policy also made the colony the destination of any slaves recaptured by the American navy. Once a ship carrying slaves was taken she then would be taken first to Liberia to off-load the recaptives, and thence to her home port in the United States for legal proceedings against ship and crew.

The *Pons* took another week to reach Monrovia, during which the bodies of 41 more slaves slipped into her wake. When early on the evening of 14 December she dropped anchor off Cape Mesurado, 764 of the original 903 were still alive. The survivors could not be simply put ashore. Boats or canoes were needed to lighter them in, and arrangements had to be made as to their disposition once ashore. It took a day for Cogdell to arrange with the local authorities for off-loading and caring for the recaptives. As part of that process a group from Monrovia boarded the *Pons* that forenoon, as sharks swarmed about the ship, drawn by the bodies of ten captives found dead that morning.[12] J. J. Roberts, the governor of Liberia, was accompanied by several individuals: one Judge S. Benedict, a Dr. James W. Lugenbeel, Rev. W. B. Hoyt, and Rev. J. B. Benham. Hoyt and Benham were Methodist Episcopal missionaries who had arrived in Liberia from the United States less than a week earlier. Lugenbeel was a young missionary doctor who had also been appointed U.S. Agent in Liberia for Recaptured Africans. The stench aboard the slaver was so awful that the visitors could bring themselves to stay aboard only a short while, observing the crowded deck and peering into the hold.

Hoyt, Benham, and Lugenbeel all wrote eyewitness accounts within twenty-four hours of boarding the *Pons*. Hoyt remarked that although he had been prepared beforehand by Cogdell, whom he describes as "the gentlemanly officer in command," the scene he encountered was "impossible for language to convey."[13] The recaptives, many emaciated and all absolutely naked, crowded the decks in various postures; swarms of flies buzzed about the suppurating sores on arms and legs. Below deck were hundreds more. The day, Hoyt noted, was warm, and the smell was overpowering:

> Here and there might be seen individuals in the last agonies of expiring nature, unknown, and apparently unnoticed. There was no offer of sympathy to alleviate in the least their misery. Their companions appeared dejected, weighed down with their own sorrows. My heart sickens at the

remembrance of that awful scene. As I came on the crowded deck, I saw directly in front of me one emaciated and worn down by long suffering to a mere skeleton, pining away and apparently near eternity. I looked over into the steerage. The hot, mephitic air almost overpowered me. At the foot of the ladder lay two of the most miserable beings I ever beheld. They were reduced, as the one above named, so that their bones almost protruded from their flesh. Large sores had been worn upon their sides and limbs, as they had been compelled to lay upon the hard plank composing the deck of the vessel. They lay directly under the hatchway, whither they had crawled, apparently to obtain a little purer air. One I thought dead, until by some slight motion of the limbs I discovered his agonies were not yet ended. The other lay with his face toward me, and such an expression of unmitigated anguish I never before saw. I cannot banish the horrid picture. These were not isolated cases, but as they were those that were first noticed they made, perhaps, a stronger impression on my mind.[14]

Like Hoyt, Benham could not bring himself to enter the hold, where the temperature was guessed to be between 100 and 120 degrees, and from which the smell was overpowering. The sights on deck were enough:

The sailors pointed me to a group of three little boys, under the bow of the long boat, on deck. One of them was probably eight years of age, and almost in a dying state, and had been pining away for the last six days. Two others, perhaps ten and twelve years of age, were sitting by him, one on either side, watching him with a great deal of apparent sympathy, and administering to him as they were able. They had procured a small quantity of oakum, with which they had made his bed, and a small piece of muslin for his pillow.

They did not leave him night or day, and the sailors always found one of them awake. Through an interpreter I commended them for their kindness to the little sufferer, and promised to take them to live with me, and that they should bring with them their sick companion. I gave each a slip of paper with my name, directing them to keep them, so that I might know them when they landed.

The elder boys are brothers, the younger was from the same tribe.[15]

The next day, 16 December, the recaptives were landed ashore. Boats and Kroo canoes took them from the *Pons* to the beach. As the boats got within wading distance of the sand the recaptives, nearly all completely naked, leaped into the surf and splashed eagerly onto Liberian soil. The little boy described above was not among them; his body with seven others had been cast overboard. The two brothers who had watched over him for two weeks came ashore clutching soggy scraps of paper, their "tickets" to be taken in by Rev. Benham. Seven hundred fifty-six came ashore alive.

Virtually the entire population of Monrovia, perhaps a thousand strong (about a quarter of the non-aboriginal population of Liberia) came down to the shore to watch. The slaver captain Gallano, who had been permitted ashore to buy warm clothing for the voyage to his trial in Philadelphia, was a spectator, too. When the Liberians saw his handiwork they turned toward him in fury. He hastily left the scene, lucky to escape unharmed.[16]

Some of the recaptives were too weak to climb out of the boats unaided. Still, freedom and the cool water of the surf seem to have reanimated many, who clapped their hands, exclaimed, and even sang in joy as they rushed onto the beach.[17] The Monrovians gave them small bits of biscuit and a little water at first, then filled a dugout canoe with water, "into which they plunged like hungry pigs into a trough—the stronger faring the best."[18] Others spotted a nearby stagnant pool and "swallowed its black contents with great avidity" until some of the Liberians, with violent benevolence, drove them away with threats and even whips. On the half-mile walk up from the beach to Monrovia some lay down to die but were picked up and carried by their stronger companions or by Monrovians.

The landward side of the disembarkation was run by Dr. Lugenbeel in his official capacity as U.S. Agent for Recaptured Africans. Aboard the *Pons* John Lawrence supervised the business of getting the recaptives into the boats and canoes and on their way ashore. Lieutenant Cogdell's "infirmity" had overwhelmed him and he had taken refuge ashore.[19]

THE NEW LIBERIANS

As quickly as possible Lugenbeel parceled out the new Liberians to the missionaries and to colonist families. The U.S. government had placed one thousand dollars at Lugenbeel's disposal for expenses. He thus had a little over a dollar per recaptive, a budget he actually managed to stay well within. (The United States had also given him two thousand dollars to construct a receiving facility, but the structure was not built until 1847, so Lugenbeel had to create a makeshift situation for the *Pons* arrivals.) Under a special act of the Liberian legislature the new arrivals were apprenticed for a set period, during which time their sponsors were to teach them a trade, the English language, and other useful skills. As almost all the recaptives were between the ages of eight and eighteen, the missionaries saw them as children in need of education. The missionaries requested and received permission to care for, to educate, and of course to convert a hundred of the children. Of these the twenty girls were especially welcome, as the missionary school had had a particularly difficult time recruiting female students from the local tribes. With what may strike a modern reader as breathtaking swiftness and assurance, the missionaries had within a day given new western names to all their recruits. Hence the *Pons* suddenly produced (no doubt before they themselves knew who they were) the likes of Silas Comfort, Benjamin Clark, Lorenzo D. Sherwood, James W. Lugenbeel, Gabriel Hoyt, and Mary Hoyt. The two boys with notes from Rev. Benham became John Wesley and David A. Shepard.

In a hastily called meeting the day before the landing the missionary group had on the spot subscribed $135 of its own money to cover temporary expenses for their planned one hundred children. Within days they had sent off to their sponsoring group in the United States a bundle of narratives and appeals—the "Circular Appeal of the Methodist Liberian Mission."[20] Lugenbeel parceled out another two hundred recaptives in a couple of days, six hundred by the end of the month, and the remaining group shortly thereafter. He required each responsible party to promise in writing to present their recaptives "well clothed" at the next probate court, scheduled for early February, for final legalities. The children were bound as apprentices and the adults were bound for seven years. Lugenbeel sent one group of seventeen identified as "Congos" and apparent "headmen" to the settlement of New Georgia (where some Congos were already established), to be looked after until they could fend for themselves.

Whether the new Liberians understood all their new obligations seems questionable, and there was also the possibility of abuse or neglect on the other side of the apprenticeship contracts.[21] It may be said the recaptives were simply being transferred from one form of servitude to another, albeit a more benign one. However, apprenticing was still practiced in the United States as it had been since earliest colonial times. On that model a system established in Liberia years before the arrival of the *Pons* had been applied to settlers from the states and recruits from local tribes, as well as to recaptives. The *Pons* strained the system, though, by injecting roughly three times as many recaptives as the *total* that had been brought to Liberia since the colony's establishment.[22] Indeed, the ratio of colonists (in all of Liberia) to new *Pons* arrivals was only about four to one. One bit of luck was that the ship *Roanoke* that had arrived from the States only days before (8 December) with Hoyt, Benham, a third minister, their wives, and 190 new settlers emancipated by the will of their late master in Virginia, had also bought supplies that could be diverted to the emergency needs of the recaptives.[23]

Dr. Lugenbeel had already been fully occupied with the arrival of the *Roanoke,* since a number of her passengers had required his medical attention. To this situation was suddenly added the staggering task of treating and generally looking after the sorely neglected recaptives from the *Pons*. Obviously many of the recaptives were in poor shape, too; sixty-five died in the next two months. Lugenbeel fortunately could rely upon the help of two Liberians he was training as physicians. Struggling against debilitating illness himself, Lugenbeel managed his manifold responsibilities remarkably well.[24]

The American recolonization societies responded to the missionaries' "Circular Appeal" with substantial shipments of clothing and other supplies. Indeed, they swiftly chartered the barque *Chatham* to carry their gathered materials to Liberia, at a total cost of over five thousand dollars.[25] Meanwhile, shortly after Bell's arrival with the *Yorktown* in January the citizens of Monrovia gave a public dinner honoring him and his officers for the capture of the *Pons.*

Unsurprisingly, not all of "Captain Bell's *protagees,*" as the *Liberia Herald* was to call them, adhered to their contracts. The following July the *Herald* lamented that "a number of these people are living wild in the woods, and at night come in town and carry off cattle &c. Within the last fortnight six milch cows and a number of sheep, hogs and goats have been carried off by these marauders."[26] In fact, many of the locals to whom they had been assigned were so impoverished and ill-prepared as to be scarcely able to take care of themselves, much less their new wards. A poor harvest that year had made things worse. By late June Governor Roberts reported that "hundreds of [*Pons* recaptives] . . . most of them emaciated, sick and in a wretched state of helplessness," were at large in the community, while "Scores of them, for the last month or two, have been hanging upon the skirts of the colonists. Indeed, the present scarcity of provisions is owing, in a great degree, to their numerous depredations upon the young crops of our farmers."[27] Fortunately the colonists were able to issue thousands of dollars worth of food, clothing, and tobacco to the new arrivals.[28] By December 1846, a year after the *Pons* landing, the *Herald* remarked that "These people or a large portion of them are becoming of value to their guardians—those remaining in the colony, show no disposition, now to wander off." Lugenbeel reported in early 1847 that, "They have generally abandoned their thievish practices, and also the practice of running away. . . . Many of them have made remarkable progress in acquiring a knowledge of the English language and the habits of civilization."[29] A more skeptical view suggests that after finding it impossible to live in the woods, most of the recaptives had surrendered to the requirements of their new and not particularly generous masters, the colonists. The *Yorktown*'s Surgeon Williams revisited Liberia in 1848, and naturally had a special interest in the *Pons* recaptives. By his observation their clothing was skimpy and, except for the girls taken in by the mission, their education neglected. As for their food, "that consists of the refuse of their masters' tables."[30] On the other hand, the pugnaciousness of some proved convenient. A correspondent from the settlement of Grand Bassa, where relations with the indigenous Fishmen had not been smooth, reported happily that "Our Congoes have really turned out manly; they have thrown more dread upon the Fishmen . . . and the surrounding tribes, than I have ever known exerted upon them before."[31] Colonist Mildred

Skipwith, writing in 1848, commented, "The surviving ones are as healthy a set of people as ever a person would wish to see, several of which has embraced the religion of our saviour—and making rapid improvements in Education. Tho I must say of a truth that they are the most savage, & blud thirsty people I ever saw or ever wishes to see."[32] In 1850 Lugenbeel reported that most of the inhabitants of New Georgia were recaptives, and that the settlement provided most of the vegetables for Monrovia.[33] Years later, too, a *Pons* survivor named John Robinson is mentioned as the manager of a coffee plantation owned by the Methodist mission.[34]

LAWRENCE'S LAST WEEKS: WITH THE *PONS*

Although Cogdell managed to impress the Reverend Hoyt as a "gentlemanly officer" when he met the delegation of Liberian leaders on the day after the *Pons* dropped anchor off Monrovia, nevertheless Cogdell saw the need to explain his condition as due to the understandable stress and fatigue of the previous two weeks aboard the prize ship. Actually Cogdell had been drinking heavily for days. Likely others of the prize crew, including Lawrence, had been imbibing more than usual, too, not without reason. Cogdell's situation, though, was extreme. He went ashore the very day they anchored and remained there, incapacitated, until shortly before the *Pons* sailed for Philadelphia two weeks later.[35] (Staying ashore for even a single night was, it will be recalled, directly contrary to orders.) Thus it fell to Lawrence not only to supervise the off-loading of the recaptives on 15 December but also to make all the preparations necessary for the transatlantic voyage. These included off-loading 195 bags of farina and beans and some rice, the "slave food"; mending sails and making other repairs; loading ballast; and ensuring sufficient food and drink was aboard to last forty-five days, the anticipated outside length of the trip to Philadelphia. Only one boat was available (apparently the *Pons* had only one and no budget to hire locally), so all of this took a while for Lawrence and the ten crewmen to accomplish. Some of the crew became ill, though none so thoroughly as Cogdell. Lawrence must have visited him more or less daily to get whatever instructions Cogdell would have been in condition to give, and to keep him informed of their progress, a task that can hardly have been easy. Not only did Lawrence by this time have strong feelings against the lieutenant, but also Cogdell was in a very poor state indeed. Dr. Proust, the local doctor contracted to look after the prize crew, spent twice as much time treating Cogdell as he did treating the other eleven combined. When Lugenbeel visited him on 18 December (four days after the arrival) he "found him laboring under some deep emotion of the mind." For days groaning and sighing deeply, Cogdell refused nourishment (at least of the solid kind). On 22 December Lugenbeel discerned clear symptoms of delirium tremens. These worsened until the day after Christmas when Lugenbeel used "powerful opiates and other means to overcome the violence of his disease."[36] Cogdell was well enough, though weak, to sail with the *Pons* on New Year's Day, 1846.

Captain Bell had directed Cogdell to remain at Monrovia no longer than necessary, but Lawrence thought the departure was too hastily made, out of a desire on Cogdell's part to get away before the arrival of the *Yorktown* or some other U.S. Navy ship: "He is making every effort to hasten us off in the most unprepared state imaginable. I have the most gloomy forebodings as to the result of our passage."[37]

Imagine Lawrence's frame of mind on the afternoon of New Year's Day, 1846, as he watched his men work the capstan and raise the anchor, and saw the wind fill the worn sails of the *Pons*. He had spent two weeks aboard ship in conditions more ghastly than he could ever have imagined, witness to incredible suffering that he and the rest of the prize crew could scarcely begin to palliate. For most of that time, too, he had been under the command of an abusive drunkard. In the two weeks after disembarking the slaves, fully occupied in dealing with Cogdell and making preparations for getting under way, he must often have glanced past Cape Mesurado in the hope of seeing a warship coming in whose captain would recognize the situation and relieve Lawrence from having to cross the Atlantic with a man he regarded as monstrous. But no such ship arrived. The *Pons* got under way with Lawrence, Cogdell, ten prize crew, and four Portuguese from the slave crew aboard. The slaver captain, Gallano, had turned his shopping trip ashore into a permanent absence, making his way to Canot's establishment at Cape Mount, where he had boarded the *Roanoke* (the same ship that had brought the missionaries and freed slaves from the United States to Monrovia) for South America.[38] In a twenty-one-year career in slaving the *Pons* was Gallano's twenty-fourth load of slaves; he had been stopped six times by the British and now once by the Americans.[39]

Upon his arrival in Philadelphia Cogdell reported that the weather had been mild the first couple of weeks. However, on 12 January Lawrence had come down with a fever. On 30 January he died, and the next day Cogdell buried him at sea.[40] Lawrence was twenty-four years old.

THE AFRICAN SQUADRON

Like all American squadrons, the U.S. African Squadron was ordered to protect American interests in its area, but specifically it was also charged with stopping slave ships leaving the African coast. It carried out this mission with some credit considering the extent of its capabilities. *Mission* and *purpose*, however, were not quite identical. The American government could hardly have expected the little squadron to stop the slave trade altogether. The squadron was expected, though, to (1) add weight to the U.S. insistence that the British leave U.S.–flag vessels alone, and (2) create sufficient risk to slavers abusing the American flag to greatly diminish or eliminate that practice. The squadron served these ends quite well.

Including the 913 recaptives aboard the *Pons,* between 1843 and early 1862 the African Squadron captured 34 ships and rescued 3,676 slaves, not all of whom lived to reach Liberia. In the comparable period between 1843 and 1861, the British African Squadron took hundreds of prizes and landed 45,612 recaptives ashore.[41] The British could draw upon a much larger navy and furthermore supported their efforts on the West African coast much more thoroughly and consistently. They could also inspect ships of all major flags except the stars and stripes, and they eventually inspected those ships, whereas the U.S. squadron was limited to ships of its own flag. The British also relied on the equipment provisions of the Quintuple Treaty and the effective operations of specialized courts they had set up in Sierra Leone to facilitate condemning slavers captured prior to loading their cargo. In contrast, the U.S. African Squadron had to send its prizes, like *Patuxent* and *Pons,* all the way across the Atlantic for sometimes dubious results.

The U.S. African Squadron operated much in the manner established by Commodore Perry, making long and necessarily inefficient patrols from its base at the Cape Verde Islands. As they came and went, the captains and commodores showed varying degrees of enthusiasm and effectiveness. By any measure, however, Captain Bell, who captured two more ships after the *Patuxent* and *Pons,* was one of the best. Under President Buchanan in the late 1850s the squadron rendezvous was moved to Loando on the African coast, where the whole operation was better supported and more efficient.[42] Then in 1862 the ships were called home for good as the Lincoln government focused its resources on the war that would end slavery in the United States.

Clearly the British squadron seized more slave ships and rescued more slaves than the U.S. squadron, but both efforts pale when compared with the massive volume of the trade: between 1843 and 1862, more than half a million slaves were successfully exported to the Western hemisphere, roughly ten times the number interdicted by the British and American squadrons.[43] The transatlantic slave trade was not actually suppressed until after the American Civil War, which was followed by a variety of political and military efforts that finally terminated the institution.

The U.S. African Squadron was a stepchild of strategy and might have been represented by a pin stuck into a map. But that pin would have represented ships of pine and wood, drenched in rain or baked in the equatorial sun; it would have represented men from Maryland and the Carolinas and New York, rocking interminably in the swells off the African coast, eating year-old beef and weevily bread and hoping to get home. It would also have stood for John C. Lawrence, a young man encountering people and things he had only read about or not even imagined.

We cannot identify the disease that killed John Lawrence, though a likely guess would be quartan malaria. Whatever the specific microbe, it found Lawrence during his time aboard the *Pons,* so it is accurate to say that, though it was not his intent, Lawrence gave his life in the struggle against slavery. His beneficiaries, the *Pons* survivors, never knew.

Epilogue

Lieutenant Cogdell did not have an easy voyage. Instead of the normal few weeks, it took him two and a half *months* to cross the Atlantic to Philadelphia. Weeks of calms and light breezes were followed, he reported later, by a month of headwinds, often of gale strength. Losing Lawrence early on, he pressed two of his senior enlisted men into service as watch officers. He finally arrived in Philadelphia on 13 March 1846.[1] The battered *Pons* and the four Portuguese sailors (one a mere fourteen years old) were delivered to the federal marshal, and legal condemnation of the ship began. Meanwhile, Cogdell, having triumphantly reported his arrival to the secretary of the navy, was ordered to report to Washington at once. He was astonished to learn that charges had been made against him, and puzzled to know who had made them. Proceeding home to Portsmouth, Virginia, he received a letter from Secretary Bancroft charging that "you indulged in drinking to such excess, as to disqualify you for the performance of your duty, and to bring on a fit of *delirium tremens;* that in consequence of the illness occasioned by your excess in drinking, the care of the vessel and the labor of superintending the landing of the recaptured Africans at Monrovia devolved on others; that a bill of expenses on account of the *Pons* certified by you to be correct, comprises articles purchased for your private use; and that a bill of

$60 paid for medical attendance on the crew of the *Pons* contains a charge of $40 for attendance on you alone. It is stated also that on the passage to Monrovia, you were abusive and insulting in your deportment to Master's Mate Lawrence."[2] Cogdell admitted he had been sick, but vehemently denied all the charges. He said the only time he could have been remotely construed as unkind to Lawrence was when he had placed a senior crewman on watch with him, and told Lawrence to heed the crewman's advice about weather. He asked who was making the charges.[3]

The accuser, surprisingly, was Lawrence himself. Two days before leaving Liberia Lawrence had written a letter detailing his complaints against Cogdell and left it to be given to Captain Bell when the *Yorktown* arrived at Monrovia. The *Yorktown* arrived 17 January. Upon receiving Lawrence's letter Bell immediately investigated and obtained corroboration from Lugenbeel. A letter from Bell, enclosing Lawrence's and one from Lugenbeel, had arrived in Washington before Cogdell arrived in Philadelphia. Both Bell and Lugenbeel vouched strongly for Lawrence's character: Bell recommended him to the secretary's special notice, describing him as "a young man of good education and excellent moral character," stating that "his conduct while under my command, has met the entire approbation of myself and the other officers of the ship." Noting that Lawrence would be without employment once the *Pons* reached port, Bell recommended him for promotion to a master's warrant, and urged that if that could not be done Lawrence should at least be given his old assignment as a master's mate aboard the receiving ship in New York. In remarking that he had not wanted Cogdell in the first place, but that the lieutenant had after all behaved well while aboard the *Yorktown,* Bell distanced himself from the problem while nevertheless supporting Lawrence.[4] Lugenbeel praised Lawrence as someone who "seemed to conduct himself with great propriety, in every thing relative to the *Pons* and her crew," and urged him to the secretary's "special consideration."[5] Of course neither Lugenbeel nor Bell could know that Lawrence would die before their letters reached the secretary's desk.

These letters from Lawrence, Bell, and Lugenbeel were undoubtedly sufficient to put Cogdell's career at serious risk, but Cogdell meanwhile had apparently gotten into an additional scrape in Portsmouth, of which the details are obscure. He was ordered to report on 13 July to the newly established Naval School (the Naval Academy) at Annapolis, Maryland. There he was to turn over his sword and face a general court-martial. Captain Bell, Boatswain George Turney (the senior enlisted man of the *Pons* prize crew), and others concerned were summoned as witnesses.

On the appointed day the court, composed of two captains, two commanders (one being Cdr. Franklin Buchanan, superintendent of the new school), and two lieutenants, convened. The judge advocate, Prof. Henry Lockwood, was ready with pens, paper, and blank legal forms. When the accused failed to appear the court adjourned. The next day the court reconvened and, since the accused was again absent, adjourned again. When apprised of the situation Bancroft ordered the commandant of the Norfolk Navy Yard to check on Cogdell. The court continued to meet at noon each day (except Sunday), and adjourn each day. Finally, on 24 July Cogdell stepped ashore in Portsmouth from the regular Baltimore boat and was immediately arrested by the local commander, David Farragut, and sent to Annapolis in the custody of a marine lieutenant. The next day Cogdell and his escort appeared before the court. There was, after all, no trial. In addition to the charges from Portsmouth and the extremely serious charges related to Lawrence and the *Pons*, Cogdell had picked up another charge of improper behavior for being publicly drunk in Washington on 17 July. When he entered the room to face the court he saw not only witnesses to all these charges—Captain Bell, Boatswain Turney, and others— but also among the adjudicating officers behind the long table directly in front was Commander Buchanan. It was Buchanan who, three years earlier as captain of the *Vincennes,* had charged Cogdell with dereliction of duty. Moreover, Cogdell's failure to report to the court as ordered was in itself sufficient grounds for dismissal. The wretched lieutenant offered up his commission as well as his sword, and it was accepted.[6] Two weeks later he was dead.[7]

THE *PONS*

The *Pons* was turned over to federal civil authorities as soon as she reached Philadelphia. Lying at Simpson and Neal's wharf in Southwark from the moment she arrived she was a cause celebre, attracting fascinated crowds. Drawn by the ship's sudden notoriety they also admired the remarkable beauty of her construction.[8] However some onlookers, like Philadelphia businessman Joseph Sill, saw nothing beautiful in her at all. After dinner late on a Sunday afternoon he walked with two friends "down to the Queen St. wharf to see the Barque 'Pons,' which has been made so infamous by being captured on the Coast of Africa with 900 slaves on board—We could only see her outside, which is dirty and small, her capacity not being greater, apparently, than about 270 tons; and yet the inhuman Owners were about to ship 400 more Slaves on board when she was Captured by the American Sloop of War 'Yorktown'—I trust the presence of this craft will arouse the feelings of the people here and make them hate the very name of Slave, or Slave Owner!"[9]

Someone published a pasteboard flyer with an anti-slavery poem on one side and a series of quotations about the *Pons* taken from letters by Captain Bell and others on the reverse. It noted that, by actual measurement while the ship was in Philadelphia, "each slave had only a square space seventeen inches in the side; and when the hatches were closed, they would breathe all the air in the hold twice in an hour. If they had laid side by side, and each occupied fifteen inches in width, and five feet in length, 268 would have filled up the hold."[10]

The four Portuguese crewmen whiled away their time in jail, and Lieutenant Cogdell reported to Washington while the legal establishment followed its prescribed ways. On 8 April, with Cogdell as the formal witness, the federal court in Philadelphia condemned the *Pons*. Not surprisingly, no one had come forward to claim ownership of the ship or put up a defense. The four Portuguese, who had been held as witnesses but could not be prosecuted because the U.S. anti-slavery statute applied only to U.S. citizens, were released to go their way.

On 29 April, once emptied of its stores and cargo, sails removed, the hold "purified" and whitewashed, and her pumps repaired, the *Pons* was sold at auction at the Philadelphia Exchange by the U.S. Marshall's office. The barque and everything aboard brought a grand total of $5,657.50. After legal costs and other expenses $5,034.97 remained.[11] By law half of the total went to the Naval Retirement Fund and the other half was distributed to the crew of the *Yorktown* as prize money, in amounts determined by rank. The distribution began in November, a year after the *Pons*'s capture. Commodore Skinner, as squadron commander, received $125.87. Captain Bell got $251.75. The lowest-ranking crewmembers each received $7.87. Lieutenant Cogdell's share, paid to his widow, Emma, was $83.92. Master's Mate Lawrence's share, paid to his father, was $41.96. Though during the hearing some of the regular *Yorktown* crew had objected, even the *Yorktown*'s Kroomen were awarded $7.87 apiece.

The real prize, though, was not the ship but its human cargo. For their recapture the government paid additional prize money, the statutory $25 for each recaptive landed alive in Liberia. For its 756 recaptives the crew of the *Yorktown* received $18,900. Captain Bell's share of *that* amount would have been $1,890, and

Commodore Skinner's half as much. Each of the lowest-ranking crewmembers and each Krooman received $56.81. Lawrence's share, sent to his father, was $315. In 1851 Congress agreed to settle the claim of the American Colonization Society for their expenses of supporting and maintaining the recaptured Africans from the *Pons*, in an amount not to exceed $50 per head.[12]

The career of the *Pons* did not continue untroubled. In early November after her sale she was on her way from Malaga to the United States. For motives now unknown, her crew of ten, led by the mate wielding an axe, drove the captain into his cabin and kept him there for the final three days of the voyage. In April 1847, by which time her owner had obtained from Congress permission to change her name to *Cordelia*, desperate Irish were fleeing the potato famine on crowded vessels that came to be called "coffin ships." The *Pons* arrived in Philadelphia from Waterford, Ireland, and was seized for being overloaded. American law permitted only two passengers for every five tons of displacement, and the *Pons* was only 196 tons. Aboard the soon-to-be *Cordelia* 110 Irish had been crammed into a space considered safe for only 80 persons—on the ship that had once held over 900 slaves![13]

Notes

Prologue

1. USS Yorktown log, 7 August 1844, National Archives, Washington, D.C.

2. Earl E. McNeilly, *The United States Navy and the Suppression of the West African Slave Trade, 1819–1862* (Ann Arbor, Mich.: University Microfilms, 1979), 102.

3. Charles Bell to James Paulding, 28 July 1840, CDL, Navy Department Correspondence, National Archives, Washington, D.C.; McNeilly, *Navy and the Suppression of the Slave Trade,* 103.

4. Bell to Paulding, 26 August 1844, CDL; John Y. Mason to Bell, 6 September 1844, LS, Navy Department Correspondence, National Archives, Washington, D.C.

5. William Cushman to Mason, 30 August 1844; Henry A. Steele to Mason, 10 August 1844; and Francis A. Roe to Mason, 29 August 1844, all MLR, Navy Department Correspondence, National Archives, Washington, D.C.

6. Mason to John C. Lawrence, 18 September 1844, MLS, Navy Department Correspondence, National Archives, Washington, D.C. Since this letter promises Lawrence will be considered for assignment, he cannot have reported to the *Yorktown* until some days after 18 September. Roe's journal, *Journal of a Cruize in the U.S. Ship of War Yorktown, Charles H. Bell Esq. Commander, During the Years 1844–45* (Roe Papers, Box 1,

Library of Congress, Manuscript Division), has a list of officers of the *Yorktown* dated simply "October" that does not include Lawrence, so it would seem Lawrence joined the ship between 1 and 11 October (when the ship left New York). A letter from Capt. Jacob Jones to Mason dated 27 July 1844 (in CL, Navy Department Correspondence, National Archives, Washington, D.C.) mentions Lawrence's earlier experience; a letter from David Henshaw (for the secretary of the navy) to Lawrence dated 26 January 1844 (MLS), refusing Lawrence's request to be advanced to master's mate, indicates Lawrence is attached to the receiving ship *North Carolina* but shows his address as No. 10 Walker St., New York.

7. According to one historian the election of 1844 "surpassed in excitement anything which had been known in American politics." James C. Ridpath, *History of the United States* (Philadelphia: Jones Brothers, 1877), 446.

8. *Illustrated London News,* 11 January 1845, 18.

Chapter 1. November 1844

1. *Yorktown* log, 9–13 November 1844.

2. Matthew C. Perry to Mason, secretary of the navy, 30 November 1844 and 23 January 1845, SL, Navy Department Correspondence, National Archives, Washington, D.C.; Surgeon Edmund DuBarry to Perry, 2 December 1844, enclosed in Perry to Mason, 2 December 1844, SL.

3. *Yorktown* log, 29 November 1844.

4. Isaac Mayo to John H. B. Latrobe, 3 January 1844, Maryland State Colonization Society Papers, Maryland Historical Society, Baltimore.

5. Mayo's resignation was not accepted, however. As with a handful of others submitted, President Lincoln specifically rejected it and instead cashiered him. Probably Mayo never knew what happened, as he was dying the very day of Lincoln's action.

Chapter 2. December 1844

1. Perry to Bell, 29 November 1844, in Letter Books of Commodore Matthew C. Perry, 10 March 1843–20 February 1845, National Archives, Washington, D.C., microfilm at Nimitz Library, U.S. Naval Academy, Annapolis, Md.

2. Mason to Perry, 20 December 1844, U.S. Navy Area Files, Area 11, National Archives, Washington, D.C.

3. For Perry's views see his letter to Secretary Mason dated 6 March 1845, with enclosed "Notes," both in SL.

4. Bell to Perry, 18 December 1844, enclosed in Perry to Mason, 28 January 1845, SL.

5. Lewis S. Williams to William Williams, 17 December 1844, Archer-Mitchell-Stump-Williams Family Papers, MS 1948, Box 11, Manuscripts Department, Maryland Historical Society Library.

6. Svend E. Holsoe, "Theodore Canot at Cape Mount, 1841–1847," *Liberian Studies Journal* 44 (1972): 168, citing "Editorial" in *Liberia Herald* 14 (1845): 3.

7. The *Yorktown* log dated 13 December notes "shipped James Worthy, American Seaman from the English brig *Arabian.*"

8. Bell to Perry, 18 December 1844, enclosed in Perry to Mason, 28 January 1844, SL.

9. Holsoe, "Canot at Cape Mount," 166, in which he cites the American Colonization Society's tables showing the number of emigrants sent to Liberia.

10. Brantz Mayer, *Captain Canot: or Twenty Years of an African Slaver* (New York: G. Appleton, 1854), 330–31; Bell to Perry, 18 December 1844, SL.

11. Lewis S. Williams to William Williams, 17 December 1844, Archer-Mitchell-Stump-Williams Family Papers.

12. Roger Pasquier, "A propos de Théodore Canot negrier en Afrique," *Rev. Français d'Histoire d'Outre-Mer* 55.200 (1968): 352–54; Roger Pasquier, "Theophile Conneau alias Theodore Canot negrier en Afrique,"

Revue d'histoire des colonies 40 (1953): 249–63; Holsoe, "Canot at Cape Mount," 163–81; Theophilus Conneau, *A Slaver's Log Book or 20 Years' Residence in Africa* (Englewood Cliffs, N.J.: Prentice-Hall, 1976), 361–62.

13. Bell to Perry, 18 December 1844, SL. Canot describes his flag as a tricolor with a white star in the center. Mayer, *Captain Canot,* 319.

14. Holsoe, "Canot at Cape Mount," 166.

15. 28th Congress, 2nd Session, SD 150, p. 321.

16. Mayer, *Captain Canot,* 295–97.

17. Roe, journal entry for 16 December 1844, *Journal of a Cruize.*

18. *Yorktown* log, 15 December 1844.

19. Commo. Charles W. Skinner to Secretary of the Navy George Bancroft, 13 August 1845, SL.

20. Skinner to Bancroft, 12 October 1845, SL, with enclosures from participants in duel; McDonough to [Bancroft], 11 February 1846, SL, in which he testifies to Hurst having deliberately aimed away from Creighton.

21. Bell to Perry, 18 December 1844, enclosed in Perry to Mason, 28 January 1845, SL.

22. Horatio Bridge, *Journal of an African Cruiser,* Intro. by Donald H. Simpson (London: Dawsons of Pall Mall, 1968), 40ff; Jay Slagle, *Ironclad Captain: Seth Ledyard Phelps and the U.S. Navy, 1841–1864* (Kent, Ohio: Kent State University Press, 1996), 30ff.

23. Skinner to [Bancroft], 16 May 1845, SL.

24. *Yorktown* log, 18–23 December 1844.

25. Roe, journal entry for 24 December 1844, *Journal of a Cruize.*

26. After composing his previous entry on Christmas morning and dating it 25 December, Lawrence writes a second entry on the evening of the same day. Instead of simply making that entry a continuation of the one for 25 December he temporarily shifts his method of dating to sea time so he can date this second entry 26 December.

27. The colony at Sinou, originally called Mississippi in Africa, was founded by the Mississippi and Louisiana State Colonization Societies. It is now Sinoe County, Liberia.

28. The following year Mrs. Sawyer married the newly arrived missionary James Connelly, and she is referred to again by Lawrence on 10 October as his wife. "Memorial of Rev. James McCullough Connelly," *Southwestern Presbyterian,* 25 November 1895.

29. Bridge, *African Cruiser,* 105–7.

Chapter 3. January 1845

1. Bridge, *African Cruiser,* 14 et seq.

2. Ibid., 79–83.

3. Oddly, Lawrence reports a number of guns in the salute that does not agree with the number reported in both Roe's journal and the ship's log (both of the latter note thirteen guns instead of twenty-one). Similar discrepancies occur elsewhere. Why would there have been thirteen instead of twenty-one? Roe describes the salute as being in honor of the governor of the town, who presumably by his rank would rate thirteen guns, whereas if the salute were rendered in honor of the British flag itself it would have been twenty-one guns. In any case, such salutes were returned from shore "gun for gun," as the log often records.

4. Bridge, *African Cruiser,* 134–35, in which he mentions seeing three alligators (one of which is seven or eight feet long) inhabiting a pond here. These creatures were identified as "fetishes." The locals fed them and allowed children to bathe in the pond.

5. Letitia Elizabeth Landon has in recent years been the subject of several books. Horatio Bridge, who visited Elmina ("El Mina") in April 1844, gives a lengthy discourse on Landon and her grave. He speaks of her as "a woman whose poetry touched him in his early youth," and remarks that "it is well established here, that her death was accidental." Bridge, *African Cruiser,* 139.

6. Neville court-martial account from Records of General Courts-Martial and Courts of Inquiry of the Navy Department, 1799–1867, M-273, Reel 60, Case 980 (Neville), National Archives, Washington, D.C.

7.Bridge, *African Cruiser,* 142.

8. The *Yorktown* took aboard from the *Rhoderick Dhu* twenty-five boxes of soap and five gallons of oil, according to the log of 29 January. That same day one Edward Loring (officers' steward) was discharged from the service.

9. Iguana.

Chapter 4. February 1845

1. Perry to Bell, 29 November 1844, SL.

2. Bridge, *African Cruiser,* 152, describes King Glass as "an old man, much inclined to drink, yet more regular than any of his subjects in attendance at church." As the salute to George Washington was fired at noon, the visit of the African dignitaries lasted a bit more than an hour.

3. *Yorktown* log, 26 February 1845; Bridge, *African Cruiser,* 149.

4. In contrast to Lawrence, Horatio Bridge quite admired both Reverend Wilson and Mrs. Wilson: "Mr. Wilson is well known in America by reputation, and is one of the most able and judicious among the three hundred missionaries, whom the American Board sends forth throughout the world. Here at Gaboon, he preaches to the natives in their own language, which he represents as being very soft, and easy of acquirement. The people frequent divine services with great regularity, and are at least attentive listeners, if not edified by what they hear. Mrs. Wilson is a lady of remarkable zeal and energy. Reared in luxury, in a Southern city, she liberated her slaves, gave up a handsome fortune to the uses of missions, and devoted herself to the same great cause, in that region of the earth where her faith and fortitude were likely to be most severely tried. It is now six years since she came to Africa" (*African Cruiser,* 151). Wilson soon published a grammar and vocabulary of the Mpongwe language, and eventually became the Presbyterians' secretary of foreign missions.

5. "Verbum sapienti suff.": a word to the wise suffices.

Chapter 7. May 1845

1. Lewis S. Williams letter, begun 30 April 1845, Archer-Mitchell-Stump-Williams Family Papers.

2. The word given here as "a-lulled" is the editor's best guess at an unclear word in the manuscript containing multiple l's.

3. Bell to Paulding, 22 June 1840, MOL, Navy Department Correspondence, National Archives, Washington, D.C.

4. Perhaps "Pati" is a nickname for a friend? The written presentation of the name appears clearly as Pati, regardless of to whom it refers.

5. *Yorktown* log, 27 May 1845.

Chapter 9. July 1845

1. Lawrence may also have produced some sort of holiday drawing for his journal. The entry for 3 July ends a few inches from the top on the recto of the leaf preceding the one headed by the all-capital "JULY THE FOURTH." The verso of the leaf, unlike any others in the journal, is left blank, and the bottom three quarters of the leaf have been neatly cut out.

2. Here Lawrence apparently took up his journal later in the day, forgetting he already had an entry for 16 July, labeling the carryover passage at the top of his page "15th cont'd," when it was actually the end of the (first) entry for the sixteenth, and this paragraph "16th."

3. Lewis S. Williams to William Williams, 30 November 1845, Archer-Mitchell-Stump-Williams Family Papers.

Chapter 10. August 1845

1. Skinner to Bancroft, 9 August 1845, SL.

2. Skinner to Bancroft, 29 August 1845, SL.

3. Ibid.

4. Franklin Buchanan to David Henshaw, 13 October 1843, CDL.

5. George W. Harrison et al. to Capt. Elie A. F. La Vallette, 15 February

1844, enclosed in La Vallette to Henshaw, 19 February 1844, CL; date of Cogdell's attachment to *Yorktown* from Roe journal entry for 26 August 1845, *Journal of a Cruize.*

6. Records of General Courts-Martial and Courts of Inquiry of the Navy Department, 1799–1867, Case C.M. 979 (M-273, Reel 60); Case C.M. 980 (M-273, Reel 60).

Chapter 11. September 1845

1. For more on sea time see note 26 of chapter two (above). According to sea time the actual morning of 5 September is recorded as the latter part of the log entry dated 5 September, since the first part of the log entry dated 5 September was the hours from noon to midnight of 4 September

2. Roe journal entry for 9 September 1845, *Journal of a Cruize; Yorktown* log, 9 September 1845.

3. Lewis S. Williams to William Williams, 10 November 1844, Archer-Mitchell-Stump-Williams Family Papers.

4. Hampden C. DuBose, *Memoirs of Rev. John Leighton Wilson, D.D.* (Richmond, Va.: Presbyterian Committee of Publication, 1895), 159–70.

5. Slaveships customarily were given a temporary second deck in the hold for slaves to lie on. Possession of lumber appropriate to building such a deck was one of the points of suspicion that could justify seizure by authorities. Others included, as Lawrence mentions, large stores of rice (or other grain) and irregular or nonexistent papers. In addition, suspicion fell upon the following: cooking pots or water supplies (or casks to hold water) significantly larger than needed for the crew; hatches with open gratings (not used by merchant ships but necessary to permit a cargo of slaves to breathe); superfluous bulkheads; excess mats or matting; and shackles or handcuffs. Under the Quintuple Treaty of 1841 (signed by England, Austria, Prussia, and Russia), any *one* of these factors sufficed for a seizure of the ship and almost certainly condemnation in court. Instructions to the U.S. African Squadron listed essentially the same grounds for suspicion, but left open whether one or more points of viola-

tion were enough to justify seizure. In addition, condemnation in U.S. courts was far from automatic. Thus Captain Bell and the other American naval commanders operated in a fuzzier legal context than did their English counterparts.

6. In the manuscript Lawrence captions the previous paragraph as "28th cont." and this one as "29th," though he already has an earlier entry for 29 September. The present editor offers no further explanation.

7. The journal really does say "31st." Comparison with the *Yorktown*'s log suggests this entry, like the correctly dated following entry, actually refers to 1 October, though, given the lack of events recorded in the entry, it scarcely matters.

Chapter 12. The *Patuxent*

1. Canot later admitted to being involved in the *Atalanta* business, though merely as an intermediary.

2. Bell to U.S. District Attorney of New York, 3 October 1845, copy in Bell to Bancroft, 4 October 1845, oddly in MOL; Bell to Bancroft, 4 October 1845, MOL; J. J. Roberts to Bell, 3 October 1845, enclosed in Bell to Bancroft, 4 October 1845, MOL.

3. *United States v. Nathaniel T. Davis,* 17 March 1846, U.S. Circuit Court for the Southern District of New York, Record Group 21, Entry 67, Criminal Case Files Box No. 1, National Archives, New York City.

4. William E. Chandler to Bancroft, 9 January 1846, MOL.

5. USNA *Record Book 1846,* 60–61. Cushman's required midshipman journals and letters were also judged inadequate.

6. Chandler, "Inventory of Items aboard *Patuxent,*" from *Patuxent* log, held in William E. Chandler Papers, New York Public Library, Manuscript Division.

7. *United States v. Nathaniel T. Davis,* 6; Bell to U.S. District Attorney for New York, 3 October 1845, MOL.

8. Chandler to Bancroft, 10 June 1846, MOL.

9. *Patuxent* log, 19 November 1846.

10. Survey report by Napoleon Smith, et al., 24 November 1844, enclosed in Chandler to Bancroft, 7 February 1846, in Letters Received by the Secretary of the Navy from Officers, Roll 173.

11. *Patuxent* log, 21 November 1846.

12. Bancroft to Chandler, 8 December 1845, LS.

13. Chandler to Bancroft, 10 December 1845, MOL.

14. Chandler to Bancroft, 7 January 1846, MOL.

15. Chandler to U.S. Attorney Benjamin F. Butler, 27 June 1846, enclosed in Chandler to Bancroft, 27 June 1846, MOL; Chandler to Bancroft, 7 January 1846, MOL.

16. Chandler to Bancroft, 27 June 1846 (enclosure), MOL.

17. Chandler to Bancroft, 7 January 1846, MOL.

18. Ibid.

19. Chandler to Bancroft, 27 January 1846, MOL.

20. Chandler to Bancroft, 8 June 1846, MOL.

21. Chandler to [Bancroft], 9 March 1846, MOL.

22. Ibid.

23. *U.S. v. Nathaniel T. Davis,* [7]; "The Claim and Answer of Thomas L. Shaw . . . to the Libel filed on the eleventh day of March . . . against the said Schooner *Patuxent,*" 29 May 1846. U.S. Circuit Court for the District of New York, Admiralty Case File 3–28 *U.S.A. v. the Schooner* Patuxent (hereafter "*Patuxent* file").

24. Chandler to Bancroft, 25 March 1846, MOL.

25. "The Petition of Nathaniel T. Davis to the District Court of the United States for the Southern District of New York: The United States of America vs. The Schooner *Patuxent* . . . 25 April 1846," *Patuxent* file.

26. Nathaniel T. Davis to Emile H. Lacombe and Achille Begoden, "Power and Assignment," 6 November 1846, *Patuxent* file.

27. "The Claim and Answer of Thomas L. Shaw," *Patuxent* file.

28. Chandler to Bancroft, 5 May 1846; Chandler to the Secretary of the Navy, 11 May 1846, both MOL.

29. Chandler to Bancroft, 27 June 1846, MOL.

30. Capt. Theophilus Conneau, *A Slaver's Logbook: or 20 Years'*

Residence in Africa, introduction by Mabel M. Smythe (Englewood Cliffs, N.J.: Prentice Hall, 1976), 347–50; Holsoe, "Canot at Cape Mount," 169–71.

31. Chandler to Bancroft, 11 February 1846, MOL.

32. *United States v. Schooner* Patuxent *and Cargo,* Motion Ret'ble, 5 May 1847 [incorrectly dated 5 May 1846], *Patuxent* file.

33. Conneau, *Slaver's Logbook,* 347–50.

Chapter 13. October 1845

1. Roe, journal entry for 13 October 1845, *Journal of a Cruize.*

Chapter 14. November 1845

1. Tony Hodges and Malyn Newitt, *São Tome and Principe: From Plantation Colony to Microstate* (Boulder: Westview Press, 1988), 56.

2. James Buchanan to Bancroft, 8 October 1846, MLR.

Chapter 15. December 1845

1. *Philadelphia Public Ledger,* 18 March 1846, 2.

2. *Philadelphia Public Ledger,* 11 April 1846, 2.

3. Bell to Bancroft, 30 November, April 1846, MLR; *African Repository,* April 1846, 118; Rev. J. B. Benham to F. Burns, *African Repository,* May 1846, 146; Steele affidavit, 1 December 1845, *Philadelphia Public Ledger,* 18 March 1846, 2.

4. Bell to Bancroft, 11 December 1845, CDL.

5. Forfeiture Petition, 1 May 1847, District Court for Eastern District of Pennsylvania, *Pons* Papers.

6. The ship's measurement is given exactly thus in legal documents, odd though the fraction may seem.

7. *Philadelphia Public Ledger,* 18 March 1846, 2.

8. *Philadelphia Public Ledger,* 17 March 1846, 2.

9. Bell to Bancroft, 11 December 1845, CDL.

10. Lewis J. Williams to William Williams, 30 November 1845, Archer-Mitchell-Stump-Williams Family Papers.

11. Bancroft to Prof. H. H. Lockwood, Judge Advocate, 17 July 1846, LS.

12. William B. Hoyt, *Land of Hope: Reminiscences of Liberia and Cape Palmas* (Hartford: Henry J. Fox & Wm. B. Hoyt, 1852), 75.

13. William B. Hoyt to "a friend," 15 December 1845, *African Repository,* May 1846, 144.

14. Ibid.

15. J. B. Benham to F. Burns, 17 December 1845, *African Repository,* May 1846, 147.

16. *Liberia Herald,* April 1846; *African Repository,* April 1846, 118.

17. Dr. J. W. Lugenbeel, 16 December 1845, letter to editor in *National Intelligencer; African Repository,* April 1846, 143.

18. Benham to Burns, 17 December 1845, *African Repository,* April 1846, 147.

19. Lugenbeel to Bell, 17 January 1846, and Lawrence to Bell, 30 December 1845, both enclosed in Bell to Bancroft, 27 January 1846, CDL.

20. *African Repository,* May 1846, 141–53.

21. *African Repository,* April 1846, 118.

22. *African Repository,* August 1846, 236.

23. *Liberia Herald,* 28 December 1845; *African Repository,* May 1846, 141.

24. Lugenbeel to W. McLain, *African Repository,* April 1846, 113.

25. J. J. Roberts to Ex. Committee N.Y. State Colonization Society, 27 June 1846, *African Repository,* October 1846, 301, and June 1846, 189.

26. *Liberia Herald,* 17 July 1846, 75.

27. Roberts to McLain, *African Repository,* October 1846, 302.

28. *African Repository,* January 1847, 25.

29. Lugenbeel to McLain, *African Repository,* May 1847.

30. Lewis S. Williams to Hon. S. Archer, 27 May 1848, in Archer-Mitchell-Stump-Williams Family Papers.

31. *Liberia Herald,* 4 December 1846, 15.

32. Matilda Skipwith quote of 4 July 1848 in R. M. Miller, *Dear Master* (Ithaca, N.Y.: Cornell University Press, 1978), 101.

33. J. W. Lugenbeel, *Sketches of Liberia* (Washington, D.C.: C. Alexander, 1850), 10.

34. *African Repository,* December 1863, quoted in Tom W. Schick, *Behold the Promised Land: A History of Afro-American Settler Society in Nineteenth-Century Liberia* (Baltimore: Johns Hopkins University Press, 1980), 115.

35. Lugenbeel to Bell, 17 January 1846; Lawrence to Bell, 30 December 1845; both enclosed in Bell to Bancroft, 27 January 1846, CDL.

36. Lugenbeel to Bell, 17 January 1846, enclosed in Bell to Bancroft, 27 January 1846, CDL.

37. Lawrence to Bell, 30 December 1845, enclosed in Bell to Bancroft, 27 January 1846, CDL.

38. Lugenbeel to McLain, 29 December 1845, in *African Repository,* April 1846, 112–13.

39. Hoyt, *Land of Hope,* 88; Lugenbeel to McLain, 29 December 1845, in *African Repository,* April 1846, 112. Hoyt says Gallano had been stopped three times, while Lugenbeel says "six times by British cruisers." As Lugenbeel is more specific and was writing almost immediately after conversing with Gallano, his figure seems more reliable.

40. Richard C. Cogdell to Bancroft, 29 April 1846, MOL. In the undated letter to Bancroft reporting his arrival with the *Pons* in Philadelphia on 13 March 1846, Cogdell says Lawrence took sick on 12 January, while in his letter of 29 April 1846 he says Lawrence became sick on 1 January.

41. Christopher Lloyd, *The Navy and the Slave Trade* (London: Frank Cass & Co., 1949), 275–76.

42. Ibid.

43. Earl E. McNeilly, *Navy and the Suppression of the Slave Trade,* 204–38.

Epilogue

1. Cogdell to Bancroft, n.d. (13 March 1846?), MOL.

2. Bancroft to Cogdell, 16 April 1846, LS.

3. Cogdell to Bancroft, 24 April 1846, MOL.

4. Bell to Bancroft, 27 January 1846, CDL.

5. Lugenbeel to Bell, 17 January 1846, enclosed in Bell to Bancroft, 27 January 1846, CDL.

6. David Farragut to Bancroft, 24 July 1846, CDL; Farragut to Bancroft, 20 July 1846, CDL; Buchanan to Bancroft, 15 July 1846, CDL.

7. Affidavit of Arthur Emmerson, 21 September 1846, in *Pons* Papers in Record Group 21, Eastern District Court of Pennsylvania, Informations 1843–1854, Box No. 10. Also, *American Beacon and Portsmouth Daily Advertiser,* 10 August 1846, gives Cogdell's death as occurring the previous Saturday, 8 August.

8. *Philadelphia Public Ledger,* 18 March 1846, 2.

9. Entry for 23 February 1846, Diary of Joseph I. Sill, Vol. 7: 1846, Historical Society of Pennsylvania, Philadelphia.

10. Pasteboard flyer in Nimitz Library Special Collections, U.S. Naval Academy, Annapolis, Md. The poem on the front of the flyer is by English poet James Hurnard.

11. Commissioner's Report, filed 13 November 1846, in *Pons* Papers, RG 21, Box 10.

12. Thirty-first Congress, Second Session (1851), in George Minot, ed., *U.S. Laws, Statutes, etc.,* vol. 9 (Boston: Charles C. Little and James Brown, 1851), chap. 45.

13. *Pons* Papers, RG 21, Box 10; Minot, *U.S. Laws,* chap. 19. The *Pons*'s new owner was Edward Harris Miles of Philadelphia.

Bibliography

Manuscripts and Archival Sources

Historical Society of Pennsylvania Library, Manuscript Division, Philadelphia
Joseph I. Sill Diary. Vol. 7: 1846

Library of Congress, Manuscript Division
Francis Asbury Roe, *Journal of a Cruize in the U. S. Ship of War Yorktown, Charles H. Bell Esq. Commander, During the Years 1844–45.* Francis A. Roe Papers, Box 1

Maryland Historical Society Library, Baltimore
Maryland Colonization Society Papers
Lewis S. Williams letters and journal in the Archer-Mitchell-Stump-Williams Family Papers, Manuscripts Department, MS 1948, Box 11

National Archives, College Park, Maryland
USS *Yorktown,* USS *Oriole,* USS *Preble* plans

National Archives, Mid-Atlantic Region, Philadelphia
U.S. District Court of the United States for the Eastern District of Pennsylvania
Pons Papers, Box 10
Informations 1843–1854 and Information Docket 1839–1862

National Archives, Northeast Region, New York City
Admiralty Case File 3-28 U.S.A. v. The Schooner *Patuxent*
U.S. Circuit Court for the Southern District of New York Criminal Case against Nathaniel T. Davis, Box 1, Entry 67

National Archives, Washington, D.C.

U.S. Navy Area Files

USS *Yorktown* logs 1844–1846

 Records of General Courts-Martial and Courts of Inquiry of the Navy Department, 1799–1867, M-273, Reel 60, Case 979 (Marin) and Case 980 (Neville)

 Letter Books of Commodore Matthew C. Perry, 10 March 1843–20 February 1845 (microfilm copy held at Nimitz Library, U.S. Naval Academy)

Navy Department Correspondence (microfilm copies located at Nimitz Library, U.S. Naval Academy). Correspondence is divided into several categories; those cited in the present volume are:

  LS Letters sent by the secretary of the navy to officers, 1798–1871

  MLS Miscellaneous letters sent by the secretary of the navy, 1798–1886

  SL Letters received by the secretary of the navy from commanding officers of squadrons ("Squadron Letters"), 1841–1886

  CL Letters received by the secretary of the navy from captains ("Captains' Letters"), 1805–1861 and 1866–1885

  CDL Letters received by the secretary of the navy from commanders, 1804–1886

  MOL Letters received by the secretary of the navy from officers below the rank of commander, 1802–1886

  MLR Miscellaneous letters received by the secretary of the navy, 1801–1884

New York Public Library, Manuscript Division

William E. Chandler Papers, including *Patuxent* log

Nimitz Library Special Collections, U.S. Naval Academy, Annapolis, Maryland

Pons / Hurnard's Pasteboard flyer

John Clarkson Lawrence's *Journal of a Cruise*

U.S. Naval Academy Archives, Annapolis, Maryland

USNA *Record Book 1846*

Printed Sources

Periodicals

African Repository
American Beacon and Portsmouth Daily Advertiser
Illustrated London News
Liberia Herald
National Intelligencer
Philadelphia Public Ledger

Books and Articles

Bridge, Horatio. *Journal of an African Cruiser.* Introduction by Donald H. Simpson. London: Dawsons of Pall Mall, 1968.

Campbell, Penelope. *Maryland in Africa: The Maryland State Colonization Society, 1831–1857.* Urbana: University of Illinois Press, 1971.

Conneau, Captain Theophilus. *A Slaver's Log Book: or 20 Years' Residence in Africa.* Introduction by Mabel M. Smythe. Englewood Cliffs, N.J.: Prentice-Hall, 1976.

DuBose, Hampden C. *Memoirs of Rev. John Leighton Wilson, D.D.* Richmond, Va.: Presbyterian Committee of Publication, 1895.

Hensley, P. H. "Memorial of Rev. James McCullough Connelly." *Southwestern Presbyterian* (21 November 1895), n.p.

Hodges, Tony, and Malyn Hewitt. *São Tome and Principe: From Plantation Colony to Microstate.* Boulder, Colo.: Westview Press, 1988.

Holsoe, Svend E. "Theodore Canot at Cape Mount, 1841–1847." *Liberian Studies Journal* 44 (1972): 163–81.

Hoyt, William B. *Land of Hope: Reminiscences of Liberia and Cape Palmas.* Hartford: Henry J. Fox and William B. Hoyt, 1852.

Lloyd, Christopher. *The Navy and the Slave Trade.* London: Frank Cass & Co., 1949.

Lugenbeel, J. W. *Sketches of Liberia.* Washington, D.C.: C. Alexander, 1850.

Mayer, Brantz. *Captain Canot: or Twenty Years of an African Slaver.* New York: G. Appleton, 1854.

McNeilly, Earl E. *The United States Navy and the Suppression of the West African Slave Trade, 1819–1862.* Ann Arbor, Mich.: University Microfilms, 1979.

Miller, R. M. *Dear Master.* Ithaca: Cornell University Press, 1978.

Minot, George, ed. *U.S. Laws, Statutes, etc.* Vol. 9. Boston: Charles C. Little and James Brown, 1851.

Pasquier, Roger. "A propos de Théodore Canot négrier en Afrique." *Revue Français d'Histoire d'Outre-Mer* 55.200 (1968): 352–54.

———. "Théophile Conneau alias Théodore Canot: négrier en Afrique." *Revue d'histoire des colonies* 40 (1953): 249–63.

Patterson, K. David. *The Northern Gabon Coast to 1875.* Oxford: Clarendon, 1975.

Ridpath, James C. *History of the United States.* Philadelphia: Jones Brothers, 1877.

Scott, Anna M. *Day Dawn in Africa.* New York: Protestant Episcopal Society for the Promotion of Evangelical Knowledge, 1858.

Shick, Tom W. *Behold the Promised Land: A History of Afro-American Settler Society in Nineteenth-Century Liberia.* Baltimore: Johns Hopkins University Press, 1980.

Slagle, Jay. *Ironclad Captain: Seth Ledyard Phelps and the U.S. Navy, 1841–1864.* Kent, Ohio: Kent State University Press, 1966.

U.S. Congress, House Committee on Commerce. *Report of Mr. Kennedy, of Maryland, from the Committee on Commerce of the House of Representatives of the United States on the African Slave Trade,* U.S. Twenty-seventh Congress, Third Session. Washington: 1843; rpt. Freeport, N.Y.: Books for Libraries, 1971.

Wilson, Rev. J. Leighton. *Western Africa: Its History, Condition and Prospects.* New York: Harper and Brothers, 1856.

Index

About the Authors

C. Herbert Gilliland grew up in Gainesville, Florida, and earned both his bachelor's and master's degrees from the University of Florida. Commissioned in the U.S. Naval Reserve in 1966, he served as communications officer on a destroyer and destroyer staff before returning to the University of Florida, where he earned his Ph.D. in English in 1976. Recalled to active duty, he was a member of the U.S. Naval Academy English department from 1982 to 1985 before leaving to join the faculty of Virginia Military Institute. He later returned to the Naval Academy as a civilian professor. After a final period of active duty in support of Operation Desert Storm in 1992, he retired from the naval service with the rank of captain. He is presently Professor of English at the Naval Academy.

John Clarkson Lawrence was born about 1821 and may have grown up on Long Island, New York. After sailing aboard various merchant and naval vessels, he became master's mate aboard the sloop USS *Yorktown* in October 1844. When that ship captured the slave ship *Pons* carrying more than nine hundred slaves, he was sent aboard as the second-ranking member of the prize crew. After taking the slaves to Liberia, Lawrence and the *Pons* headed for Philadelphia. En route, Lawrence died of fever on 30 January 1846.

The Naval Institute Press is the book-publishing arm of the U.S. Naval Institute, a private, nonprofit, membership society for sea service professionals and others who share an interest in naval and maritime affairs. Established in 1873 at the U.S. Naval Academy in Annapolis, Maryland, where its offices remain today, the Naval Institute has members worldwide.

Members of the Naval Institute support the education programs of the society and receive the influential monthly magazine *Proceedings* and discounts on fine nautical prints and on ship and aircraft photos. They also have access to the transcripts of the Institute's Oral History Program and get discounted admission to any of the Institute-sponsored seminars offered around the country.

The Naval Institute also publishes *Naval History* magazine. This colorful bimonthly is filled with entertaining and thought-provoking articles, first-person reminiscences, and dramatic art and photography. Members receive a discount on *Naval History* subscriptions.

The Naval Institute's book-publishing program, begun in 1898 with basic guides to naval practices, has broadened its scope to include books of more general interest. Now the Naval Institute Press publishes about one hundred titles each year, ranging from how-to books on boating and navigation to battle histories, biographies, ship and aircraft guides, and novels. Institute members receive significant discounts on the Press's more than eight hundred books in print.

Full-time students are eligible for special half-price membership rates. Life memberships are also available.

For a free catalog describing Naval Institute Press books currently available, and for further information about subscribing to *Proceedings* magazine or about joining the U.S. Naval Institute, please write to:

Membership Department
U.S. Naval Institute
291 Wood Road
Annapolis, MD 21402-5034
Telephone: (800) 233-8764
Fax: (410) 269-7940
Web address: www.navalinstitute.org